Official TOEFL iBT® Tests Volume

Using the Digital Resources

Authentic TOEFL iBT test questions are used in this book. When you take the actual TOEFL iBT® test, you may notice some variations in how the questions are presented to you on screen.

Installation

First, go to **www.mhprofessional.com/totvol2**. Once on the site, you'll be prompted to enter your access code—you can find your unique code in an envelope at the end of the book or on your eBook confirmation in your ETS account. Please note that this code is redeemable only by you and a maximum of two times.

Once you enter your access code, a download will automatically begin. This download will contain the audio files you need as well as files that contain the tests in both PC and Mac® format.

Main Menu for Practice Tests

When you launch the program, the following screen will appear:

 Official TOEFL iBT® Tests Volume 2, 4th Edition

| Options | Main Menu |

Application Overview

Practice Test 1 Test Sections

Practice Test 2 Test Sections

Practice Test 3 Test Sections

Practice Test 4 Test Sections

Practice Test 5 Test Sections

Taking TOEFL iBT Tests on Your Computer

From the **Main Menu**, choose Test 1, 2, 3, 4, or 5. Then select the test section you wish to take: **Reading, Listening, Speaking**, or **Writing**. Note that you can take each section more than once.

When you open a test section, you will first be provided with instructions for that section. A timer on the screen shows how many minutes and seconds you have left for that section. You can hide the timer if you find it distracting.

If you must take a break during the test, select **Main Menu** at the top of the screen. This will take you back to the main menu. When you are ready to resume, open the test section again, and select the **Continue** button. Your work will not be lost, and when you resume, you will begin exactly where you left off. The timer clock will stop while you are on your break and will restart immediately when you resume the test. There are no breaks during the actual test.

Answering Questions

To answer the questions in the Reading and Listening sections, select the best answer or follow the instructions given. For some questions, you will need to select more than one answer. Select the **Next** button to move forward to the next question. In the Listening section, the **Next** button is only enabled after you select an answer choice or choices. In the Reading section, you can select the **Next** button at any time to move forward to the next question, and you can select the **Back** button to move back to the previous question.

For the Speaking section, you should record your response to each question using a recording device after you hear the instruction telling you to begin speaking. Stop recording once the response time expires.

For the Writing section, write your response to each question in the space provided within the time allowed.

When all the questions in a section have been answered, select the **Next** button to complete the section.

Playing Audio Tracks

In the Listening, Speaking, and Writing sections, you will listen to audio tracks. Audio controls are available at the bottom of the screen. At the end of a track, select the **Next** button to start answering questions.

Your Performance

On the **Main Menu**, select any test you have taken. The percentage of questions answered correctly for the Reading and Listening sections only will be displayed. By selecting a test section and then selecting **Review**, you will be able to review the questions from that section. For the Reading and Listening sections, you will see the correct answer for each question. For the Speaking section, you will be provided with important points for each question, sample responses, and rater comments on the responses. Use these to evaluate your performance on the Speaking section. For the Writing section, you will be given topic notes, sample essays, and rater comments on the essays. Use these to evaluate your performance on the Writing section.

Audio Files for Working Through the Tests in the Book

You may choose to work with the tests printed in the book rather than with the tests you download to your computer. If so, you will still need to listen to the audio tracks. Once you download the folder named "Audio Files" to your computer, you can select the audio tracks by number as you proceed through the book. As you work through the tests in the book, a headphones symbol 🎧 will indicate each time you need to play a track. Select the number of the track as instructed in the book.

Official
TOEFL iBT® Tests

VOLUME 2

FOURTH EDITION

1 2 3 4 5 6 7 8 9 LON 29 28 27 26 25 24

Domestic Edition
ISBN   978-1-265-48163-6
MHID   1-265-48163-6

e-ISBN 978-1-265-48172-8
e-MHID   1-265-48172-5

McGraw Hill books are available at special quantity discounts to use as premiums and sales promotions or for use in corporate training programs. To contact a representative, please visit the Contact Us pages at www.mhprofessional.com.

McGraw Hill is committed to making our products accessible to all learners. To learn more about the available support and accommodations we offer, please contact us at accessibility@ mheducation.com. We also participate in the Access Text Network (www.accesstext.org), and ATN members may submit requests through ATN.

Contents

Introduction

About the TOEFL iBT Test

The TOEFL iBT® test measures your ability to use and understand the English language as it is read, heard, spoken, and written in the university classroom. More than 12,000 universities, agencies, and other institutions in more than 160 countries—including Australia, Canada, New Zealand, the United States, the United Kingdom, and countries all across Europe and Asia—accept TOEFL scores as part of their admissions criteria, making the TOEFL iBT test the most widely accepted English-language test in the world.

Each TOEFL iBT® test contains four sections: Reading, Listening, Speaking, and Writing. The questions in these sections measure how well you **read, listen, speak, and write in English**. They also measure how well you use these skills together, so in some cases you will be asked to integrate your skills. For example, you may read a passage or listen to a lecture and then write or speak about what you learned. Here are brief descriptions of each section, including what the section measures and the types of questions it contains.

Reading Section

This section measures your ability to understand academic passages in English. The passages are excerpts from textbooks and other books suitable for use in introductory university courses.

You do not need any background knowledge about the topics contained in the passages in order to successfully answer the questions. All the information you need to answer the questions can be found in the passages. The questions measure your ability to understand stated information, make inferences, and distinguish main ideas from less important information.

Here are the types of Reading questions, with an explanation of each type:

Basic Comprehension questions	
Factual Information	These questions ask you to identify factual information that was explicitly presented in the passage.
Negative Factual Information	These questions ask you to distinguish information that is true from information that is not true or is not included in the passage.
Vocabulary	These questions ask you to identify the meanings of individual words or phrases *as they are used in the passage*.
Reference	These questions measure your ability to identify relationships between ideas mentioned in the passage and expressions that refer to the ideas. For example, an idea could be presented and another sentence could refer to "This idea." A question might ask what the phrase "This idea" refers to.
Sentence Simplification	These questions ask you to choose a sentence that has the same essential meaning as a particular sentence from the passage.
Inferencing questions	
Inference	These questions ask about information that is implied but not explicitly presented in the passage.
Rhetorical Purpose	These questions ask about the rhetorical function of specific information presented in a passage. These questions ask *why* or *how* the author mentions or includes a specific piece of information in the passage. Some questions of this type ask how an author organized information in the passage.

Insert Text	These questions provide a new sentence and ask you to place that sentence into the passage where it would best fit.
Reading-to-Learn questions	
Prose Summary	These questions ask you to identify major ideas from the passage and distinguish them from minor ideas or from ideas that are not presented in the passage. To select the correct answers, you need to both understand the relative importance of various pieces of information from the passage and identify the combination of answer choices that cover the major ideas presented in the passage. This question is always the last question in a Reading set. This question is worth up to 2 points. Test takers receive 2 points if all three correct answers are selected, and 1 point if only 2 correct answers are selected.

Listening Section

This section measures your ability to understand conversations and academic lectures in English.

You will listen to two conversations. One conversation takes place in a professor's office and may include discussion of academic material or course requirements. The other conversation takes place on a university campus and includes discussion of nonacademic content that is related to university life. Each conversation is followed by five questions.

You will also listen to three lectures on a variety of topics. In some lectures, only the professor speaks. In others, students contribute to the discussion; the professor may ask students questions about the topic being discussed or may answer students' questions. Each lecture is followed by six questions.

Each conversation and lecture is heard only once. Each contains a context photograph depicting the speaker(s). Some conversations and lectures contain other visuals, such as blackboards that present technical vocabulary or uncommon names.

Here are the types of Listening questions, with an explanation of each type:

Basic Comprehension questions	
Gist-Content	These questions ask you to identify the main idea of a lecture or conversation.
Gist-Purpose	These questions ask about the main purpose of a lecture or conversation.
Detail questions	These questions ask about important details from a lecture or conversation.
Pragmatic Understanding questions	
Function or Purpose	These questions ask you to identify a speaker's purpose in making a statement or how a statement functions in a lecture or conversation.
Speaker Attitude	These questions ask you to identify a speaker's attitude, opinion, or degree of certainty.
Connecting Information questions	
Understanding Organization	These questions ask you about the organization of information in a lecture.
Connecting Content	These questions ask you about the relationships among ideas in a lecture or conversation or to make inferences based on important points that were discussed.

Most questions are multiple choice with one correct answer. Some questions require more than one answer. You may also encounter questions that ask you to place the steps of a process in order, place check marks in a grid, or listen again to a portion of a conversation or lecture.

Speaking Section

This section measures your ability to speak in English about a variety of topics.

For each question, you will be given a short time to prepare your response. When the preparation time is up, answer the question as completely as possible in the time indicated for that question. For the tests in this book, you should record your responses on a recording device. That way, you can review them later and compare them with the notes in the Answers section and rubrics.

For the first question, Paired Choice, you will give your opinion about a familiar topic. You will need to explain what your opinion is and explain the reasons you have for holding that opinion.

For the second question, Fit and Explain, you will first read a short passage and then listen to or read a transcript of a conversation on the same topic. You will then be asked a question about both. You will need to combine appropriate information from the passage and the conversation to provide a complete answer to the question. Your response is scored on your ability to speak clearly and coherently and on your ability to accurately convey information about the passage and the conversation.

For the third question, General/Specific, you will first read a short passage on an academic subject and then listen to or read a transcript of a talk on the same subject. You will then be asked a question about both. Your response is scored on your ability to speak clearly and coherently and on your ability to integrate and convey key information from the passage and the talk.

For the last question, Summary, you will listen to or read a transcript of part of a lecture. You will then be asked a question about it. Your response is scored on your ability to speak clearly and coherently and on your ability to accurately convey information from the lecture.

Speaking responses are scored in terms of three important dimensions: delivery, language use, and topic development. When raters evaluate responses, they consider all three dimensions equally. No single dimension is weighted more heavily than another.

Writing Section

This section measures your ability to write in English to communicate in an academic environment.

For Writing question 1, you will read a passage and listen to or read a transcript of a lecture. Then you will respond to a question that asks you about the relationship between the reading passage and the lecture. Try to answer as completely as possible using information from both the reading passage and the lecture. The question does *not* ask you to express your personal opinion. You may consult the reading passage again when it is time for you to write. Typically, an effective response will contain a minimum of 150 words. Your response is judged on the quality of your writing and on the completeness and accuracy of the content.

For Writing question 2 you will read a question from a professor and responses from other students in an online discussion. You will write a response that contributes to the discussion. An effective response typically contains at least 100 words.

How to Use This Book/Digital Resources

Official TOEFL iBT® Tests Volume 2, can help you prepare for the test. It contains five TOEFL iBT tests. All the test questions are authentic TOEFL iBT questions, but some are presented differently than on the real test. (Please note that you should use a recording device for the Speaking section.) You can take each test in two ways:

- **In the book**, using a pen or pencil to mark your answers or to write your responses. Whenever you need to listen to an audio track, you will see the headphones icon 🎧 printed on the page. The audio tracks are provided with the digital download. On the **Main Menu**, select **Audio Tracks**, and you will see the tracks listed by number. Select each one when you are instructed to do so in the book.

- **On your computer**, using the interactive versions of the tests provided on the digital download. Follow the instructions provided on the first page of this book, titled "Using the Digital Resources." Select your answers and enter your written responses as instructed. The audio tracks will play automatically as the test questions are presented to you on screen.

Written transcripts of the audio tracks are located in Appendix B. If you do not have access to the audio tracks but do have access to people with good English pronunciation, ask them to read the transcripts aloud to you. Listening to the transcripts is better practice than reading them to yourself. If someone reads the transcripts to you, make sure you see the pictures.

If you are using the print versions of the tests, listen to each audio track only one time. As in the real test, you may take notes while you listen and use your notes to help you answer the questions.

Answers

An Answers section for each test in this book is provided at the end of the test.

For the Reading and Listening sections, Answer Keys are provided.

For the Speaking and Writing sections, there is no single correct answer for each question. The Answers section has descriptions of what you need to do to get a high score. You can also evaluate your responses using the scoring rubrics provided in Appendix A.

In the Speaking section, if you have recorded your responses on a recording device, you can compare them with the descriptions in the Answers section and with the rubrics.

If you are using the computerized tests, follow the on-screen instructions to see the Reading and Listening answers and the answer descriptions for Speaking and Writing.

Rubrics

Rubrics are used to guide raters in evaluating Speaking and Writing section responses. All TOEFL iBT® test rubrics can be found in Appendix A.

Speaking scores represent an overall judgment of how well a response communicates its intended message. **Delivery** and **language use** are two key categories that raters consider when scoring responses to all four of the Speaking questions. **Topic development** is a third key category. For the Independent Speaking question, topic development is characterized by the *fullness* of the content provided in the response as well as its overall *coherence*. Using memorized responses or examples is strongly discouraged and could lower your score. It is very easy for ETS raters to distinguish memorized responses from those that are natural and spontaneous. For Integrated Speaking questions, topic development is characterized by the *accuracy* and *completeness* of the content provided in the response as well as its overall *coherence*.

Writing scores also represent an overall judgment of how well a response communicates its intended message. The **quality of the writing** is a key characteristic that raters consider when scoring responses to the Integrated Writing question (question 1) and the Writing for an Academic Discussion question (question 2). For the Integrated Writing question, high-quality writing is characterized by appropriate and precise use of grammar and vocabulary. For the Writing for an Academic Discussion question, you should also make sure that your ideas are well-supported by reasons and examples and are expressed clearly. Since your response represents an online post, it does not need to be organized into separate paragraphs. However, your ideas need to be **well-connected, coherent, and clear.** If you use a lot of words and sentences that are not well-connected and do not support each other, you'll receive a low score. Do not try to add words to your response by using long memorized introductory or concluding phrases and sentences. They represent neither authentic writing nor the type of writing used in online discussions.

The **completeness and accuracy of the content** is a key characteristic of responses that raters consider when scoring responses to an Integrated Writing question. A complete and accurate response presents the relevant main points from both the lecture and the reading, demonstrates the relationship between each of these main points, includes supporting details, and does not include information from sources other than the lecture and the reading. For a Writing for an Academic Discussion question, **contribution to the discussion** is a very important criterion used to evaluate your response. The discussion includes a professor's question as well as posts by other students. Contributing to a discussion does not necessarily mean coming up with a lot of new ideas. One can also contribute to a discussion by agreeing or disagreeing with what someone else has already written and then explaining why in your own words. Make sure that you don't just repeat what someone else has written—use your own words, your own voice, and elaborate on the ideas in your own way.

More Official Resources

ETS has many official resources to help you prepare for the TOEFL iBT® test, including:

- *The Official Guide to the TOEFL® Test, Seventh Edition*
- *TOEFL® Practice Online*
- *"Inside the TOEFL® Test"* Video Series
- *TOEFL® Test Preparation: The Insider's Guide (MOOC)*
- *Official TOEFL iBT® Prep Course*

For information about these resources and more, and to register for the test, visit **www.ets.org/toefl.**

TOEFL iBT® Test 1

READING

In this section, you will be able to demonstrate your ability to understand academic passages in English. You will read and answer questions about **two passages**.

In the actual test, you will have 36 minutes total to read both passages and answer the questions. A clock will indicate how much time remains.

Some passages may include one or more notes explaining words or phrases. The words or phrases are marked with footnote numbers and the notes explaining them appear at the end of the passage.

Most questions are worth 1 point, but the last question for each passage is worth 2 points.

You may review and revise your answers in this section as long as time remains.

At the end of this practice test, you will find an answer key.

Directions: Read the passage. Then answer the questions. You have 18 minutes to answer the questions.

THE ARRIVAL OF PLANT LIFE IN HAWAII

When the Hawaiian Islands emerged from the sea as volcanoes, starting about five million years ago, they were far removed from other landmasses. Then, as blazing sunshine alternated with drenching rains, the harsh, barren surfaces of the black rocks slowly began to soften. Winds brought a variety of life-forms.

Spores light enough to float on the breezes were carried thousands of miles from more ancient lands and deposited at random across the bare mountain flanks. A few of these spores found a toehold on the dark, forbidding rocks and grew and began to work their transformation upon the land. Lichens were probably the first successful flora. These are not single individual plants; each one is a symbiotic combination of an alga and a fungus. The algae capture the Sun's energy by photosynthesis and store it in organic molecules. The fungi absorb moisture and mineral salts from the rocks, passing these on in waste products that nourish algae. It is significant that the earliest living things that built communities on these islands are examples of symbiosis, a phenomenon that depends upon the close cooperation of two or more forms of life and a principle that is very important in island communities.

Lichens helped to speed the decomposition of the hard rock surfaces, preparing a soft bed of soil that was abundantly supplied with minerals that had been carried in the molten rock from the bowels of Earth. Now, other forms of life could take hold: ferns and mosses (two of the most ancient types of land plants) that flourish even in rock crevices. These plants propagate by producing spores—tiny fertilized cells that contain all the instructions for making a new plant—but the spores are unprotected by any outer coating and carry no supply of nutrient. Vast numbers of them fall on the ground beneath the mother plants. Sometimes they are carried farther afield by water or by wind. But only those few spores that settle down in very favorable locations can start new life; the vast majority fall on barren ground. By force of sheer numbers, however, the mosses and ferns reached Hawaii, survived, and multiplied. Some species developed great size, becoming tree ferns that even now grow in the Hawaiian forests.

Many millions of years after ferns evolved (but long before the Hawaiian Islands were born from the sea), another kind of flora evolved on Earth: the seed-bearing plants. This was a wonderful biological invention. The seed has an outer coating that surrounds the genetic material of the new plant, and inside this covering is a concentrated supply of nutrients. Thus, the seed's chances of survival are greatly enhanced over those of the naked spore. One type of seed-bearing plant, the angiosperm, includes all forms of blooming vegetation. In the angiosperm the seeds are wrapped in an additional layer of covering. Some of these coats are hard—like the shell of a nut—for extra protection. Some are soft and tempting, like a peach or a cherry. In some angiosperms the seeds are equipped with gossamer wings, like the dandelion and milkweed seeds. These new characteristics offered better ways for the seeds to move to new habitats. They could travel through the air, float in water, and lie dormant for many months.

Plants with large, buoyant seeds—like coconuts—drift on ocean currents and are washed up on the shores. Remarkably resistant to the vicissitudes of ocean travel, they can survive prolonged immersion in salt water. When they come to rest on warm beaches and the conditions are favorable, the seed coats soften. Nourished by their imported supply of nutrients, the young plants push out their roots and establish their place in the sun.

By means of these seeds, plants spread more widely to new locations, even to isolated islands like the Hawaiian archipelago, which lies more than 2,000 miles west of California and 3,500 miles east of Japan. The seeds of grasses, flowers, and blooming trees made the long trips to these islands. (Grasses are simple forms of angiosperms that bear their encapsulated seeds on long stalks.) In a surprisingly short time, angiosperms filled many of the land areas on Hawaii that had been bare.

Directions: Now answer the questions.

PARAGRAPH 2

Spores light enough to float on the breezes were carried thousands of miles from more ancient lands and deposited **at random** across the bare mountain flanks. A few of these spores found a toehold on the dark, forbidding rocks and grew and began to work their transformation upon the land. Lichens were probably the first successful flora. These are not single individual plants; each one is a symbiotic combination of an alga and a fungus. The algae capture the Sun's energy by photosynthesis and store it in organic molecules. The fungi absorb moisture and mineral salts from the rocks, passing these on in waste products that nourish algae. **It is significant that the earliest living things that built communities on these islands are examples of symbiosis, a phenomenon that depends upon the close cooperation of two or more forms of life and a principle that is very important in island communities.**

1. The phrase "**at random**" in the passage is closest in meaning to
   (A) finally
   (B) over a long period of time
   (C) successfully
   (D) without a definite pattern

2. Which of the sentences below best expresses the essential information in the highlighted sentence in the passage? Incorrect choices change the meaning in important ways or leave out essential information.
   (A) Some of the earliest important examples of symbiosis—the close cooperation of two or more living things—occur in island communities.
   (B) Symbiosis—the close cooperation of pairs or small groups of living organisms—is especially important in these island environments.
   (C) The first organisms on these islands worked together closely in a relationship known as symbiosis, which is particularly important on islands.
   (D) It is significant to note that organisms in the beginning stages of the development of island life cannot survive without close cooperation.

3. It can be inferred from paragraph 2 that the fungi in lichens benefit from their symbiotic relationship with algae in what way?

(A) The algae help the fungi meet some of their energy needs.
(B) The algae protect the fungi from the Sun's radiation.
(C) The algae provide the fungi with greater space for absorbing water.
(D) The fungi produce less waste in the presence of algae.

P A R A G R A P H 3

Lichens helped to speed the decomposition of the hard rock surfaces, preparing a soft bed of soil that was abundantly supplied with minerals that had been carried in the molten rock from the bowels of Earth. Now, other forms of life could take hold: ferns and mosses (two of the most ancient types of land plants) that flourish even in rock crevices. These plants propagate by producing spores—tiny fertilized cells that contain all the instructions for making a new plant—but the spores are unprotected by any outer coating and carry no supply of nutrient. Vast numbers of them fall on the ground beneath the mother plants. Sometimes they are carried farther afield by water or by wind. But only those few spores that settle down in very favorable locations can start new life; the vast majority fall on barren ground. By force of sheer numbers, however, the mosses and ferns reached Hawaii, survived, and multiplied. Some species developed great size, becoming tree ferns that even now grow in the Hawaiian forests.

4. According to paragraph 3, what was the relationship between lichens and ferns in the development of plant life on Hawaii?

(A) Ferns were able to grow because lichens created suitable soil.
(B) The decomposition of ferns produced minerals that were used by lichens.
(C) Lichens and ferns competed to grow in the same rocky environments.
(D) Lichens and ferns were typically found together in volcanic areas.

P A R A G R A P H 4

Many millions of years after ferns evolved (but long before the Hawaiian Islands were born from the sea), another kind of flora evolved on Earth: the seed-bearing plants. This was a wonderful biological invention. The seed has an outer coating that surrounds the genetic material of the new plant, and inside this covering is a concentrated supply of nutrients. Thus, the seed's chances of survival are greatly enhanced over those of the naked spore. One type of seed-bearing plant, the angiosperm, includes all forms of blooming vegetation. In the angiosperm the seeds are wrapped in an additional layer of covering. Some of these coats are hard—like the shell of **a nut**—for extra protection. Some are soft and tempting, like **a peach** or **a cherry**. In some angiosperms the seeds are equipped with gossamer wings, like the dandelion and milkweed seeds. These new characteristics offered better ways for the seeds to move to new habitats. They could travel through the air, float in water, and lie **dormant** for many months.

5. Why does the author mention "**a nut**," "**a peach**," and "**a cherry**"?

(A) To indicate that some seeds are less likely to survive than others
(B) To point out that many angiosperms can be eaten
(C) To provide examples of blooming plants
(D) To illustrate the variety of coverings among angiosperm seeds

6. The word "**dormant**" in the passage is closest in meaning to

Ⓐ hidden
Ⓑ inactive
Ⓒ underground
Ⓓ preserved

7. According to paragraph 4, why do seeds have a greater chance of survival than spores do? To receive credit, you must select TWO answer choices.

☐ A Seeds need less water to grow into a mature plant than spores do.
☐ B Seeds do not need to rely on outside sources of nutrients.
☐ C Seeds are better protected from environmental dangers than spores are.
☐ D Seeds are heavier than spores and are therefore more likely to take root and grow.

PARAGRAPH 5

Plants with large, buoyant seeds—like coconuts—drift on ocean currents and are washed up on the shores. Remarkably resistant to the vicissitudes of ocean travel, they can survive prolonged immersion in salt water. When they come to rest on warm beaches and the conditions are favorable, the seed coats soften. Nourished by their imported supply of nutrients, the young plants push out their roots and establish their place in the sun.

8. According to paragraph 5, a major reason that coconuts can establish themselves in distant locations is that their seeds can

Ⓐ survive long exposure to heat on island beaches
Ⓑ float and survive for long periods in ocean water
Ⓒ use salt water for maintenance and growth
Ⓓ maintain hard, protective coats even after growing roots

   Lichens helped to speed the decomposition of the hard rock surfaces, preparing a soft bed of soil that was abundantly supplied with minerals that had been carried in the molten rock from the bowels of Earth. Now, other forms of life could take hold: ferns and mosses (two of the most ancient types of land plants) that flourish even in rock crevices. **(A)** These plants propagate by producing spores—tiny fertilized cells that contain all the instructions for making a new plant—but the spores are unprotected by any outer coating and carry no supply of nutrient. **(B)** Vast numbers of them fall on the ground beneath the mother plants. **(C)** Sometimes they are carried farther afield by water or by wind. **(D)** But only those few spores that settle down in very favorable locations can start new life; the vast majority fall on barren ground. By force of sheer numbers, however, the mosses and ferns reached Hawaii, survived, and multiplied. Some species developed great size, becoming tree ferns that even now grow in the Hawaiian forests.

9. Look at the part of the passage that is displayed above. The letters **(A)**, **(B)**, **(C)**, and **(D)** indicate where the following sentence could be added.

   So since the chances of survival for any individual spore are small, the plants have to produce many spores in order to reproduce.

   Where would the sentence best fit?
   - (A) Choice A
   - (B) Choice B
   - (C) Choice C
   - (D) Choice D

10. **Directions:** An introductory sentence for a brief summary of the passage is provided below. Complete the summary by selecting the THREE answer choices that express the most important ideas in the passage. Some sentences do not belong in the summary because they express ideas that are not presented in the passage or are minor ideas in the passage. **This question is worth 2 points.**

Write your answer choices in the spaces where they belong. You can either write the letter of your answer choice or you can copy the sentence.

> **After the formation of the Hawaiian Islands, much time passed before conditions were suitable for plant life.**
>
> ●
>
> ●
>
> ●

Answer Choices

[A] Algae are classified as symbiotic because they produce energy through the process of photosynthesis.

[B] The first successful plants on Hawaii were probably lichens, which consist of algae and fungi living in a symbiotic relationship.

[C] Lichens helped create favorable conditions for the growth of spore-producing plants such as ferns and mosses.

[D] Seed-bearing plants evolved much later than spore-producing plants, but both types of plants had evolved well before the formation of the Hawaiian Islands.

[E] Unlike spores, seeds must move to new habitats in order to have a strong chance of survival and growth.

[F] Seed-bearing plants arrived and spread quickly in Hawaii, thanks to characteristics that increased their seeds' ability to survive and to move to different areas.

Directions: Read the passage. Then answer the questions. You have 18 minutes on average to answer the questions.

THE IMPACT OF INDUSTRIALIZATION ON LABOR SYSTEMS

Industrialization during the eighteenth and nineteenth centuries was a complex process that consisted of many components. Three of these are important for the discussion of labor systems. One is the specialization of labor, giving each individual a specific task that can be done quickly and efficiently before passing on the product to the next individual for the next task. The second is the use of machines in the production of goods. Machines proved much faster, more powerful, and more efficient than humans or animals, who could not generate the sustained operation, the amount of force, or the accuracy of the new steam-driven engines. Finally, industrial work moved out of the home. This development had a major impact on women's relationship to labor during the nineteenth century. It also placed strain on men, now separated from their families for lengthy periods of time. Children, though sometimes able to work near relatives in the early days of the factories, also found their work-family relationship redefined by the movement of industrial work out of the home, and here the ultimate solution was to pull children out of the labor force altogether.

These three developments had huge implications. Growing specialization meant that most workers did not see a finished product. Their skill levels declined. While skilled workers remained essential, the typical factory hand was semiskilled. He or she required a few months of training to attain peak efficiency but, by the same token, could be relatively easily replaced. Job security and a sense of purpose in work both declined. Introduction of new technology had significant effects, beginning simply with priorities: machines became more important than ordinary workers to the production process. A French manufacturer in the 1830s regularly decorated the week's most productive machine with a garland of flowers; he offered nothing to the workers involved. Work became organized around technological requirements—and these frequently changed because of recurrent improvements and a demand for faster production. Finally, the gap between family and work meant that workers, already subjected to laboring in larger settings than they were accustomed to, had to deal with strangers. While camaraderie might develop, the social atmosphere of work was growing less familiar.

Industrialization did not take shape overnight, and its gradual unfolding may have helped some workers to adapt. In textiles, initially one of the key sectors to be mechanized, a process called proto-industrialization developed in the seventeenth to eighteenth centuries. In Europe and elsewhere, some manufacturing had long been accomplished by rural workers using fairly simple equipment in their homes. Merchants brought raw materials and orders for goods, then picked up the work when it was completed. The system was called the putting-out system. With proto-industrialization, these operations simply expanded and intensified. Far more workers came to be involved, particularly when population growth began to reduce the availability of agricultural land. Operations became somewhat more specialized, with a focus on spinning thread, weaving cloth, or carding wool. Most important, proto-industrialization gave workers experience in wage work and in working for someone else—a profit-minded someone else, based outside the village community. This was not industrial work, but it was a foretaste.

The initial move toward working permanently in places other than home occurred only when changes in rural production and urban migration as a result of overpopulation in the countryside created a class of people who had only their labor to sell in order to provide for their livelihood. As Europe's population almost doubled in the eighteenth century, the need for jobs off the land became desperate, leading to a willingness to accept unfamiliar work settings. The change in rural production occurred first in England and then spread to much of the rest of western Europe. In England, wealthy individuals began to fence off their land and purchase common lands from the villages. As fewer owners controlled more land, many villagers lost access to farm ownership. Many could not even work the land as occasional laborers or renters, since the new owners turned much of the land to raising sheep, a much less labor-intensive activity than farming. Thus numerous villagers had no place to go other than the cities, where some began to work in factories.

Directions: Now answer the questions.

PARAGRAPH 1

Industrialization during the eighteenth and nineteenth centuries was a complex process that consisted of many **components**. Three of these are important for the discussion of labor systems. One is the specialization of labor, giving each individual a specific task that can be done quickly and efficiently before passing on the product to the next individual for the next task. The second is the use of machines in the production of goods. Machines proved much faster, more powerful, and more efficient than humans or animals, who could not generate the sustained operation, the amount of force, or the accuracy of the new steam-driven engines. Finally, industrial work moved out of the home. This development had a major impact on women's relationship to labor during the nineteenth century. It also placed strain on men, now separated from their families for lengthy periods of time. **Children, though sometimes able to work near relatives in the early days of the factories, also found their work-family relationship redefined by the movement of industrial work out of the home, and here the ultimate solution was to pull children out of the labor force altogether.**

11. The word "**components**" in the passage is closest in meaning to
    - Ⓐ developments
    - Ⓑ variations
    - Ⓒ pieces
    - Ⓓ achievements

12. Which of the sentences below best expresses the essential information in the highlighted sentence in the passage? Incorrect choices change the meaning in important ways or leave out essential information.
    - Ⓐ Once industrial work moved out of the home, children could not work near their relatives and eventually lost interest in work.
    - Ⓑ Moving industrial work out of the home and into factories also changed children's relationship to family life and to work, which eventually led to children being removed from the labor force.
    - Ⓒ When industrial work moved out of the home, children's family relationships were sometimes redefined to allow them to live with relatives near the factories.
    - Ⓓ Children were unwilling to be pulled out of the labor force until industrial work moved out of the home.

Industrialization during the eighteenth and nineteenth centuries was a complex process that consisted of many components. Three of these are important for the discussion of labor systems. One is the specialization of labor, giving each individual a specific task that can be done quickly and efficiently before passing on the product to the next individual for the next task. The second is the use of machines in the production of goods. Machines proved much faster, more powerful, and more efficient than humans or animals, who could not generate the sustained operation, the amount of force, or the accuracy of the new steam-driven engines. Finally, industrial work moved out of the home. This development had a major impact on women's relationship to labor during the nineteenth century. It also placed strain on men, now separated from their families for lengthy periods of time. Children, though sometimes able to work near relatives in the early days of the factories, also found their work-family relationship redefined by the movement of industrial work out of the home, and here the ultimate solution was to pull children out of the labor force altogether.

These three developments had huge implications. Growing specialization meant that most workers did not see a finished product. Their skill levels declined. While skilled workers remained essential, the typical factory hand was semiskilled. He or she required a few months of training to attain peak efficiency but, by the same token, could be relatively easily replaced. Job security and a sense of purpose in work both declined. Introduction of new technology had significant effects, beginning simply with priorities: machines became more important than ordinary workers to the production process. A French manufacturer in the 1830s regularly decorated the week's most productive machine with a garland of flowers; he offered nothing to the workers involved. Work became organized around technological requirements—and these frequently changed because of recurrent improvements and a demand for faster production. Finally, the gap between family and work meant that workers, already subjected to laboring in larger settings than they were accustomed to, had to deal with strangers. While camaraderie might develop, the social atmosphere of work was growing less familiar.

13. Paragraphs 1 and 2 suggest that before industrialization, work was generally

    Ⓐ much more difficult both to find and to keep

    Ⓑ carried out with little concern for accuracy or efficiency

    Ⓒ performed almost entirely by the adult males in a family

    Ⓓ part of family life and shared by all family members

P
A
R
A
G
R
A
P
H

1
&
2

**P
A
R
A
G
R
A
P
H

2**

These three developments had huge implications. Growing specialization meant that most workers did not see a finished product. Their skill levels declined. While skilled workers remained essential, the typical factory hand was semiskilled. He or she required a few months of training to attain peak efficiency but, by the same token, could be relatively easily replaced. Job security and a sense of purpose in work both declined. Introduction of new technology had significant effects, beginning simply with priorities: machines became more important than ordinary workers to the production process. A French manufacturer in the 1830s regularly decorated the week's most productive machine with a garland of flowers; he offered nothing to the workers involved. Work became organized around technological requirements—and these frequently changed because of recurrent improvements and a demand for faster production. Finally, the gap between family and work meant that workers, already subjected to laboring in larger settings than they were accustomed to, had to deal with strangers. While camaraderie might develop, the social atmosphere of work was growing less familiar.

14. According to paragraph 2, which of the following was a consequence of the fact that factory workers did not have to be highly skilled?

Ⓐ Typical factory workers were semiskilled and then trained to become fully skilled.

Ⓑ Firing workers and replacing them with newly hired workers cost factory owners relatively little.

Ⓒ Workers were not always told the purpose of the tasks that they were assigned to do.

Ⓓ Individual workers were able to perform more than one kind of job in the production process.

15. In paragraph 2, why does the author mention the French manufacturer and his garlands?

Ⓐ To give an example of how some manufacturers fully participated in the production process

Ⓑ To illustrate the idea that machines came to be regarded as more important than workers

Ⓒ To demonstrate how some manufacturers effectively enforced goals for production

Ⓓ To suggest that French manufacturers were particularly advanced in their use of technology

Industrialization did not take shape overnight, and its gradual unfolding may have helped some workers to **adapt**. In textiles, initially one of the key sectors to be mechanized, a process called proto-industrialization developed in the seventeenth to eighteenth centuries. In Europe and elsewhere, some manufacturing had long been accomplished by rural workers using fairly simple equipment in their homes. Merchants brought raw materials and orders for goods, then picked up the work when it was completed. The system was called the putting-out system. With proto-industrialization, these operations simply expanded and intensified. Far more workers came to be involved, particularly when population growth began to reduce the availability of agricultural land. Operations became somewhat more specialized, with a focus on spinning thread, weaving cloth, or carding wool. Most important, proto-industrialization gave workers experience in wage work and in working for someone else—a profit-minded someone else, based outside the village community. This was not industrial work, but it was a foretaste.

16. The word "**adapt**" in the passage is closest in meaning to

  Ⓐ advance
  Ⓑ adjust
  Ⓒ survive
  Ⓓ plan ahead

17. It can be inferred from paragraph 3 that an important factor that contributed to the expansion of the putting-out system was

  Ⓐ the desire of workers to market their own goods
  Ⓑ an increase in the number of rural people who were unable to practice farming
  Ⓒ a sharp increase in the demand for textiles
  Ⓓ the large number of merchants who moved into village communities

The initial move toward working permanently in places other than home occurred only when changes in rural production and urban migration as a result of overpopulation in the countryside created a class of people who had only their labor to sell in order to provide for their livelihood. As Europe's population almost doubled in the eighteenth century, the need for jobs off the land became desperate, leading to a willingness to accept unfamiliar work settings. The change in rural production occurred first in England and then spread to much of the rest of western Europe. In England, wealthy individuals began to fence off their land and purchase common lands from the villages. **(A)** As fewer owners controlled more land, many villagers lost access to farm ownership. **(B)** Many could not even work the land as occasional laborers or renters, since the new owners turned much of the land to raising sheep, a much less labor-intensive activity than farming. **(C)** Thus, numerous villagers had no place to go other than the cities, where some began to work in factories. **(D)**

18. According to paragraph 4, all of the following contributed to the trend of laborers leaving their homes to work EXCEPT

  Ⓐ the shift from cultivating of crops to raising sheep
  Ⓑ the substantial growth in population
  Ⓒ the use of common lands for urban rather than rural purposes
  Ⓓ the loss of farm ownership by ordinary people

19. Look at the part of the passage that is displayed above. The letters **(A)**, **(B)**, **(C)**, and **(D)** indicate where the following sentence could be added.

But losing their family farms was not the only reason rural residents felt pressured to move to cities.

Where would the sentence best fit?

  Ⓐ Choice A
  Ⓑ Choice B
  Ⓒ Choice C
  Ⓓ Choice D

20. **Directions:** An introductory sentence for a brief summary of the passage is provided below. Complete the summary by selecting the THREE answer choices that express the most important ideas in the passage. Some sentences do not belong in the summary because they express ideas that are not presented in the passage or are minor ideas in the passage. **This question is worth 2 points.**

Write your answer choices in the spaces where they belong. You can either write the letter of your answer choice or you can copy the sentence.

> **Industrialization in Europe changed the nature of both work and family life.**
>
> ●
>
> ●
>
> ●

Answer Choices

A   The specialization of labor and the use of machines reduced the value of individual workers in the production process while speeding up production and increasing stress on workers.

B   Before industrialization, rural people sometimes manufactured goods in their homes for merchants, using raw materials supplied by the merchants.

C   People were initially reluctant to work in factories because they had no previous experience of having to work for wages.

D   Although full industrialization came early to the textile profession, it took a longer time to spread throughout the economy, partly because it was difficult to train enough workers to use the new machines.

E   The loss of farmworkers to cities and factory jobs at a time of growing demand for wool from manufacturers led many landowners to switch from farming to less labor-intensive sheep raising.

F   Overpopulation in the countryside and changes in the ownership and use of land made the factory system possible by forcing villagers to seek new kinds of work in cities.

LISTENING

In this section, you will be able to demonstrate your ability to understand conversations and lectures in English.

In the actual test, the section is divided into two separately timed parts. You will hear each conversation or lecture only one time. A clock will indicate how much time remains. The clock will count down only while you are answering questions, not while you are listening. You may take up to 16.5 minutes to answer the questions.

In this practice test, there is no time limit for answering questions.

You may take notes while you listen. You may use your notes to help you answer the questions. Your notes will not be scored.

Answer the questions based on what is stated or implied by the speakers.

In some questions, you will see this icon: . This means that you will hear, but not see, part of the question.

Answer each question before moving on. Do not return to previous questions.

At the end of this practice test, you will find an answer key.

Directions: Listen to Track 1.

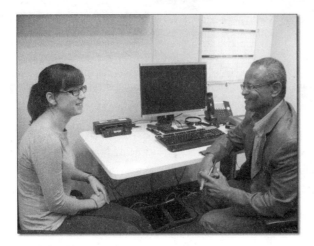

Directions: Now answer the questions.

1. Why does the woman go to see the professor?

   Ⓐ To get advice on the topic of a term paper
   Ⓑ To discuss different types of food packaging
   Ⓒ To find out if the university will offer courses in food packaging
   Ⓓ To ask about jobs in the food industry

2. Why does the professor mention his previous jobs?

   Ⓐ To explain why the woman should study physics, math, and chemistry
   Ⓑ To recommend that the woman get a summer job on a fishing boat
   Ⓒ To point out that industry jobs can lead to a teaching career
   Ⓓ To confirm an assumption the woman made about finding a job

3. The woman mentions a research study of milk packaging. What was the finding of the study?

   Ⓐ Plastic containers may change the flavor of milk.
   Ⓑ Light may negatively affect the quality of milk.
   Ⓒ People prefer to buy milk in see-through containers.
   Ⓓ Opaque containers are effective in protecting milk from bacteria.

4. What does the professor imply about the dairy in Chelsea?

   Ⓐ It has plans to start bottling milk in opaque containers.
   Ⓑ Some of its employees attended the university.
   Ⓒ Employees there might be able to provide useful information.
   Ⓓ He worked there before joining the university faculty.

5. *Listen again to part of the conversation by playing Track 2.* *Then answer the question.*

    What does the woman mean when she says this?

    (A) She has read conflicting information.
    (B) She has been too busy to begin her research.
    (C) The topic she is researching is too broad.
    (D) The information she needs is not available.

Directions: Listen to Track 3.

Environmental Science

Directions: Now answer the questions.

6. What is the lecture mainly about?

　Ⓐ Factors involved in the increased growth of shrubs in Arctic Alaska

　Ⓑ How temperature increases might be affecting the permafrost in Arctic Alaska

　Ⓒ Why nutrient production of microbes in the soil in Arctic Alaska is declining

　Ⓓ Reasons that grasslands are turning into tundra in Arctic Alaska

7. According to the professor, what are two features of shrubs that allow them to grow well in Arctic regions? *Select 2 answers.*

　Ⓐ They have roots that can penetrate permafrost.

　Ⓑ Their height allows them to absorb more sunlight.

　Ⓒ They absorb nutrients from the soil efficiently.

　Ⓓ They have a shallow root system.

8. What is one reason for the increase in shrub growth in Arctic Alaska?

　Ⓐ Decreases in grass and moss growth have altered the balance of nutrients in the soil.

　Ⓑ Increases in ground temperature have led to increased microbial activity.

　Ⓒ Increases in average winter temperatures have made permafrost permeable to water.

　Ⓓ Increases in snowfall have provided more water for shrubs.

9. Why are nutrients in the soil NOT carried away by spring runoff?

　Ⓐ The roots of shrubs prevent nutrient-filled soil from being washed away.

　Ⓑ Most nutrients are not in the area of the soil most affected by runoff.

　Ⓒ Most nutrients remain frozen in the permafrost when spring runoff is at its peak.

　Ⓓ Most nutrients have been absorbed by vegetation before the runoff period begins.

10. Why does the professor mention shrub expansion into other environments, such as semiarid grasslands?

    (A) To suggest that new shrubland may not convert back to tundra

    (B) To explain how shrubland can expand in a warm climate

    (C) To cite a similarity between the types of shrubs in semiarid grassland and tundra environments

    (D) To explain how a biological loop can cause shrub expansion

11. *Listen to Track 4 to answer the question.*

    What does the professor imply when she says this?

    (A) The information she gave is important enough to be repeated.

    (B) Climate scientists are asking the wrong questions.

    (C) The phenomenon she is describing is more complex than it appears.

    (D) Students should be able to solve the puzzle easily.

Directions: Listen to Track 5.

Directions: Now answer the questions.

12. What are the speakers mainly discussing?

    Ⓐ A book that the man is trying to find in the library

    Ⓑ A book that the man already returned to the library

    Ⓒ A book that the man is using to write his senior thesis

    Ⓓ A book that the man lent to his sociology professor

13. What does the woman offer to do for the man?

    Ⓐ Let the man know when a book he needs is returned to the library

    Ⓑ Photocopy a chapter of a book for him

    Ⓒ Ask a professor to return a book the man needs

    Ⓓ Find a copy of a book for him at another library

14. What is the woman trying to explain when she mentions students who have lost their borrowing privileges?

    Ⓐ Why the man should not photocopy part of the book

    Ⓑ The reasons for one of the library's policies

    Ⓒ What will happen if the man does not return the book

    Ⓓ The reason the man has to fill out a form

15. How does the man probably feel at the end of the conversation?

    Ⓐ Annoyed that he has to pay a fine on the book

    Ⓑ Upset that he will lose his library privileges

    Ⓒ Glad that he can keep the book for two more weeks

    Ⓓ Appreciative that the woman is helping him

16. *Listen again to part of the conversation by playing Track 6.* *Then answer the question.*

   Why does the woman say this?

   (A) To make sure she understands what the man's problem is
   (B) To encourage the man to return the book to the library soon
   (C) To check whether the man has already returned the book
   (D) To explain to the man a change in the library's policies

Directions: Listen to Track 7.

Directions: Now answer the questions.

17. What is the lecture mainly about?

    Ⓐ Reasons that geologists study lake fossils in desert regions
    Ⓑ A comparison of ancient and present-day lakes in desert environments
    Ⓒ Geological evidence for the formation of ancient sand dunes
    Ⓓ A hypothesis for how some ancient desert lakes formed

18. What is the professor's opinion about the conclusions of the recent study of the limestone formations in the Empty Quarter?

    Ⓐ They have changed the way geologists study desert environments.
    Ⓑ They contradict findings about similar desert lakes.
    Ⓒ They explain the causes of monsoons in the desert.
    Ⓓ They need to be confirmed by additional studies.

19. According to the professor, what feature of the sand dunes made the formation of the lakes possible?

    Ⓐ The degree of slope of the sides of the dunes
    Ⓑ The presence of clay and silt particles in the dunes
    Ⓒ The position of the dunes relative to the wind and rain
    Ⓓ The narrowness of the valleys between the dunes

20. How is it possible to determine in which rainy period a lake was formed?
    Select 2 answers.

    Ⓐ By examining the location of the lake bed
    Ⓑ By measuring the amount of sand covering the lake bed
    Ⓒ By examining the color of the limestone formation
    Ⓓ By identifying the types of fossils found in the limestone

21. What does the professor imply about the lack of water buffalo and hippopotamus fossils in the more recent lakes?

    Ⓐ The level of water in the lakes was not sufficient for these animals.
    Ⓑ The bottoms of the lakes were too sandy for these animals to stand in.
    Ⓒ The location of the lakes made them too difficult for these animals to reach.
    Ⓓ The vegetation near the lakes did not attract these animals.

22. What possible explanation does the professor give for the apparent absence of fish in the most ancient lakes?

    Ⓐ The presence of predators
    Ⓑ Lack of appropriate food
    Ⓒ Lack of suitable water
    Ⓓ Extreme desert temperatures

Directions: Listen to Track 8.

Linguistics

Directions: Now answer the questions.

23. What does the professor mainly discuss?

    (A) The findings of a study on prairie dog communication

    (B) The way that mammals learn to make warning cries

    (C) Features that distinguish language from animal communication systems

    (D) Various types of signals used by animals to communicate with each other

24. Why does the student mention a research project she studied in a biology class?

    (A) To point out similarities in the behavior of rodents and monkeys

    (B) To explain how she first became interested in animal communication

    (C) To introduce an instance of an animal species that might have language

    (D) To show how she applied her knowledge of linguistics in another course

25. What is the professor's opinion of a recent study of prairie dogs?

   Ⓐ She finds the study interesting but is not convinced that prairie dogs can communicate.
   Ⓑ She thinks that some claims made by the researchers are not supported by their findings.
   Ⓒ She sees the study as proof that mammals other than humans possess a form of language.
   Ⓓ She thinks the researchers misinterpreted the high-pitched barks as warning signals.

26. What does the professor say about the individual units that make up human languages?

   Ⓐ They can be combined to create an infinite number of new messages.
   Ⓑ They are not capable of being reproduced by members of any other species.
   Ⓒ They function in the same way as the signals all animals use to communicate.
   Ⓓ They are acquired instinctively without having to be learned.

27. The professor uses the sentence, "Move the large coyote fast," in order to illustrate two features of language. What are they? *Select 2 answers.*

   A   Displacement
   B   Learnability
   C   Productivity
   D   Discreteness

28. *Listen again to part of the lecture by playing Track 9.* 🎧 *Then answer the question.*

   Why does the professor say this?

   Ⓐ To see if anyone knows the answer to the student's question
   Ⓑ To suggest that the student is using the wrong terminology
   Ⓒ To express frustration because she has already answered a similar question
   Ⓓ To determine whether she has been speaking clearly enough

SPEAKING

In this section, you will be able to demonstrate your ability to speak about a variety of topics.

In the actual test, the Speaking section will last approximately 16 minutes. You will answer four questions by speaking into the microphone. You may take notes while you listen. You may use your notes to help you answer the questions. Your notes will not be scored. For each question, you will have time to prepare before giving your response. You should answer the questions as completely as possible in the time allowed.

For this practice test, you may want to use a personal recording device to record and play back your responses.

For each question, play the audio track listed and follow the directions to complete the task.

At the end of this practice test, you will find important points for each question, sample responses, and comments on those responses by official raters.

1. You will now give your opinion about a familiar topic. After you hear the question, you should give yourself 15 seconds to prepare and 45 seconds to speak.

Listen to Track 10.

> Some people think that family members are the most important influence on young adults. Others believe that friends are the most important influence. Which do you agree with? Explain why.
>
> **Preparation Time: 15 seconds**
> **Response Time: 45 seconds**

2. Now you will read a passage about a campus situation and then listen to a conversation about the same topic. You will then answer a question, using information from both the reading passage and the conversation. You should give yourself 30 seconds to prepare and 60 seconds to speak.

Listen to Track 11.

Reading Time: 45 seconds

Required Work Experience

The Business Studies Department at State University will now require all students enrolled in its program to complete one semester of work experience in a local corporation or small business. It is felt that students will benefit from this work experience by developing leadership and organizational skills that would not normally be learned in a classroom or campus setting. Furthermore, the relationships that students establish with the company that they work for may help them to secure permanent employment with that company once they have completed the program and graduated.

Listen to Track 12.

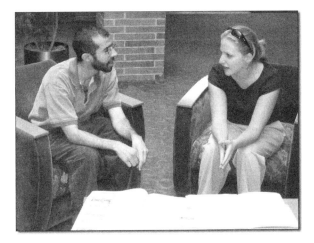

> The woman expresses her opinion of the university's new policy. State her opinion and explain the reasons she gives for holding that opinion.
>
> | Preparation Time: 30 seconds |
> |:---:|
> | Response Time: 60 seconds |

3. Now you will read a passage about an academic subject and then listen to a lecture on the same topic. You will then answer a question, using information from both the reading passage and the lecture. You should give yourself 30 seconds to prepare and 60 seconds to speak.

Listen to Track 13.

Reading Time: 50 seconds

> ### The Establishing Shot
>
> Film directors use different types of camera shots for specific purposes. An establishing shot is an image shown briefly at the beginning of a scene, usually taken from far away, that is used to provide context for the rest of the scene. One purpose of the establishing shot is to communicate background information to the viewer, such as the setting—where and when the rest of the scene will occur. It also establishes the mood or feeling of the scene. Due to the context that the establishing shot provides, the characters and events that are shown next are better understood by the viewer.

Listen to Track 14.

Using the professor's example, explain what an establishing shot is and how it is used.

Preparation Time: 30 seconds
Response Time: 60 seconds

4. Now you will listen to a lecture. You will then be asked to summarize the lecture. You should give yourself 20 seconds to prepare and 60 seconds to speak.

Listen to Track 15.

Using points from the lecture, explain how the passion plant and the potato plant defend themselves from insects.

Preparation Time: 20 seconds
Response Time: 60 seconds

WRITING

In this section, you will be able to demonstrate your ability to use writing to communicate in an academic environment. There will be two writing tasks.

At the end of this practice test, you will find topic notes for each question.

Turn the page to see the directions for the first writing task.

Writing Based on Reading and Listening

For this task, you will read a passage about an academic topic. Then you will listen to a lecture about the same topic. You may take notes while you listen.

In your response, provide a detailed summary of the lecture and explain how the lecture relates to the reading passage.

In the actual test, you will have 3 minutes to read the passage and 20 minutes to write your response. While you write, you will be able to see the reading passage. If you finish your response before time is up, you may go on to the second writing task.

Reading Time: 3 minutes

Archaeologists have recently found a fossil of a 150-million-year-old mammal known as *Repenomamus robustus* (*R. robustus*). Interestingly, the mammal's stomach contained the remains of a psittacosaur dinosaur. Some researchers have therefore suggested that *R. robustus* was an active hunter of dinosaurs. However, a closer analysis has made the hypothesis that *R. robustus* was an active hunter unlikely. It was probably just a scavenger that sometimes fed on dinosaur eggs containing unhatched dinosaurs.

First, *R. robustus*, like most mammals living 150 million years ago, was small—only about the size of a domestic cat. It was much smaller than psittacosaurs, which were almost two meters tall when full grown. Given this size difference, it is unlikely that *R. robustus* would have been able to successfully hunt psittacosaurs or similar dinosaurs.

Second, the legs of *R. robustus* appear much more suited for scavenging than hunting: they were short and positioned somewhat to the side rather than directly underneath the animal. These features suggest that *R. robustus* did not chase after prey. Psittacosaurs—the type of dinosaur found in the stomach of *R. robustus*—were fast moving. It is unlikely that they would have been caught by such short-legged animals.

Third, the dinosaur bones inside the stomach of the *R. robustus* provide no evidence to support the idea that the dinosaur had been actively hunted. When an animal has been hunted and eaten by another animal, there are usually teeth marks on the bones of the animal that was eaten. But the bones of the psittacosaur inside the *R. robustus* stomach do not have teeth marks. This suggests that *R. robustus* found an unguarded dinosaur nest with eggs and simply swallowed an egg with the small psittacosaur still inside the eggshell.

Listen to Track 16.

Directions: You have 20 minutes to plan and write your response. Your response will be judged on the basis of the quality of your writing and on how well your response presents the points in the lecture and their relationship to the reading passage. Typically, an effective response will contain a minimum of 150 words.

Listen to Track 17.

Response Time: 20 minutes

Question 1

Summarize the points made in the lecture, being sure to explain how they respond to the specific points made in the reading passage.

_____

_____

_____

_____

_____

_____

_____

_____

_____

_____

_____

_____

_____

_____

_____

_____

_____

_____

_____

Writing for an Academic Discussion

For this task, you will read an online discussion. A professor has posted a question about a topic, and some classmates have responded with their ideas.

In the actual test, you will have 10 minutes to write a response that contributes to the discussion.

Question 2

Your professor is teaching a class on environmental policy. Write a post responding to the professor's question.

In your response, you should do the following.

- Express and support your opinion.
- Make a contribution to the discussion in your own words.

An effective response will contain at least 100 words.

Dr. Diaz

Many common agricultural practices today are harmful to the environment. But while these practices cause ecological damage, many people argue that they are necessary to feed the world's growing population. Governments in some countries have nevertheless passed laws restricting agricultural practices known to cause ecological harm. Do you agree that governments should pass laws to limit or ban farming practices that may harm the environment? Why or why not?

Claire

I agree that governments should pass laws to protect the environment from harm caused by agriculture. Whether it's the use of pesticides that harm important insects—for example, pollinators such as bees—or the clearing of forest wildlife habitats to make way for farmlands, any activity that harms the environment should be restricted.

Paul

We must be careful about banning practices that farmers rely on to produce food for their communities and the world. Using less harmful practices is obviously preferable, but only if we can maintain our food supply. Feeding the human population should be the priority. We should ban a particular agricultural practice only if it is not necessary to produce crops.

Response Time: 10 minutes

ANSWERS

Reading Section

1. D
2. C
3. A
4. A
5. D
6. B
7. B, C
8. B
9. B
10. B, C, F

11. C
12. B
13. D
14. B
15. B
16. B
17. B
18. C
19. B
20. A, B, F

Listening Section

1.	A	15.	D
2.	D	16.	A
3.	B	17.	D
4.	C	18.	D
5.	C	19.	B
6.	A	20.	A, D
7.	C, D	21.	A
8.	B	22.	C
9.	B	23.	C
10.	A	24.	C
11.	C	25.	B
12.	C	26.	A
13.	B	27.	C, D
14.	C	28.	B

Speaking Section

Prompts, Important Points, and Sample Responses with Rater Comments

Use the sample Independent and Integrated Speaking Rubrics in Appendix A to see how responses are scored. The raters who listen to your responses will analyze them in three general categories. These categories are delivery, language use, and topic development. All three categories have equal importance.

This section includes important points that should be covered when answering each question. All of these points must be present in a response in order for it to receive the highest score in the Topic Development category. These important points are guides to the kind of information raters expect to hear in a high-level response.

This section also refers to sample responses, which can be found on the audio tracks. Some responses were scored at the highest level, while others were not. The responses are followed by comments from certified ETS raters.

1: Paired Choice

Prompt

Some people think that family members are the most important influence on young adults. Others believe that friends are the most important influence. Which do you agree with? Explain why.

Important Points

In this question, you need to say whether you think family members or friends are the most important influence on young adults. Then you must explain why this is your preference. You should try to explain it fully; you should not just give a list of reasons. Instead, you should try to pick one or two reasons and explain your opinion in more detail. Add examples when appropriate. If you think family members are the most important influence, for example, you could explain by discussing reasons such as the amount of time young adults spend with family versus friends, which gives family members more opportunities to influence them.

Sometimes test takers would like to choose both options, saying, for example, that one might be true in some circumstances and the other might be true in different circumstances. This approach is acceptable; however, it can be difficult to fully explain your opinion if you choose both options, and it might lower your score if you don't finish or don't sufficiently support both choices during your response time. Only very fluent speakers should use the approach of choosing both options.

High-Level Response:
Listen to Track 18.
Rater Comments

The speaker states her view that both family members and friends influence young adults depending on the stage of life they're in, and then supports this view fully by describing the stages of life when family and when friends have an influence. She provides examples of when family members are more influential and when friends are, and discusses the importance of friends when you're separated from your family, such as when you're away at college. Her pronunciation is clear and she does not need to pause to think of how to say her ideas in English. Sometimes her vocabulary choices are not perfect—for example, she says *"how you wear"* instead of "how you dress," but these errors are minor and the listener can still easily understand her ideas.

Low-Level Response:
Listen to Track 19.
Rater Comments

The speaker's pronunciation of individual words is fairly clear, but he pauses and hesitates often to think of the next word to say. His hesitations cause him to run out of time before he can finish what he would like to say. This shows that he still needs to improve his fluency in English. Also, while he states which view he agrees with—that friends are the most important influence—he does not develop this idea with much detail. He says *"they spend much of their time with their friends,"* but he doesn't explain why this causes friends to have more influence, possibly because he lacks the vocabulary to talk more about it. Instead, he

simply repeats that friends are the most important influence.

2: Fit and Explain
Prompt

The woman expresses her opinion of the university's new policy. State her opinion and explain the reasons she gives for holding that opinion.

Important Points

When answering this question, it is important to include information from both the reading passage and the conversation between students. You should indicate that the woman disagrees with the Business Studies Department's new policy, which requires students in the Business Studies Department to spend one semester working in a local corporation or small business. You should also explain the two reasons she gives for disagreeing with this policy: she doesn't think students will actually develop leadership and/or organizational skills at the jobs they would have to work, since they would be doing basic tasks that won't be meaningful; and she doesn't think that this experience will help students find permanent jobs in the future, since many other universities have similar programs and so there will be too much competition with other students.

High-Level Response:
Listen to Track 20.
Rater Comments

This speaker clearly states the woman's opinion of the policy (*"The woman believe that this policy is not a positive move"*), a brief explanation of the policy, and the two reasons why she disagrees with the policy. The speaker makes a few very minor errors (*"the woman believe"; "the abundance of university who"; "offered to student"*), but these do not prevent listeners from understanding what the speaker is communicating. The speaker has very clear pronunciation and speaks at an even pace, making use of appropriate pauses and intonation. He is also able to use advanced vocabulary and grammatical structures effectively (*"she believes that job that would be offered to student would be really low-level and low-responsibility jobs which will not allow them to grow into and develop the qualities of leadership"; "contrary to what the policy says").*

Low-Level Response:
Listen to Track 21. 🎧
Rater Comments

This speaker addresses the question but does not provide a complete answer, and her response is overall somewhat difficult to follow. She states the woman's opinion but does not explain what the woman is disagreeing with, since she only makes a vague reference to the policy *"Girl says, say, say that uh recruiting proposed by university is not a good uh, um, uh, a good statement. . . ."* While she does use some sophisticated vocabulary (*"particular skills," "permanent employment"*), she does not fully explain her ideas. For example, when she says, *"he didn't give any particular skills in leadership or organization,"* she does not make it clear that she is talking about the woman's brother or his job experience and does not say how that relates to the new policy. Her pronunciation is clear, but her control of grammar is weak, which makes it difficult to understand her meaning: *"when the student um attain graduation, have to compete with older students . . . so there's no any. . . ."*

3: General/Specific
Prompt

Using the professor's example, explain what an establishing shot is and how it is used.

Important Points

In this item, you should explain that in a movie or film, an establishing shot is used at the beginning of a scene to provide context, such as place, time, and mood. The shot in the professor's example showed a detective's office in a city in the past (1940s), so the viewer knows that the rest of the scene takes place in the city in the 1940s. The shot in the example is filmed with darkness, rain, and shadows that give it a gloomy or mysterious feeling, so the viewer knows that the events which follow will be dark and mysterious. A high-level response will communicate in a coherent and organized way the purpose of the establishing shot (to let viewers know where and when the scene is taking place and to set a mood) and explain how the establishing shot in the professor's example carries out this purpose.

High-Level Response:
Listen to Track 22. 🎧
Rater Comments

The speaker clearly describes what an establishing shot is: *"shown at the beginning of the movie, it gives like a sense of what the feeling is like in the movie."* The professor's example is described accurately, with all important points included and connected clearly to the concept (*"it describes the movie beforehand, so he could tell that the movie was in the 1940s"*). The speaker uses sophisticated language fluently (*"by that he could tell that the movie was going to have a dark setting"*). The speaker pauses several times to organize her thoughts, but the pauses are located at natural places and do not seriously interrupt the response. Although the speaker is rushed at the end, she remains understandable and successfully includes all points.

Low-Level Response:
Listen to Track 23. 🎧
Rater Comments

The speaker does manage to express the central idea of the establishing shot and partially describe the shot used in the professor's example. However, he does not have very strong control of grammar or vocabulary, often resulting in vague ideas (*"gives several, some examples using, eh, lights, or, or in an office, if a, it's a very old office"*) or confusing statements (*"that the director's, like, that the people concern about it"*). Although the speaker connects the example to the concept, important parts of the example are left out (that the scene gave a gloomy and mysterious feeling, that it showed a city). The speaker's unclear pronunciation also requires the listener to work hard to understand his speech. Several important words cannot be understood at all, leaving the listener to guess at their meaning.

4: Summary

Prompt

Using points from the lecture, explain how the passion plant and the potato plant defend themselves from insects.

Important Points

For this task, you should use the examples from the lecture to explain how plants defend themselves from insects. You should explain that plants can use both physical and chemical defenses. The passion plant uses a physical defense. This plant has spiky hairs on its leaves that prevent insects from landing on the plant and eating the leaves. The potato plant, on the other hand uses a chemical defense. This plant releases a chemical through its leaves when an insect eats it. The chemical makes the insect feel full, so it stops eating the plant.

High-Level Response:
Listen to Track 24.
Rater Comments

The speaker gives a well-organized, clear response and is able to summarize all of the important information from the lecture. He jumps immediately into a summary of the examples, but he shows a clear connection between the two examples to the main concept. Consider his sentence: *"On the other side, potato plants uses chemical features to prevent being eaten by insects."* Though there are some grammatical errors in this sentence, he uses a transitional phrase *"on the other side,"* and he stresses the word *"chemical"* to emphasize the contrast between the two examples. He does speak very quickly at times, but he shows that he is able to communicate without too many pauses to search for words. He makes occasional pronunciation errors but has the ability to correct himself. For instance, he describes the chemical defenses that the potato plant uses *"to prevent being eaten."* At first, "being eaten" is pronounced incorrectly, but he quickly corrects his pronunciation and continues with the response.

Mid-Level Response:
Listen to Track 25.
Rater Comments

This speaker is able to convey all of the important points from the lecture, but her response takes some effort to understand. She pauses frequently, searching for words. She clearly understood and is able to explain both examples, but her vocabulary is sometimes vague (*"the potato plant has some, like, chemical things"*) or inaccurate. For instance, in the first point about the passion plant, she describes the spikes *"which prevent him from the insect"* instead of *"which protect it from the insect."* Her pronunciation is mostly easy to understand, but she does make a few mistakes that confuse her meaning. For example, while describing the chemical defenses of the potato plant, she says that *"the insect doesn't feel hungry,"* but her pronunciation of "hungry" sounds more like "angry."

Writing Section

Prompts, Topic Notes, and Sample Responses with Rater Comments

Use the sample Integrated Writing and Writing for an Academic Discussion Rubrics in Appendix A to see how responses are scored.

This section includes topic notes that are guides to the kind of information raters expect to read in a high-level response.

This section also refers to sample responses. These responses were scored at the highest level.

The responses are followed by comments from certified ETS raters.

Question 1
Prompt

Summarize the points made in the lecture, being sure to explain how they respond to the specific points made in the reading passage.

Topic Notes

The reading discusses three reasons to believe that a small mammal, R. robustus, could not have been an active hunter (perhaps it was a scavenger that sometimes fed on unhatched eggs of the psitticosaur dinosaur), but the lecturer presents reasons why each of these three reasons are unconvincing.

Responses with scores of 4 and 5 typically discuss all three points in the table with good accuracy and level of detail.

Point made in the reading	Corresponding point from the lecture
R. robustus was smaller than psitticosaurs so given their size, R. robustus was not likely to be a successful hunter of psitticosaurs or similar dinosaurs.	R. robustus was too small to hunt adult psitticosaurs, but it could have hunted baby psitticosaurs or other similarly sized dinosaurs—prey that was smaller than or had less mass than R. robustus.
R. robustus would not have been able to move fast enough to catch prey because it had short legs positioned to the side.	There is a modern day mammal, the Tasmanian Devil, that has the same leg features as R. robustus but can achieve speeds fast enough to make it an effective predator.
The lack of teeth marks on the bones found in the stomach of R. robustus indicates it was not an active hunter (and that it probably just swallowed a dinosaur egg whole).	R. robustus probably swallowed its prey whole or in large pieces; R. robustus had no marks on its back teeth, which were probably not used for chewing.

Sample Response

The lecture completely refutes the reading passage. The professor use the following points to indicate that R. robustus could have been actively hunting baby psittacosaur and similar sized baby dinosaurs.

First, although R. robustus was small, it was much bigger than baby psittacosaurs dinosaur, more than twice in size. This means R. robustus was big enough to hunt baby psittacosaurs.

Second, even though R. robustus had short legs and they were positioned somewhat to the side, these features are not sufficient indications that R. robustus could not run as fast enough to be successful predator. The professor pointed out that Tasmanian Devil, a morden-day successful predator whose legs share similar "disadvantages", can run as fast as 50 KM/H and is an active and very successful hunter today. So its possible R. robustus could run just as fast and therefore be as successful in hunting.

Last but not the least, lack of teeth marks on the dinosaur bones is not enough evidence to support conclusion that the dinosaur was not actively hunted. Studies of fossil records show that though R. robustus had powerful jaws but also, it did not use its back-teeth for chewing because its back teeth had no wear and tear. So we can also guess that R. robustus could had swallowed the baby dinosaur whole and therefore not leaving any teeth marks.

Rater Comments

This response earns a score of 5. Grammatical errors are few and minor. "This response clearly conveys the three main points from the lecture, includes the important supporting details, and shows how those points challenge the information from the three points in the reading passage. Note that the response does not discuss the dinosaur egg to get the point across as to why the bones of the prey did not contain teeth marks; although this would have been helpful, it could be argued that this is not essential information for conveying the point clearly. Therefore, even though this last sentence is not quite as clear as the rest of this response, holistically, it still conveys all of the relevant information with sufficient clarity to rate a score of 5.

Question 2

Prompt

Refer to page 45 to review the Writing for an Academic Discussion question.

Topic Notes

To earn a top score, you should develop a response that contributes to the discussion about the idea of governments regulating farming practices that may harm the environment. An effective response will contain at least 100 words.

One discussion participant argues that any activity that harms the environment should be restricted. Another discussion participant mostly disagrees, arguing that producing sufficient amounts of food is the top priority and that governments should only ban harmful agricultural practices that could be replaced with less harmful practices. In your response, you might seize on the ideas already stated and develop them in greater detail or introduce entirely new ideas. You may argue, for example, that in order to feed the growing human population, we may need to continue some undesirable agricultural practices while scientists work on developing less harmful alternatives. You may add an original argument, such as recommending that, rather than governments, farmers themselves develop their own regulating council to ensure best practices are followed for both the environment and food production.

You should make sure that your ideas are well-supported by reasons and examples and are expressed clearly. Since your response represents an online post, it does not need to be organized into separate paragraphs. However, your ideas need to be well-connected, coherent, and clear. Your response is scored using the Writing for an Academic Discussion rubric (see Appendix A).

Sample Response

In my opinion, any practice that harms the environment should not be continued. It is high time that we realize the damage we have caused to the enviroment. As humans our primary responsibility should be to take care of the earth that we walk on. Commercial agriculture has destroyed the soil, air, water, space to a great extent. Due to current agricultural practices, food is getting less nutritious every day. The nutrition provided by eating an orange 100 years ago is way higher than what it is now. Which means we need to eat more to get the same amount of nutrition. Also the soil fertility is going down day by day which means soil is getting converted to sand i.e. organic matter is getting reduced. It is actually more profitable and feeds humanity better if we explore sustainable agricultural practices. This will help our future generations to have food or else there will be food crisis and wars caused by lack of food.

Rater Comments

This is a 5-level response. The writer provides a very clearly expressed, relevant contribution to the discussion and displays consistently high-level facility in the use of language. The writer largely agrees with Claire that any activity—agricultural or otherwise—that harms the environment should be discontinued, but the writer expands on this idea with an original, nuanced argument supported by plenty of detail. The writer points out ways in which harming the environment through current agricultural practices is actually threatening our food supply, nutrition, and soil, so that exploring sustainable agricultural practices actually "feeds humanity better." The writer makes effective use of a variety of grammatical structures and uses precise, idiomatic language throughout, such as "it is high time," "to a great extent," "organic matter," and "sustainable agricultural practices." There are almost no grammatical or lexical errors in the response, other than a few very minor ones that would be expected from a competent writer when writing under timed conditions.

TOEFL iBT® Test 2

READING

In this section, you will be able to demonstrate your ability to understand academic passages in English. You will read and answer questions about **two passages**.

In the actual test, you will have 36 minutes total to read both passages and answer the questions. A clock will indicate how much time remains.

Some passages may include one or more notes explaining words or phrases. The words or phrases are marked with footnote numbers, and the notes explaining them appear at the end of the passage.

Most questions are worth 1 point, but the last question for each passage is worth 2 points.

You may review and revise your answers in this section as long as time remains.

At the end of this practice test, you will find an answer key.

Directions: Read the passage. Then answer the questions. You have 18 minutes to answer the questions.

CHINESE POTTERY

China has one of the world's oldest continuous civilizations—despite invasions and occasional foreign rule. A country as vast as China with so long-lasting a civilization has a complex social and visual history, within which pottery and porcelain play a major role.

The function and status of ceramics in China varied from dynasty to dynasty, so they may be utilitarian, burial, trade, collectors', or even ritual objects, according to their quality and the era in which they were made. The ceramics fall into three broad types—earthenware, stoneware, and porcelain—for vessels, architectural items such as roof tiles, and modeled objects and figures. In addition, there was an important group of sculptures made for religious use, the majority of which were produced in earthenware.

The earliest ceramics were fired to earthenware temperatures, but as early as the fifteenth century B.C.E, high-temperature stonewares were being made with glazed surfaces. During the Six Dynasties period (265–589 C.E), kilns[1] in north China were producing high-fired ceramics of good quality. Whitewares produced in Hebei and Henan provinces from the seventh to the tenth centuries evolved into the highly prized porcelains of the Song dynasty (960–1279 C.E), long regarded as one of the high points in the history of China's ceramic industry. The tradition of religious sculpture extends over most historical periods but is less clearly delineated than that of stonewares or porcelains, for it embraces the old custom of earthenware burial ceramics with later religious images and architectural ornament. Ceramic products also include lead-glazed tomb models of the Han dynasty, three-color lead-glazed vessels and figures of the Tang dynasty, and Ming three-color temple ornaments, in which the motifs were outlined in a raised trail of slip,[2] as well as the many burial ceramics produced in imitation of vessels made in materials of higher intrinsic value.

Trade between the West and the settled and prosperous Chinese dynasties introduced new forms and different technologies. One of the most far-reaching examples is the impact of the fine ninth-century C.E Chinese porcelain wares imported into the Arab world. So admired were these pieces that they encouraged the development of earthenware made in imitation of porcelain and instigated research into the method of their manufacture. From the Middle East the Chinese acquired a blue pigment—a purified form of cobalt oxide unobtainable at that time in China—that contained only a low level of manganese. Cobalt ores found in China have a high manganese content, which produces a more muted blue-gray color. In the seventeenth century, the trading activities of the Dutch East India Company resulted in vast quantities of decorated Chinese porcelain being brought to Europe, which stimulated and influenced the work of a wide variety of wares, notably Delft. The Chinese themselves adapted many specific vessel forms from the West, such as bottles with long spouts, and designed a range of decorative patterns especially for the European market.

Just as painted designs on Greek pots may seem today to be purely decorative, whereas in fact they were carefully and precisely worked out so that at the time, their meaning was clear, so it is with Chinese pots. To twentieth-century eyes, Chinese pottery may appear merely decorative, yet to the Chinese the form of each object and its adornment had meaning and significance. The dragon represented the emperor, and the phoenix, the empress; the pomegranate indicated fertility, and a pair of fish, happiness; mandarin ducks stood for wedded bliss; the pine tree, peach, and crane are emblems of long life; and fish leaping from waves indicated success in the civil service examinations. Only when European decorative themes were introduced did these meanings become obscured or even lost.

From early times pots were used in both religious and secular contexts. The imperial court commissioned work and in the Yuan dynasty (1279–1368 C.E) an imperial ceramic factory was established at Jingdezhen. Pots played an important part in some religious ceremonies. Long and often lyrical descriptions of the different types of ware exist that assist in classifying pots, although these sometimes confuse an already large and complicated picture.

[1]**kilns:** enclosed ovens used to heat and harden clay objects
[2]**slip:** a mixture of clay and water used to decorate pottery

Directions: Now answer the questions.

PARAGRAPH 2

The function and status of ceramics in China varied from dynasty to dynasty, so they may be utilitarian, burial, trade, collectors', or even ritual objects, according to their quality and the era in which they were made. The ceramics fall into three broad types—earthenware, stoneware, and porcelain—for vessels, architectural items such as roof tiles, and modeled objects and figures. In addition, there was an important group of sculptures made for religious use, the majority of which were produced in earthenware.

1. According to paragraph 2, which of the following is true of Chinese ceramics?

    (A) The function of ceramics remained the same from dynasty to dynasty.
    (B) The use of ceramics as trade objects is better documented than the use of ceramics as ritual objects.
    (C) There was little variation in quality for any type of ceramics over time.
    (D) Some religious sculptures were made using the earthenware type of ceramics.

P A R A G R A P H 3

The earliest ceramics were fired to earthenware temperatures, but as early as the fifteenth century B.C.E, high-temperature stonewares were being made with glazed surfaces. During the Six Dynasties period (265–589 C.E), kilns in north China were producing high-fired ceramics of good quality. Whitewares produced in Hebei and Henan provinces from the seventh to the tenth centuries evolved into the highly prized porcelains of the Song dynasty (960–1279 C.E), long regarded as one of the high points in the history of China's ceramic industry. **The tradition of religious sculpture extends over most historical periods but is less clearly delineated than that of stonewares or porcelains, for it embraces the old custom of earthenware burial ceramics with later religious images and architectural ornament**. Ceramic products also include lead-glazed tomb models of the Han dynasty, three-color lead-glazed vessels and figures of the Tang dynasty, and Ming three-color temple ornaments, in which the motifs were outlined in a raised trail of slip, as well as the many burial ceramics produced in imitation of vessels made in materials of higher intrinsic value.

2. Which of the sentences below best expresses the essential information in the highlighted sentence in the passage? Incorrect choices change the meaning in important ways or leave out essential information.

   Ⓐ While stonewares and porcelains are found throughout most historical periods, religious sculpture is limited to the ancient period.

   Ⓑ Religious sculpture was created in most periods, but its history is less clear than that of stonewares or porcelains because some old forms continued to be used even when new ones were developed.

   Ⓒ While stonewares and porcelains changed throughout history, religious sculpture remained uniform in form and use.

   Ⓓ The historical development of religious sculpture is relatively unclear because religious sculptures sometimes resemble earthenware architectural ornaments.

3. Paragraph 3 supports all of the following concerning the history of the ceramic industry in China EXCEPT:

   Ⓐ The earliest high-fired ceramics were of poor quality.

   Ⓑ Ceramics produced during the Tang and Ming dynasties sometimes incorporated multiple colors.

   Ⓒ Earthenware ceramics were produced in China before stonewares were.

   Ⓓ The Song dynasty period was notable for the production of high-quality porcelain ceramics.

P
A
R
A
G
R
A
P
H

4

Trade between the West and the settled and prosperous Chinese dynasties introduced new forms and different technologies. One of the most far-reaching examples is the impact of the fine ninth-century C.E Chinese porcelain wares imported into the Arab world. So admired were these pieces that they encouraged the development of earthenware made in imitation of porcelain and **instigated** research into the method of their manufacture. From the Middle East the Chinese acquired a blue pigment—a purified form of cobalt oxide unobtainable at that time in China— that contained only a low level of manganese. Cobalt ores found in China have a high manganese content, which produces a more muted blue-gray color. In the seventeenth century, the trading activities of the Dutch East India Company resulted in vast quantities of decorated Chinese porcelain being brought to Europe, which stimulated and influenced the work of a wide variety of wares, notably Delft. The Chinese themselves adapted many specific vessel forms from the West, such as bottles with long spouts, and designed a range of decorative patterns especially for the European market.

4. The word "**instigated**" in the passage is closest in meaning to

   Ⓐ improved
   Ⓑ investigated
   Ⓒ narrowed
   Ⓓ caused

5. According to paragraph 4, one consequence of the trade of Chinese ceramics was

   Ⓐ the transfer of a distinctive blue pigment from China to the Middle East
   Ⓑ an immediate change from earthenware production to porcelain production in European countries
   Ⓒ Chinese production of wares made for the European market
   Ⓓ a decreased number of porcelain vessels available on the European market

P
A
R
A
G
R
A
P
H

5

Just as painted designs on Greek pots may seem today to be purely decorative, whereas in fact they were carefully and precisely worked out so that at the time, their meaning was clear, so it is with Chinese pots. To twentieth-century eyes, Chinese pottery may appear merely decorative, yet to the Chinese the form of each object and its adornment had meaning and significance. The dragon represented the emperor, and the phoenix, the empress; the pomegranate indicated fertility, and a pair of fish, happiness; mandarin ducks stood for wedded bliss; the pine tree, peach, and crane are emblems of long life; and fish leaping from waves indicated success in the civil service examinations. Only when European decorative themes were introduced did these meanings become obscured or even lost.

6. In paragraph 5, the author compares the designs on Chinese pots to those on Greek pots in order to

   (A) emphasize that while Chinese pots were decorative, Greek pots were functional
   (B) argue that the designs on Chinese pots had specific meanings and were not just decorative
   (C) argue that twentieth-century scholars are better able to understand these designs than were ancient scholars
   (D) explain how scholars have identified the meaning of specific images on Chinese pots

7. Which of the following is mentioned in paragraph 5 as being symbolically represented on Chinese ceramics?

   (A) Chinese rulers
   (B) love of homeland
   (C) loyalty to friends
   (D) success in trade

8. Paragraph 5 suggests which of the following about the decorations on Chinese pottery?

   (A) They had more importance for aristocrats than for ordinary citizens.
   (B) Their significance may have remained clear had the Chinese not come under foreign influence.
   (C) They contain some of the same images that appear on Greek pots.
   (D) Their significance is now as clear to twentieth-century observers as it was to the early Chinese.

P A R A G R A P H 4

Trade between the West and the settled and prosperous Chinese dynasties introduced new forms and different technologies. One of the most far-reaching examples is the impact of the fine ninth-century c.e. Chinese porcelain wares imported into the Arab world. **(A)** So admired were these pieces that they encouraged the development of earthenware made in imitation of porcelain and instigated research into the method of their manufacture. **(B)** From the Middle East the Chinese acquired a blue pigment—a purified form of cobalt oxide unobtainable at that time in China—that contained only a low level of manganese. Cobalt ores found in China have a high manganese content, which produces a more muted blue-gray color. **(C)** In the seventeenth century, the trading activities of the Dutch East India Company resulted in vast quantities of decorated Chinese porcelain being brought to Europe, which stimulated and influenced the work of a wide variety of wares, notably Delft. **(D)** The Chinese themselves adapted many specific vessel forms from the West, such as bottles with long spouts, and designed a range of decorative patterns especially for the European market.

9. Look at the part of the passage that is displayed above. The letters **(A)**, **(B)**, **(C)**, and **(D)** indicate where the following sentence could be added.

    Foreign trade was also responsible for certain innovations in coloring.

    Where would the sentence best fit?
    Ⓐ Choice A
    Ⓑ Choice B
    Ⓒ Choice C
    Ⓓ Choice D

10. **Directions:** An introductory sentence for a brief summary of the passage is provided below. Complete the summary by selecting the THREE answer choices that express the most important ideas in the passage. Some sentences do not belong in the summary because they express ideas that are not presented in the passage or are minor ideas in the passage. **This question is worth 2 points.**

Write your answer choices in the spaces where they belong. You can either write the letter of your answer choice or you can copy the sentence.

Ceramics have been produced in China for a very long time.

-
-
-

Answer Choices

A The Chinese produced earthenware, stoneware, and porcelain pottery, and they used their ceramics for a variety of utilitarian, architectural, and ceremonial purposes.

B The shape and decoration of ceramics produced for religious use in China were influenced by Chinese ceramics produced for export.

C As a result of trade relations, Chinese ceramic production changed, and Chinese ceramics influenced the ceramic production of other countries.

D Chinese burial ceramics have the longest and most varied history of production and were frequently decorated with written texts that help scholars date them.

E Before China had contact with the West, the meaning of various designs used to decorate Chinese ceramics was well understood.

F Ceramics made in imperial factories were used in both religious and nonreligious contexts.

Directions: Read the passage. Then answer the questions. You have 18 minutes on average to answer the questions.

BEGGING BY NESTLINGS

Many signals that animals make seem to impose on the signalers costs that are overly damaging. A classic example is noisy begging by nestling songbirds when a parent returns to the nest with food. These loud cheeps and peeps might give the location of the nest away to a listening hawk or raccoon, resulting in the death of the defenseless nestlings. In fact, when tapes of begging tree swallows were played at an artificial swallow nest containing an egg, the egg in that "noisy" nest was taken or destroyed by predators before the egg in a nearby quiet nest in 29 of 37 trials.

Further evidence for the costs of begging comes from a study of differences in the begging calls of warbler species that nest on the ground versus those that nest in the relative safety of trees. The young of ground-nesting warblers produce begging cheeps of higher frequencies than do their tree-nesting relatives. These higher-frequency sounds do not travel as far, and so may better conceal the individuals producing them, who are especially vulnerable to predators in their ground nests. Biologist David Haskell created artificial nests with clay eggs and placed them on the ground beside a tape recorder that played the begging calls of either tree-nesting or of ground-nesting warblers. The eggs "advertised" by the tree-nesters' begging calls were found bitten significantly more often than the eggs associated with the ground-nesters' calls.

The hypothesis that begging calls have evolved properties that reduce their potential for attracting predators yields a prediction: baby birds of species that experience high rates of nest predation should produce softer begging signals of higher frequency than nestlings of other species less often victimized by nest predators. This prediction was supported by data collected in one survey of 24 species from an Arizona forest, more evidence that predator pressure favors the evolution of begging calls that are hard to detect and pinpoint.

Given that predators can make it costly to beg for food, what benefit do begging nestlings derive from their communications? One possibility is that a noisy baby bird provides accurate signals of its real hunger and good health, making it worthwhile for the listening parent to give it food in a nest where several other offspring are usually available to be fed. If this hypothesis is true, then it follows that nestlings should adjust the intensity of their signals in relation to the signals produced by their nestmates, who are competing for parental attention. When experimentally deprived baby robins are placed in a nest with normally fed siblings, the hungry nestlings beg more loudly than usual—but so do their better-fed siblings, though not as loudly as the hungrier birds.

If parent birds use begging intensity to direct food to healthy offspring capable of vigorous begging, then parents should make food delivery decisions on the basis of their offspring's calls. Indeed, if you take baby tree swallows out of a nest for an hour, feeding half the set and not feeding the other half, when the birds are replaced in the nest, the unfed youngsters beg more loudly than the fed birds, and the parent birds feed the active beggars more than those who beg less vigorously.

As these experiments show, begging apparently provides a signal of need that parents use to make judgments about which offspring can benefit most from a feeding. But the question arises, why don't nestlings beg loudly when they aren't all that hungry? By doing so, they could possibly secure more food, which should result in more rapid growth or larger size, either of which is advantageous. The answer lies apparently not in the increased energy costs of exaggerated begging—such energy costs are small relative to the potential gain in calories—but rather in the damage that any successful cheater would do to its siblings, which share genes with one another. An individual's success in propagating its genes can be affected by more than just its own personal reproductive success. Because close relatives have many of the same genes, animals that harm their close relatives may in effect be destroying some of their own genes. Therefore, a begging nestling that secures food at the expense of its siblings might actually leave behind fewer copies of its genes overall than it might otherwise.

Directions: Now answer the questions.

PARAGRAPH 1

Many signals that animals make seem to impose on the signalers costs that are overly damaging. A classic example is noisy begging by nestling songbirds when a parent returns to the nest with food. These loud cheeps and peeps might give the location of the nest away to a listening hawk or raccoon, resulting in the death of the defenseless nestlings. In fact, when tapes of begging tree swallows were played at an artificial swallow nest containing an egg, the egg in that "noisy" nest was taken or destroyed by predators before the egg in a nearby quiet nest in 29 of 37 trials.

11. According to paragraph 1, the experiment with tapes of begging tree swallows establishes which of the following?

   Ⓐ Begging by nestling birds can attract the attention of predators to the nest.
   Ⓑ Nest predators attack nests that contain nestlings more frequently than they attack nests that contain only eggs.
   Ⓒ Tapes of begging nestlings attract predators to the nest less frequently than real begging calls do.
   Ⓓ Nest predators have no other means of locating bird nests except the begging calls of nestling birds.

PARAGRAPH 2

Further evidence for the costs of begging comes from a study of differences in the begging calls of warbler species that nest on the ground versus those that nest in the relative safety of trees. The young of ground-nesting warblers produce begging cheeps of higher frequencies than do their tree-nesting relatives. These higher-frequency sounds do not travel as far, and so may better conceal the individuals producing them, who are especially vulnerable to predators in their ground nests. Biologist David Haskell created artificial nests with clay eggs and placed them on the ground beside a tape recorder that played the begging calls of either tree-nesting or of ground-nesting warblers. The eggs "advertised" by the tree-nesters' begging calls were found bitten significantly more often than the eggs associated with the ground-nesters' calls.

12. Paragraph 2 indicates that the begging calls of tree-nesting warblers

   Ⓐ put them at greater risk than ground-nesting warblers
   Ⓑ can be heard from a greater distance than those of ground-nesting warblers
   Ⓒ are more likely to conceal the signaler than those of ground-nesting warblers
   Ⓓ have higher frequencies than those of ground-nesting warblers

13. The experiment described in paragraph 2 supports which of the following conclusions?

   (A) Predators are unable to distinguish between the begging cheeps of ground-nesting warblers and those of tree-nesting warblers except by the differing frequencies of the calls.

   (B) When they can find them, predators prefer the eggs of tree-nesting warblers to those of ground-nesting warblers.

   (C) The higher frequencies of the begging cheeps of ground-nesting warblers are an adaptation to the threat that ground-nesting birds face from predators.

   (D) The danger of begging depends more on the frequency of the begging cheep than on how loud it is.

PARAGRAPH 3

The hypothesis that begging calls have evolved properties that reduce their potential for attracting predators yields a prediction: baby birds of species that experience high rates of nest predation should produce softer begging signals of higher frequency than nestlings of other species less often victimized by nest predators. This prediction was supported by data collected in one survey of 24 species from an Arizona forest, more evidence that predator pressure favors the evolution of begging calls that are hard to detect and **pinpoint**.

14. The word "**pinpoint**" in the passage is closest in meaning to

   (A) observe
   (B) locate exactly
   (C) copy accurately
   (D) recognize

PARAGRAPH 4

Given that predators can make it costly to beg for food, what benefit do begging nestlings **derive** from their communications? One possibility is that a noisy baby bird provides accurate signals of its real hunger and good health, making it worthwhile for the listening parent to give it food in a nest where several other offspring are usually available to be fed. If this hypothesis is true, then it follows that nestlings should adjust the intensity of their signals in relation to the signals produced by their nestmates, who are competing for parental attention. When experimentally deprived baby robins are placed in a nest with normally fed siblings, the hungry nestlings beg more loudly than usual—but so do their better-fed siblings, though not as loudly as the hungrier birds.

15. The word "**derive**" in the passage is closest in meaning to

   (A) require
   (B) gain
   (C) use
   (D) produce

Given that predators can make it costly to beg for food, what benefit do begging nestlings derive from their communications? One possibility is that a noisy baby bird provides accurate signals of its real hunger and good health, making it worthwhile for the listening parent to give it food in a nest where several other offspring are usually available to be fed. If this hypothesis is true, then it follows that nestlings should adjust the intensity of their signals in relation to the signals produced by their nestmates, who are competing for parental attention. When experimentally deprived baby robins are placed in a nest with normally fed siblings, the hungry nestlings beg more loudly than usual—but so do their better-fed siblings, though not as loudly as the hungrier birds.

If parent birds use begging intensity to direct food to healthy offspring capable of vigorous begging, then parents should make food delivery decisions on the basis of their offspring's calls. Indeed, if you take baby tree swallows out of a nest for an hour, feeding half the set and not feeding the other half, when the birds are replaced in the nest, the unfed youngsters beg more loudly than the fed birds, and the parent birds feed the active beggars more than those who beg less vigorously.

16. In paragraphs 4 and 5, what evidence supports the claim that the intensity of nestling begging calls is a good indicator of which offspring in a nest would most benefit from a feeding?

   Ⓐ When placed in a nest with hungry robins, well-fed robins did not beg for food.
   Ⓑ Among robin nestlings, the intensity of begging decreased the more the nestlings were fed.
   Ⓒ Hungry tree swallow nestlings begged louder than well-fed nestlings in the same nest.
   Ⓓ Hungry tree swallow nestlings continued to beg loudly until they were fed, whereas well-fed nestlings soon stopped begging.

As these experiments show, begging apparently provides a signal of need that parents use to make judgments about which offspring can benefit most from a feeding. But the question arises, why don't nestlings beg loudly when they aren't all that hungry? By doing so, they could possibly secure more food, which should result in more rapid growth or larger size, either of which is advantageous. The answer lies apparently not in the increased energy costs of exaggerated begging—such energy costs are small relative to the potential gain in calories—but rather in the damage that any successful cheater would do to its siblings, which share genes with one another. An individual's success in propagating its genes can be affected by more than just its own personal reproductive success. Because close relatives have many of the same genes, animals that harm their close relatives may in effect be destroying some of their own genes. Therefore, a begging nestling that secures food at the expense of its siblings might actually leave behind fewer copies of its genes overall than it might otherwise.

17. In paragraph 6, the author compares the energy costs of vigorous begging with the potential gain in calories from such begging in order to

   Ⓐ explain why begging for food vigorously can lead to faster growth and increased size
   Ⓑ explain how begging vigorously can increase an individual's chances of propagating its own genes
   Ⓒ point out a weakness in a possible explanation for why nestlings do not always beg vigorously
   Ⓓ argue that the benefits of vigorous begging outweigh any possible disadvantages

18. According to paragraph 6, which of the following explains the fact that a well-fed nestling does not beg loudly for more food?

    Ⓐ There is no benefit for a nestling to get more food than it needs to survive.

    Ⓑ By begging loudly for food it does not need, a nestling would unnecessarily expose itself to danger from predators.

    Ⓒ If a nestling begs loudly when it is not truly hungry, then when it is truly hungry its own begging may be drowned out by that of its well-fed siblings.

    Ⓓ More of a nestling's genes will be passed to the next generation if its hungry siblings get enough food to survive.

PARAGRAPH 1

Many signals that animals make seem to impose on the signalers costs that are overly damaging. **(A)** A classic example is noisy begging by nestling songbirds when a parent returns to the nest with food. **(B)** These loud cheeps and peeps might give the location of the nest away to a listening hawk or raccoon, resulting in the death of the defenseless nestlings. **(C)** In fact, when tapes of begging tree swallows were played at an artificial swallow nest containing an egg, the egg in that "noisy" nest was taken or destroyed by predators before the egg in a nearby quiet nest in 29 of 37 trials. **(D)**

19. Look at the part of the passage that is displayed above. The letters **(A)**, **(B)**, **(C)**, and **(D)** indicate where the following sentence could be added.

    The cheeping provides important information to the parent, but it could also attract the attention of others.

    Where would the sentence best fit?

    Ⓐ Choice A

    Ⓑ Choice B

    Ⓒ Choice C

    Ⓓ Choice D

20. **Directions:** An introductory sentence for a brief summary of the passage is provided below. Complete the summary by selecting the THREE answer choices that express the most important ideas in the passage. Some sentences do not belong in the summary because they express ideas that are not presented in the passage or are minor ideas in the passage. **This question is worth 2 points.**

Write your answer choices in the spaces where they belong. You can either write the letter of your answer choice or you can copy the sentence.

Experiments have shed much light on the begging behaviors of baby songbirds.

-
-
-

Answer Choices

A Songbird species that are especially vulnerable to predators have evolved ways of reducing the dangers associated with begging calls.

B Songbird parents focus their feeding effort on the nestlings that beg loudest for food.

C It is genetically disadvantageous for nestlings to behave as if they are really hungry when they are not really hungry.

D The begging calls of songbird nestlings provide a good example of the overly damaging cost to signalers of signaling.

E The success with which songbird nestlings communicate their hunger to their parents is dependent on the frequencies of the nestlings' begging calls.

F Songbird nestlings have evolved several different ways to communicate the intensity of their hunger to their parents.

LISTENING

In this section, you will be able to demonstrate your ability to understand conversations and lectures in English.

In the actual test, the section is divided into two separately timed parts. You will hear each conversation or lecture only one time. A clock will indicate how much time remains. The clock will count down only while you are answering questions, not while you are listening. You may take up to 16.5 minutes to answer the questions.

In this practice test, there is no time limit for answering questions.

You may take notes while you listen. You may use your notes to help you answer the questions. Your notes will not be scored.

Answer the questions based on what is stated or implied by the speakers.

In some questions, you will see this icon: 🎧. This means that you will hear, but not see, part of the question.

Answer each question before moving on. Do not return to previous questions.

At the end of this practice test, you will find an answer key.

Directions: Listen to Track 26.

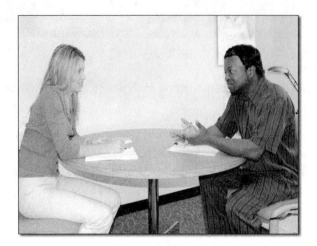

Directions: Now answer the questions.

1. Why does the student go to see the professor?

   (A) To discuss the latest trends in photography shows
   (B) To find out why some of her work was not selected for a show
   (C) To discuss how to get her photographs exhibited
   (D) To find out about a student photography show on campus

2. According to the professor, what is the best way to create work that is likely to be chosen for a show?

   (A) By taking photographs that fit with current trends
   (B) By following one's own artistic views
   (C) By consulting experienced photographers
   (D) By learning what gallery owners are interested in

3. What does the professor imply about photography created outside of the classroom?

   (A) It is usually technically stronger than work created for a class.
   (B) It tends to be more interesting than class work.
   (C) It faces increased pressure to be trendy.
   (D) It is more likely to be exhibited than is work created for a class.

4. According to the professor, what are two ways young photographers can market their work?
   Select 2 answers.

   [A] Share examples of their work with others
   [B] Hire a professional agent to sell their work
   [C] Display their work in places other than galleries
   [D] Ask a professor to recommend their work to gallery owners

5. *Listen again to part of the conversation by playing Track 27.* *Then answer the question.*

Why does the student say this?

(A) To ask the professor to reevaluate her work

(B) To indicate that she understands the importance of sharing her work

(C) To show that she disagrees with the professor's opinion

(D) To suggest that her work has met the professor's criteria

Directions: Listen to Track 28.

European History

Directions: Now answer the questions.

6. What is the main purpose of the lecture?

    (A) To describe the trade in food crops between Europe and the Americas
    (B) To describe the introduction of American food crops to Europeans
    (C) To describe the influence of American food crops on traditional European dishes
    (D) To describe the difficulties of growing American food crops in European climates

7. What does the professor imply about certain plants in the nightshade family?

    (A) They grow best in Mediterranean climates.
    (B) Their leaves are high in nutritional value.
    (C) They were mistakenly believed to be related to potatoes.
    (D) They are dangerous when eaten by human beings.

8. What does the professor imply about Thomas Jefferson's attitude toward tomatoes?

   Ⓐ It was typical of his unconventional way of thinking.
   Ⓑ It helped to advance his political career.
   Ⓒ It changed the eating habits of North Americans.
   Ⓓ It helped to make tomatoes popular in Europe.

9. According to the professor, what was the long-term effect of the introduction of American corn and potatoes to Europe?

   Ⓐ It had a negative effect on the nutritional intake of people living near the Mediterranean Sea.
   Ⓑ It contributed to a shift in the balance of power from southern Europe to northern Europe.
   Ⓒ It encouraged the development of new types of cuisine in southern Europe.
   Ⓓ It led to the failure of many native European grain crops.

10. According to the professor, what is one of the reasons why potatoes became popular in Ireland?

    Ⓐ Potatoes were more nourishing than native Irish food crops.
    Ⓑ Potatoes grew better at higher altitudes than native Irish crops.
    Ⓒ Political leaders in Ireland encouraged the cultivation of potatoes.
    Ⓓ People in Ireland were not aware that potatoes are members of the nightshade family.

11. *Listen again to part of the lecture by playing Track 29.* *Then answer the question.*

    What can be inferred about the professor when she says this?

    Ⓐ She expects the student to provide an answer to her question.
    Ⓑ She is surprised by the student's question.
    Ⓒ She thinks that she knows what the student was going to ask.
    Ⓓ She expects other students in the class to express their opinions.

Directions: Listen to Track 30.

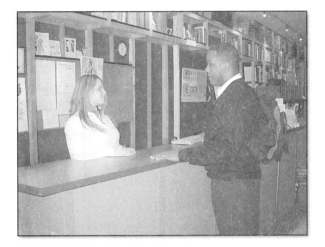

Directions: Now answer the questions.

12. Why does the student go to the bookstore?

    (A) To purchase a book by Jane Bowles

    (B) To find out which books he needs for a course

    (C) To return a book that was originally assigned for a course

    (D) To find out how to order a book for a course

13. What is the store's policy about giving refunds on books? *Select 2 answers.*

    [A] Books that are not for a specific course will receive a store credit instead of a refund.

    [B] Course textbooks can be returned for a full refund early in the school semester.

    [C] All books must be returned within two weeks to be eligible for a full refund.

    [D] Only books that are in new condition will get a full refund.

14. Why is the professor not going to discuss the book by Jane Bowles in the class?

    (A) There is not enough time left in the semester.

    (B) Not all of the students were able to get a copy of the book.

    (C) The professor miscalculated the difficulty level of the book.

    (D) The book was not on the course syllabus.

15. What does the woman imply about the book written by Jane Bowles?

    (A) It is worth reading.

    (B) It focuses on a serious topic.

    (C) She is not familiar with it.

    (D) She read it for a literature class.

16. *Listen to Track 31 to answer the question.*

What does the man mean when he says this?

(A) He thinks the store's policy is too strict.

(B) He is happy that the woman has agreed to his request.

(C) He is surprised at the woman's suggestion.

(D) He is annoyed that he needs to give the woman more information.

Directions: Listen to Track 32.

Directions: Now answer the questions.

17. What is the main purpose of the lecture?

  Ⓐ To discuss environmental phenomena that have changed the phosphorus cycle
  Ⓑ To illustrate how interrupting the phosphorus cycle can affect the environment
  Ⓒ To describe how phosphorus ends up in the atmosphere
  Ⓓ To explain how phosphorus gets recycled in the environment

18. Which human activities that influence the phosphorus cycle does the professor mention?
  Select 2 answers.

  A Fishing
  B Building dams on rivers
  C Polluting the oceans
  D Making and using fertilizer

19. Why does the professor discuss underwater volcanoes?

  Ⓐ To describe the location of most of the phosphorus on Earth
  Ⓑ To point out the difficulty of studying the phosphorus cycle
  Ⓒ To describe a step in the phosphorus cycle
  Ⓓ To illustrate the differences between two phases in the phosphorus cycle

20. What can be inferred about the professor's view on phosphorus getting washed into rivers?

  Ⓐ She is unconcerned because phosphorus is a beneficial nutrient.
  Ⓑ She is concerned about the quantity of phosphorus entering the waterways.
  Ⓒ She thinks that the amount of research conducted on the topic is excessive.
  Ⓓ She is frustrated that most of her students are unaware of the phenomenon.

21. What comparison does the professor make involving phosphorus and nitrogen?

(A) Sediment on the ocean floor contains more nitrogen than phosphorus.

(B) The atmosphere contains more nitrogen than phosphorus.

(C) Nitrogen requires more time to get recycled than phosphorus does.

(D) Phosphorus is more important than nitrogen to the development of fish.

22. *Listen again to part of the lecture by playing Track 33.* *Then answer the question.*

What does the professor mean when she says this?

(A) She realizes that the students are struggling with the concept.

(B) She is surprised that the student knew the answer to her question.

(C) She thinks that the answer to the question is obvious.

(D) She thinks that this phase of the cycle has an unusual name.

Directions: Listen to Track 34.

Psychology

childhood amnesia

Directions: Now answer the questions.

23. What is the main purpose of the lecture?
    - (A) To discuss possible explanations for childhood amnesia
    - (B) To describe key features of childhood amnesia
    - (C) To explain methods of testing memory in children of different ages
    - (D) To discuss why the ability to recall memories diminishes as a person ages

24. Why does the professor ask students about their earliest memories?
    - (A) To help students relate to the topic she is about to discuss
    - (B) To establish that people vary in the time of their earliest memory
    - (C) To introduce the connection between language and memory
    - (D) To point out a common theme in the earliest memories of most people

25. What does the professor imply about some of the explanations for childhood amnesia that she describes?
    - (A) They can never be proved or disproved.
    - (B) They were formed without proper evidence.
    - (C) They explain only certain types of childhood amnesia.
    - (D) They are contradicted by her own research.

26. The professor mentions some commonly held explanations for childhood amnesia. Indicate whether each of the following is one of the explanations she mentions.
Put a check (✓) in the correct boxes.

	Yes	No
Early memories are repressed.		
Young children have few experiences to remember.		
Young children are unable to form memories.		
Children lose memories at a faster rate than adults.		
Young children do not make an effort to remember events.		

27. How was recall tested in children without language ability?

   Ⓐ By recording children's responses to familiar faces
   Ⓑ By observing children's reactions to a repeated series of actions
   Ⓒ By having children imitate each other's actions
   Ⓓ By having children imitate an ordered sequence of actions

28. The professor mentions a study in the 1980s that tested memory in children under age 3. What did the researchers conclude from this study?

   Ⓐ Young children do not develop the capacity for recall until after age 3.
   Ⓑ Piaget's theory linking language development to memory was incorrect.
   Ⓒ Young children typically remember events for about nine months.
   Ⓓ The formation of memories is dependent upon language development.

SPEAKING

In this section, you will be able to demonstrate your ability to speak about a variety of topics.

In the actual test, the Speaking section will last approximately 16 minutes. You will answer four questions by speaking into the microphone. You may take notes while you listen. You may use your notes to help you answer the questions. Your notes will not be scored. For each question, you will have time to prepare before giving your response. You should answer the questions as completely as possible in the time allowed.

For this practice test, you may want to use a personal recording device to record and play back your responses.

For each question, play the audio track listed and follow the directions to complete the task.

At the end of this practice test, you will find important points for each question, sample responses, and comments on those responses by official raters.

1. You will now give your opinion about a familiar topic. After you hear the question, you should give yourself 15 seconds to prepare and 45 seconds to speak.

   Listen to Track 35.

   Do you agree or disagree with the following statement? Use details and examples to explain your answer.

   All children should be required to learn a second language in school.

Preparation Time: 15 seconds
Response Time: 45 seconds

2. Now you will read a passage about a campus situation and then listen to a conversation about the same topic. You will then answer a question, using information from both the reading passage and the conversation. You should give yourself 30 seconds to prepare and 60 seconds to speak.

   Listen to Track 36.

Reading Time: 45 seconds

   Student Art Display

   The university is currently considering possible locations on campus for displaying paintings and other artwork by students. I think the lobby at the entrance to the student center would be a great location. Since many students pass through the student center every day, artwork displayed in the lobby would be viewed by hundreds of people. Also, because the whole front of the building is made of glass windows, the lobby is filled with natural light. This makes it perfect for displaying artwork, which should have plenty of light to be seen and appreciated.

   Sincerely,

   Paul Sands

Listen to Track 37.

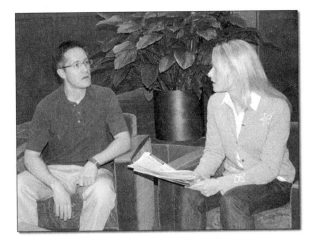

Briefly summarize the proposal in the student's letter. Then state the woman's opinion about the proposal and explain the reasons she gives for holding that opinion.

Preparation Time: 30 seconds
Response Time: 60 seconds

3. Now you will read a passage about an academic subject and then listen to a lecture on the same topic. You will then answer a question, using information from both the reading passage and the lecture. You should give yourself 30 seconds to prepare and 60 seconds to speak.

Listen to Track 38.

Reading Time: 50 seconds

Entertainment Merchandising

An effective, widely used marketing practice in the entertainment industry is entertainment merchandising. Entertainment merchandising is a form of marketing in which the brand or image from one product is also used to sell another. The practice of entertainment merchandising often occurs in connection with movies and television shows, especially those associated with children. For example, the success of a popular children's television show may result in the marketing of toys that are designed to look like characters in the show. Or the situation may be reversed when a children's television show is written to include characters that are based on already-popular toys.

Listen to Track 39.

Using the examples from the lecture, explain the concept of entertainment merchandising.

| **Preparation Time: 30 seconds** |
| **Response Time: 60 seconds** |

4. Now you will listen to a lecture. You will then be asked to summarize the lecture. You should give yourself 20 seconds to prepare and 60 seconds to speak.

Listen to Track 40.

Using the points from the lecture, explain why researchers think that babies may feel empathy.

| Preparation Time: 20 seconds |
| Response Time: 60 seconds |

WRITING

In this section, you will be able to demonstrate your ability to use writing to communicate in an academic environment. There will be two writing tasks.

At the end of this practice test, you will find topic notes for each question.

Turn the page to see the directions for the first writing task.

Writing Based on Reading and Listening

For this task, you will read a passage about an academic topic. Then you will listen to a lecture about the same topic. You may take notes while you listen.

In your response, provide a detailed summary of the lecture and explain how the lecture relates to the reading passage.

In the actual test, you will have 3 minutes to read the passage and 20 minutes to write your response. While you write, you will be able to see the reading passage. If you finish your response before time is up, you may go on to the second writing task.

Reading Time: 3 minutes

The sea otter is a small mammal that lives in waters along the western coast of North America from California to Alaska. When some sea otter populations off the Alaskan coast started rapidly declining a few years ago, it caused much concern because sea otters play an important ecological role in the coastal ecosystem. Experts started investigating the cause of the decline and quickly realized that there were two possible explanations: environmental pollution or attacks by predators. Initially, the pollution hypothesis seemed the more likely of the two.

The first reason why pollution seemed the more likely cause was that there were known sources of it along the Alaskan coast, such as oil rigs and other sources of industrial chemical pollution. Water samples from the area revealed increased levels of chemicals that could decrease the otters' resistance to life-threatening infections and thus could indirectly cause their deaths.

Second, other sea mammals such as seals and sea lions along the Alaskan coast were also declining, indicating that whatever had endangered the otters was affecting other sea mammals as well. This fact again pointed to environmental pollution, since it usually affects the entire ecosystem rather than a single species. Only widely occurring predators, such as the orca (a large predatory whale), could have the same effect, but orcas prefer to hunt much larger prey, such as other whales.

Third, scientists believed that the pollution hypothesis could also explain the uneven pattern of otter decline: at some Alaskan locations the otter populations declined greatly, while at others they remained stable. Some experts explained these observations by suggesting that ocean currents or other environmental factors may have created uneven concentrations of pollutants along the coast.

Listen to Track 41.

Directions: You have 20 minutes to plan and write your response. Your response will be judged on the basis of the quality of your writing and on how well your response presents the points in the lecture and their relationship to the reading passage. Typically, an effective response will contain a minimum of 150 words.

Listen to Track 42.

> **Response Time: 20 minutes**

Question 1

Summarize the points made in the lecture, being sure to explain how they respond to the specific points made in the reading passage.

_____

_____

_____

_____

_____

_____

_____

_____

Writing for an Academic Discussion

For this task, you will read an online discussion. A professor has posted a question about a topic, and some classmates have responded with their ideas.

In the actual test, you will have 10 minutes to write a response that contributes to the discussion.

Question 2

Your professor is teaching a class on communications. Write a post responding to the professor's question.

In your response, you should do the following.

- Express and support your opinion.
- Make a contribution to the discussion in your own words.

An effective response will contain at least 100 words.

Dr. Gupta

This week we will be learning about nonverbal communication—that is, communication that happens without words. It can be physical gestures, body language, eye contact, facial expressions, or other forms. On the discussion board, I want you to share with one another what, in your opinion, is the most important kind of nonverbal communication. Why do you think this form of communication is most important?

Claire

One form of nonverbal communication that hasn't been mentioned is the emoji. Emojis are tremendously important because they allow you to communicate very efficiently when texting. For example, instead of writing out that you think something is really funny, you can just include a laughing smiley face. Shortening the message might increase the impact it has on the reader.

Paul

I think that facial expressions are the most important kind of nonverbal communication. Seeing a person's face lets you know whether that person is sincere in what they are saying. That's why written communication and even telephone conversations can sometimes fail or at least seem to be inadequate—one person cannot see whether the other person is sincere.

Response Time: 10 minutes

ANSWERS

Reading Section

1. D
2. B
3. A
4. D
5. C
6. B
7. A
8. B
9. B
10. A, C, E

11. A
12. B
23. C
14. B
25. B
26. C
17. C
18. D
19. B
20. A, B, C

Listening Section

1. C
2. B
3. C
4. A, C
5. D
6. B
7. D
8. A
9. B
10. A
11. C
12. C
13. B, D
14. A
15. A
16. C
17. D
18. A, D
19. C

20. B
21. B
22. C
23. A
24. A
25. B
26.

	Yes	No
Early memories are repressed.	X	
Young children have few experiences to remember.		X
Young children are unable to form memories.	X	
Children lose memories at a faster rate than adults.	X	
Young children do not make an effort to remember events.		X

27. D
28. B

Speaking Section

Prompts, Important Points, and Sample Responses with Rater Comments

Use the sample Independent and Integrated Speaking Rubrics in Appendix A to see how responses are scored. The raters who listen to your responses will analyze them in three general categories. These categories are delivery, language use, and topic development. All three categories have equal importance.

This section includes important points that should be covered when answering each question. All of these points must be present in a response in order for it to receive the highest score in the topic development category. These important points are guides to the kind of information raters expect to hear in a high-level response.

This section also refers to sample responses, which can be found on the audio tracks. Some responses were scored at the highest level, while others were not. The responses are followed by comments from certified ETS raters.

1: Paired Choice
Prompt

Do you agree or disagree with the following statement? Use details and examples to explain your answer.

All children should be required to learn a second language in school.

Important Points

When you answer this question, you should take a stance and state whether you agree or disagree that all children should be required to learn a second language in school. In order to support your opinion, you should provide at least one specific reason why children should or should not be required to learn a second language, along with information to elaborate on and explain that reason. It is acceptable to talk about more than one reason for agreeing or disagreeing with the statement, but you should not simply provide a list of reasons without any explanation of them.

High-Level Response:
Listen to Track 43.
Rater Comments

In this response, the speaker states that she agrees with the statement, and although she doesn't explicitly say what the statement is, she implicitly refers to it throughout her response (*"let's say, if children don't know English, all degrees now required um a second language"* and *"so I believe Eng—like a second language it's a benefit and it's a plus for kids"*). She supports her agreement with the statement by explaining specific scenarios in which children would benefit from being required to learn a second language in school; she uses the example of English and the job market, saying that most degrees and jobs now require English, and also talks about how English will help kids communicate when they travel. Although her speech is not always smooth (she says *"um"* and hesitates somewhat frequently) and she makes some small grammatical errors (*"general speaking"*; *"all degrees now required"*; *"can able to communicate"*), it is still easy for the listener to understand her.

Mid-Level Response:
Listen to Track 44.
Rater Comments

In this response, the speaker states his agreement with the statement but does not provide full support for his opinion. Rather than choosing one or two reasons and explaining them in detail (using a personal experience, hypothetical situation, etc.), he lists many different and somewhat vague reasons but does not provide explanations for them: *"because it helps really to uh thinks about other stuff"*; *"you're just smarter and you can just have better job"*; *"it's really hard to learn second language."* The speaker

has mostly clear pronunciation and uses some sophisticated grammatical structures (*"not only the language but also other cultures"*), but his vague explanations make it somewhat difficult for a listener to follow his response.

2: Fit and Explain
Prompt

Briefly summarize the proposal in the student's letter. Then state the woman's opinion about the proposal and explain the reasons she gives for holding that opinion.

Important Points

When answering this question, it is important to include information from both the reading passage and the conversation between students. Begin by summarizing the student's proposal, which is that the lobby of the student center should be selected as the location for a student art display. Then indicate the woman's opinion of the proposal and why she feels that way. In this item, you would say that the woman disagrees that the lobby is a good place for the art displays. She says that because there are so many people passing through the lobby, it will make it difficult to view the artwork. Also, the natural light in the lobby is sometimes too bright or too dark for viewing artwork (and it is better to have controlled electric light).

High-Level Response:
Listen to Track 45.
Rater Comments

The speaker accurately and effectively covers all the important points. She explains the proposal clearly and efficiently, and covers the woman's opinion about the natural light with great detail. She does a particularly good job of organizing her response. For example, after she summarizes the letter-writer's proposal, she says *"these last two points are actually exactly the points the woman is criticizing . . ."* before continuing on to the woman's opinion, and this transition makes her ideas easy to follow. She does not talk as much about how crowding in the lobby makes the artwork difficult to view, but she does mention it in sufficient detail.

She has a wide vocabulary range and is able to summarize ideas in her own words, such as saying *"the light is dependent on the weather"* to summarize the woman's point about natural light. Her pronunciation, pacing, and intonation are also clear and effective, so it is not difficult for listeners to understand her.

Low-Level Response:
Listen to Track 46. 🎧
Rater Comments

The speaker's response contains relevant points, such as using a lobby to display artwork, the fact that the woman doesn't agree, and an explanation for why she doesn't agree. He makes some factual errors, however, such as claiming the newspaper itself is recommending the new location for the artwork. Most importantly, the response contains some major grammar problems that make it difficult to understand. For example, the speaker says *"the one who is going to just appreciate artwork will be know it,"* which does not make much sense. Sometimes the speaker's pronunciation of individual words is difficult to understand as well, such as the word "proposal."

3: General/Specific
Prompt

Using the examples from the lecture, explain the concept of entertainment merchandising.

Important Points

For this task, the prompt asks you to use the examples from the lecture to explain the concept described in the reading. You should begin your response by briefly explaining entertainment merchandising (a type of marketing where a popular brand or image of one product is used to sell another product). For the first example from the lecture, you could begin by mentioning that entertainment merchandising often occurs when children's toys are created based on popular characters in a television program or movie. For example, the professor and his friends bought Action-hero toys because they liked the Action-hero TV show. For the second example from the

lecture, you could explain that entertainment merchandising can also work in a reverse way from the first example—sometimes TV shows or movies become popular because they are based on well-known children's toys. For instance, the professor's daughter enjoys playing with a doll named Rosa. So, when a TV show about Rosa is created, she and her friends begin watching it.

High-Level Response:
Listen to Track 47. 🎧
Rater Comments

At the beginning, the speaker's explanation of the concept is a little unclear (*"brand or images are used to sell"*). However, her summary of the examples shows that she fully understood how the lecture relates to the reading. She does not confuse any details, remembering that Action-hero was first a television show and then a toy but that the Rosa doll was first a toy and then a television show. Her pronunciation is easy to understand, and she speaks without pausing or hesitating. She uses complex sentences (*"And then, they create a television show which has the doll Rosa as the main character"*) and shows a good range of vocabulary.

Mid-Level Response:
Listen to Track 48. 🎧
Rater Comments

The speaker mostly does a good job of explaining all the main points of the reading and the lecture. Her first sentence, explaining the concept of entertainment merchandising, is very clear. Her explanation of the Action-hero example is also good, but she has significant difficulty explaining the example of the Rosa doll. For example, she says, *"after she was bought from all the kids' society,"* which is unclear. It can be inferred from the rest of the response that she understands the basic ideas in the lecture, but parts of her response are a little confusing. Overall, her pronunciation is clear and she speaks fluently. She has some minor grammatical errors, but she is still easy to understand.

4: Summary

Prompt

Using the points from the lecture, explain why researchers think that babies may feel empathy.

Important Points

In this item, your summary of the key ideas from the lecture should include that researchers believe that babies are capable of feeling empathy. They think this because they did an experiment where a baby listened to other babies crying. The baby cried when he heard the other babies crying (which is what they expected). However, when the researchers played the baby a tape of his own crying, he didn't cry. This told researchers that noise wasn't the cause of the crying. Rather, it suggested that the baby cried because he felt empathy or concern for the other babies.

High-Level Response:
Listen to Track 49. 🎧

Rater Comments

The speaker gives a clear summary of the lecture, starting with a statement of what researchers believed until now and then explaining what was found in the experiment. She doesn't say explicitly that the researchers played a recording or tape of babies crying, and she also mispronounces the word "*experiment.*"

These are minor errors, however, and do not prevent the listener from understanding what happened in the experiment. One of the speaker's particular strengths is that she places emphasis on certain words to help communicate the difference between the two parts of the experiment ("*. . . it's not the actual* **noise** *that triggers the baby's reflex to cry, but actually an emotional* **feeling**").

Mid-Level Response:
Listen to Track 50. 🎧

Rater Comments

In this response, the speaker gives a basic summary of both parts of the experiment. Her pronunciation is also quite clear. However, she hesitates often while searching for words to describe what happened in the experiment. These pauses and the limits in her vocabulary prevent her from making the final connection and explaining *why* the results of the experiment led researchers to believe that babies feel empathy. The point isn't, as the speaker says, that babies can "differentiate" between their own cries and those of other babies. The point is that the baby only cried when he heard the other babies cry, which made researchers think that *noise* wasn't an issue, but rather that he felt concern for the other babies. Overall, the response is slightly confusing to the listener because of these missing pieces and lack of organization.

Writing Section

Prompts, Topic Notes, and Sample Responses with Rater Comments

Use the sample Integrated Writing and Writing for an Academic Discussion Rubrics in Appendix A to see how responses are scored.

This section includes topic notes that are guides to the kind of information raters expect to read in a high-level response.

This section also refers to sample responses. These responses were scored at the highest level. The responses are followed by comments from certified ETS raters.

Question 1

Prompt

Summarize the points made in the lecture, being sure to explain how they respond to the specific points made in the reading passage.

Topic Notes

The reading discusses three reasons to believe it is because of pollution that there has been a decline of sea otters off of Alaska and California, while the lecture discusses why predation, especially by orcas, is a better explanation of the evidence presented in the reading.

Point made in the reading	Corresponding point from the lecture
The passage argues that increased levels of pollution detected along the Alaskan coast could cause the deaths of sea otters by making them vulnerable to infections.	No dead sea otters have been found washed up on shore; this weakens the pollution theory but supports the predator theory, since the predators would eat the otters as they caught them, leaving no remains.
The decline of other sea mammals (seals and sea lions) points to a systemic cause such as pollution; the orca, a predator that could conceivably hunt several sea mammal species, is not the likely cause because it prefers larger prey such as whales.	Since the population of whales that orcas prefer to hunt has declined, orcas started hunting smaller prey, such as otters, as well as seals and sea lions.
The decline of sea otter populations is greater in some locations than in others, which again seems consistent with the pollution theory since varying concentrations of pollutants could account for such an uneven pattern.	The uneven pattern of sea otter decline can be explained by the fact that some locations where sea otters live are accessible to orcas and some are not; the accessible areas experience decline, while the populations in the inaccessible areas remain steady.

Responses with scores of 4 and 5 typically discuss all three points in the table with good accuracy and level of detail.

Sample Response

The topic discussed here is the investigation of the causes of the disappearance of the sea otter, which is a small mammal that lives in waters along the western coast of North America from California to Alaska. The woman in the lecture argues that the cause of their disappearance is the presence of the predators, especially orcas, and not pollution as the reading says.

Firstly, she argues that one of the proofs of their being attacked by the predators is the fact that no one can find any dead sea otters. If the cause was the pollution, many dead sea otters would be found along the shores. In addition, a predator will immediately eat its prey so this is why no dead sea otters were found.

Secondly, the woman in the lecture argues there is another explanation than pollution why smaller sea mammals are all disappearing. She says that, since the whales tend to disappear because of the humans hunting them, the orcas had to adapt their food habits to the sea conditions and as a result they have started eating the smaller sea animals available among them sea otters being included.

Thirdly, she argues that the orcas cannot access the shallow locations. This is why there are some areas where the sea otters are numerous. It's not because of uneven concentrations of pollutants.

Rater Comments

This response earns a score of 5. The response clearly conveys the three points from the lecture showing why predation by orcas is a better explanation than pollution for why no remains of the sea otters are found, for why a number of small animals including the sea otter started declining at the same time, and for why sea otter decline seems to have occurred to a lesser extent or not at all in some places, and to a greater extent in others. Grammatical errors are few and minor.

Question 2

Refer to page 95 to review the Writing for an Academic Discussion question.

Topic Notes

To earn a top score, you should develop a response that contributes to the discussion about the most important type of nonverbal communication. An effective response will contain at least 100 words.

One discussion participant chooses emojis and gives an example of how efficient they can be in communicating a message. Another discussion participant chooses facial expressions and compares them to other forms of communication to claim that facial expressions are necessary to express sincerity. You may seize on the ideas already stated and develop them in greater detail or may introduce entirely new ideas. You may, for example, expand the notion of nonverbal communication to include types not listed in the professor's post, such as certain images or sounds. You may describe conditions under which one or another form of nonverbal communication is most important, or you may describe the relative importance of particular forms of nonverbal communication in different cultures.

You should make sure that your ideas are well-supported by reasons and examples and are expressed clearly. Since your response represents an online post, it does not need to be organized into separate paragraphs. However, your ideas need to be well-connected, coherent, and clear. Your response is scored using the Writing for an Academic Discussion rubric (see Appendix A).

Sample Response

I think overall body language is the most important form of communication. Body movements can give many clues about a person's attitude, emotions etc. You can tell when the person is not interested in talking to you by seeing their body posture, even though they engage in a conversation. Sometimes, you can even learn if a person is anxious or feel at ease by seeing how tense their body is. Also, when verbal communication can't happen properly, such as when there are language barriers, body motions such as hand movements and facial expressions can still effectively convey a message. Therefore, I believe body language is the most significant form of nonverbal communication.

Rater Comments

This writer has composed a very clearly expressed contribution to the online discussion, demonstrating consistent facility in the use of language. The writer clearly identifies body language as the most important nonverbal communication and gives a well-elaborated rationale for this position. The writer explains that body language can both supplement verbal communication (by expressing emotion and attitude) and compensate for a lack of verbal communication ("such as when there are language barriers"). The writer displays effective use of a range of grammar and vocabulary and makes only the errors that can be expected from a competent writer writing under timed conditions (e.g. "feel at ease" should be "feeling at ease").

TOEFL iBT® Test 3

READING

In this section, you will be able to demonstrate your ability to understand academic passages in English. You will read and answer questions about **two passages**.

In the actual test, you will have 36 minutes total to read both passages and answer the questions. A clock will indicate how much time remains.

Some passages may include one or more notes explaining words or phrases. The words or phrases are marked with footnote numbers and the notes explaining them appear at the end of the passage.

Most questions are worth 1 point, but the last question for each passage is worth 2 points.

You may review and revise your answers in this section as long as time remains.

At the end of this practice test, you will find an answer key.

Directions: Read the passage. Then answer the questions. You have 18 minutes on average to answer the questions.

ANCIENT EGYPTIAN SCULPTURE

In order to understand ancient Egyptian art, it is vital to know as much as possible of the elite Egyptians' view of the world and the functions and contexts of the formal art produced for them. Without this knowledge, we can appreciate only the formal content of Egyptian art, and we will fail to understand why it was produced or the concepts that shaped it and caused it to adopt its distinctive forms. In fact, a lack of understanding concerning the purposes of Egyptian art has often led it to be compared unfavorably with the art of other cultures: Why did the Egyptians not develop sculpture in which the body turned and twisted through space like classical Greek statuary? Why do the artists seem to get left and right confused? And why did they not discover the geometric perspective as European artists did in the Renaissance? The answer to such questions has nothing to do with a lack of skill or imagination on the part of Egyptian artists and everything to do with the purposes for which they were producing their art.

The majority of three-dimensional representations, whether standing, seated, or kneeling, exhibit what is called frontality: they face straight ahead, neither twisting nor turning. When such statues are viewed in isolation, out of their original context and without knowledge of their function, it is easy to criticize them for their rigid attitudes that remained unchanged for three thousand years. Frontality is, however, directly related to the functions of Egyptian statuary and the contexts in which the statues were set up. Statues were created not for their decorative effect but to play a primary role in the cults of the gods, the king, and the dead. They were designed to be put in places where these beings could manifest themselves in order to be the recipients of ritual actions. Thus it made sense to show the statue looking ahead at what was happening in front of it so that the living performer of the ritual could interact with the divine or deceased recipient. Very often, such statues were enclosed in rectangular shrines or wall niches whose only opening was at the front, making it natural for the statue to display frontality. Other statues were designed to be placed within an architectural setting—for instance, in front of the monumental entrance gateways to temples known as pylons or in pillared courts where they would be placed against or between pillars; their frontality worked perfectly within the architectural context.

Statues were normally made of stone, wood, or metal. Stone statues were worked from single rectangular blocks of material and retained the compactness of the original shape. The stone between the arms and the body and between the legs in standing figures or the legs and the seat in seated ones was not normally cut away. From a practical aspect, this protected the figures against breakage and psychologically gives the images a sense of strength and power, usually enhanced by a supporting back pillar. By contrast, wooden statues were carved from several pieces of wood that were pegged together to form the finished work, and metal statues were either made by wrapping sheet metal around a wooden core or cast by the lost-wax process[1]. The arms could be held away from the body and carry separate items in their hands; there is no back pillar. The effect is altogether lighter and freer than that achieved in stone, but because both perform the same function, formal wooden and metal statues still display frontality.

Apart from statues representing deities, kings, and named members of the elite that can be called formal, there is another group of three-dimensional representations that depicts generic figures, frequently servants, from the nonelite population. The function of these is quite different. Many are made to be put in the tombs of the elite in order to serve the tomb owners in the afterlife.

Unlike formal statues that are limited to static poses of standing, sitting, and kneeling, these figures depict a wide range of actions, such as grinding grain, baking bread, producing pots, and making music, and they are shown in appropriate poses, bending and squatting as they carry out their tasks.

¹**lost-wax process:** an ancient method of casting using a wax model and clay mold

Directions: Now answer the questions.

PARAGRAPH 1

In order to understand ancient Egyptian art, it is vital to know as much as possible of the elite Egyptians' view of the world and the functions and contexts of the formal art produced for them. Without this knowledge we can appreciate only the formal content of Egyptian art, and we will fail to understand why it was produced or the concepts that shaped it and caused it to adopt its distinctive forms. In fact, a lack of understanding concerning the purposes of Egyptian art has often led it to be compared unfavorably with the art of other cultures: Why did the Egyptians not develop sculpture in which the body turned and twisted through space like classical Greek statuary? Why do the artists seem to get *left* and *right* confused? And why did they not discover the geometric perspective as European artists did in the Renaissance? The answer to such questions has nothing to do with a lack of skill or imagination on the part of Egyptian artists and everything to do with the purposes for which they were producing their art.

1. Paragraph 1 suggests that one reason ancient Egyptian art has been viewed less favorably than other art is that ancient Egyptian art lacks

   Ⓐ a realistic sense of human body proportion
   Ⓑ a focus on distinctive forms of varying sizes
   Ⓒ the originality of European art
   Ⓓ examples of formal art that show the human body in motion

2. In paragraph 1, the author mentions all of the following as necessary in appreciating Egyptian art EXCEPT an understanding of

   Ⓐ the reasons why the art was made
   Ⓑ the nature of aristocratic Egyptian beliefs
   Ⓒ the influences of Egyptian art on later art such as classical Greek art
   Ⓓ how the art was used

The majority of three-dimensional representations, whether standing, seated, or kneeling, exhibit what is called frontality: they face straight ahead, neither twisting nor turning. When such statues are viewed in isolation, out of their original context and without knowledge of their function, it is easy to criticize them for their rigid attitudes that remained unchanged for three thousand years. Frontality is, however, directly related to the functions of Egyptian statuary and the contexts in which the statues were set up. Statues were created not for their decorative effect but to play a primary role in the cults of the gods, the king, and the dead. They were designed to be put in places where these beings could manifest themselves in order to be the recipients of ritual actions. Thus it made sense to show the statue looking ahead at what was happening in front of it so that the living performer of the ritual could interact with the divine or deceased recipient. Very often, such statues were enclosed in rectangular shrines or wall niches whose only opening was at the front, making it natural for the statue to display frontality. Other statues were designed to be placed within **an architectural setting**—for instance, in front of the monumental entrance gateways to temples known as pylons or in pillared courts where they would be placed against or between pillars; their frontality worked perfectly within the architectural context.

3. According to paragraph 2, why are Egyptian statues portrayed frontally?

  (A) To create a psychological effect of distance and isolation
  (B) To allow them to fulfill their important role in ceremonies of Egyptian life
  (C) To provide a contrast to statues with a decorative function
  (D) To suggest the rigid, unchanging Egyptian philosophical attitudes

4. The author mentions "**an architectural setting**" in the passage in order to

  (A) suggest that architecture was as important as sculpture to Egyptian artists
  (B) offer a further explanation for the frontal pose of Egyptian statues
  (C) explain how the display of statues replaced other forms of architectural decoration
  (D) illustrate the religious function of Egyptian statues

Statues were normally made of stone, wood, or metal. Stone statues were worked from single rectangular blocks of material and retained the compactness of the original shape. The stone between the arms and the body and between the legs in standing figures or the legs and the seat in seated ones was not normally cut away. From a practical aspect, this protected the figures against breakage and psychologically gives the images a sense of strength and power, usually enhanced by a supporting back pillar. By contrast, wooden statues were carved from several pieces of wood that were pegged together to form the finished work, and metal statues were either made by wrapping sheet metal around a wooden core or cast by the lost-wax process. The arms could be held away from the body and carry separate items in their hands; there is no back pillar. The effect is altogether lighter and freer than that achieved in stone, but because both perform the same function, formal wooden and metal statues still display frontality.

5. According to paragraph 3, why were certain areas of a stone statue left uncarved?

    (A) To prevent damage by providing physical stability

    (B) To emphasize that the material was as important as the figure itself

    (C) To emphasize that the figure was not meant to be a real human being

    (D) To provide another artist with the chance to finish the carving

6. According to paragraph 3, which of the following statements about wooden statues is true?

    (A) Wooden statues were usually larger than stone statues.

    (B) Wooden statues were made from a single piece of wood.

    (C) Wooden statues contained pieces of metal or stone attached to the front.

    (D) Wooden statues had a different effect on the viewer than stone statues.

P A R A G R A P H 4

Apart from statues representing deities, kings, and named members of the elite that can be called formal, there is another group of three-dimensional representations that **depicts** generic figures, frequently servants, from the nonelite population. The function of these is quite different. Many are made to be put in the tombs of the elite in order to serve the tomb owners in the afterlife. Unlike formal statues that are limited to static poses of standing, sitting, and kneeling, these figures depict a wide range of actions, such as grinding grain, baking bread, producing pots, and making music, and they are shown in appropriate poses, bending and squatting as they carry out their tasks.

7. The word "**depicts**" in the passage is closest in meaning to

    (A) imagines

    (B) classifies

    (C) elevates

    (D) portrays

8. According to paragraph 4, what is the difference between statues that represent the Egyptian elite and statues that represent the nonelite classes?

    (A) Statues of the elite are included in tombs, but statues of the nonelite are not.

    (B) Statues of the elite are in motionless poses, while statues of the nonelite are in active poses.

    (C) Statues of the elite are shown standing, while statues of the nonelite are shown sitting or kneeling.

    (D) Statues of the elite serve an important function, while statues of the nonelite are decorative.

P
A
R
A
G
R
A
P
H

4

Apart from statues representing deities, kings, and named members of the elite that can be called formal, there is another group of three-dimensional representations that depicts generic figures, frequently servants, from the nonelite population. **(A)** The function of these is quite different. **(B)** Many are made to be put in the tombs of the elite in order to serve the tomb owners in the afterlife. **(C)** Unlike formal statues that are limited to static poses of standing, sitting, and kneeling, these figures depict a wide range of actions, such as grinding grain, baking bread, producing pots, and making music, and they are shown in appropriate poses, bending and squatting as they carry out their tasks. **(D)**

9. Look at the part of the passage that is displayed above. The letters **(A)**, **(B)**, **(C)**, and **(D)** indicate where the following sentence could be added.

In fact, it is the action and not the figure itself that is important.

Where would the sentence best fit?

Ⓐ Choice A
Ⓑ Choice B
Ⓒ Choice C
Ⓓ Choice D

10. **Directions:** An introductory sentence for a brief summary of the passage is provided below. Complete the summary by selecting the THREE answer choices that express the most important ideas in the passage. Some sentences do not belong in the summary because they express ideas that are not presented in the passage or are minor ideas in the passage. **This question is worth 2 points.**

Write your answer choices in the spaces where they belong. You can either write the letter of your answer choice or you can copy the sentence.

> **The distinctive look of ancient Egyptian sculpture was determined largely by its function.**
>
> ●
>
> ●
>
> ●

Answer Choices

A The twisted forms of Egyptian statues indicate their importance in ritual actions.
B The reason Egyptian statues are motionless is linked to their central role in cultural rituals.
C Stone, wood, and metal statues all display the feature of frontality.
D Statues were more often designed to be viewed in isolation rather than placed within buildings.
E The contrasting poses used in statues of elite and nonelite Egyptians reveal their difference in social status.
F Although the appearances of formal and generic statues differ, they share the same function.

Directions: Read the passage. Then answer the questions. You have 18 minutes on average to answer the questions.

ORIENTATION AND NAVIGATION

To South Americans, robins are birds that fly north every spring. To North Americans, the robins simply vacation in the south each winter. Furthermore, they fly to very specific places in South America and will often come back to the same trees in North American yards the following spring. The question is not why they would leave the cold of winter so much as how they find their way around. The question perplexed people for years, until, in the 1950s, a German scientist named Gustave Kramer provided some answers and, in the process, raised new questions.

Kramer initiated important new kinds of research regarding how animals orient and navigate. Orientation is simply facing in the right direction; navigation involves finding one's way from point A to point B.

Early in his research, Kramer found that caged migratory birds became very restless at about the time they would normally have begun migration in the wild. Furthermore, he noticed that as they fluttered around in the cage, they often launched themselves in the direction of their normal migratory route. He then set up experiments with caged starlings and found that their orientation was, in fact, in the proper migratory direction except when the sky was overcast, at which times there was no clear direction to their restless movements. Kramer surmised, therefore, that they were orienting according to the position of the Sun. To test this idea, he blocked their view of the Sun and used mirrors to change its apparent position. He found that under these circumstances, the birds oriented with respect to the new "Sun." They seemed to be using the Sun as a compass to determine direction. At the time, this idea seemed preposterous. How could a bird navigate by the Sun when some of us lose our way with road maps? Obviously, more testing was in order.

So, in another set of experiments, Kramer put identical food boxes around the cage, with food in only one of the boxes. The boxes were stationary, and the one containing food was always at the same point of the compass. However, its position with respect to the surroundings could be changed by revolving either the inner cage containing the birds or the outer walls, which served as the background. As long as the birds could see the Sun, no matter how their surroundings were altered, they went directly to the correct food box. Whether the box appeared in front of the right wall or the left wall, they showed no signs of confusion. On overcast days, however, the birds were disoriented and had trouble locating their food box.

In experimenting with artificial suns, Kramer made another interesting discovery. If the artificial Sun remained stationary, the birds would shift their direction with respect to it at a rate of about 15 degrees per hour, the Sun's rate of movement across the sky. Apparently, the birds were assuming that the "Sun" they saw was moving at that rate. When the real Sun was visible, however, the birds maintained a constant direction as it moved across the sky. In other words, they were able to compensate for the Sun's movement. This meant that some sort of biological clock was operating— and a very precise clock at that.

What about birds that migrate at night? Perhaps they navigate by the night sky. To test the idea, caged night-migrating birds were placed on the floor of a planetarium during their migratory period. A planetarium is essentially a theater with a domelike ceiling onto which a night sky can be projected for any night of the year. When the planetarium sky matched the sky outside, the birds fluttered in the direction of their normal migration. But when the dome was rotated, the birds changed their direction to match the artificial sky. The results clearly indicated that the birds were orienting according to the stars.

There is accumulating evidence indicating that birds navigate by using a wide variety of environmental cues. Other areas under investigation include magnetism, landmarks, coastlines, sonar, and even smells. The studies are complicated by the fact that the data are sometimes contradictory and the mechanisms apparently change from time to time. Furthermore, one sensory ability may back up another.

Directions: Now answer the questions.

PARAGRAPH 3

Early in his research, Kramer found that caged migratory birds became very restless at about the time they would normally have begun migration in the wild. Furthermore, he noticed that as they fluttered around in the cage, they often launched themselves in the direction of their normal migratory route. **He then set up experiments with caged starlings and found that their orientation was, in fact, in the proper migratory direction except when the sky was overcast, at which times there was no clear direction to their restless movements.** Kramer surmised, therefore, that they were orienting according to the position of the Sun. To test this idea, he blocked their view of the Sun and used mirrors to change its apparent position. He found that under these circumstances, the birds oriented with respect to the new "Sun." They seemed to be using the Sun as a compass to determine direction. At the time, this idea seemed preposterous. How could a bird navigate by the Sun when some of us lose our way with road maps? Obviously, more testing was in order.

11. Which of the sentences below best expresses the essential information in the highlighted sentence in the passage? Incorrect choices change the meaning in important ways or leave out essential information.

   Ⓐ Experiments revealed that caged starlings displayed a lack of directional sense and restless movements.

   Ⓑ Experiments revealed that caged starlings were unable to orient themselves in the direction of their normal migratory route.

   Ⓒ Experiments revealed that the restless movement of caged starlings had no clear direction.

   Ⓓ Experiments revealed that caged starlings' orientation was accurate unless the weather was overcast.

12. According to paragraph 3, why did Kramer use mirrors to change the apparent position of the Sun?

   Ⓐ To test the effect of light on the birds' restlessness

   Ⓑ To test whether birds were using the Sun to navigate

   Ⓒ To simulate the shifting of light the birds would encounter along their regular migratory route

   Ⓓ To cause the birds to migrate at a different time than they would in the wild

13. According to paragraph 3, when do caged starlings become restless?

    (A) When the weather is overcast

    (B) When they are unable to identify their normal migratory route

    (C) When their normal time for migration arrives

    (D) When mirrors are used to change the apparent position of the Sun

PARAGRAPH 4

So, in another set of experiments, Kramer put identical food boxes around the cage, with food in only one of the boxes. The boxes were stationary, and the one containing food was always at the same point of the compass. However, its position with respect to the surroundings could be changed by revolving either the inner cage containing the birds or the outer walls, which served as the background. As long as the birds could see the Sun, no matter how their surroundings were altered, they went directly to the correct food box. Whether the box appeared in front of the right wall or the left wall, they showed no signs of confusion. On overcast days, however, the birds were disoriented and had trouble locating their food box.

14. Which of the following can be inferred from paragraph 4 about Kramer's reason for filling one food box and leaving the rest empty?

    (A) He believed the birds would eat food from only one box.

    (B) He wanted to see whether the Sun alone controlled the birds' ability to navigate toward the box with food.

    (C) He thought that if all the boxes contained food, this would distract the birds from following their migratory route.

    (D) He needed to test whether the birds preferred having the food at any particular point of the compass.

PARAGRAPH 5

In experimenting with artificial suns, Kramer made another interesting discovery. If the artificial Sun remained stationary, the birds would shift their direction with respect to it at a rate of about 15 degrees per hour, the Sun's rate of movement across the sky. Apparently, the birds were assuming that the "Sun" they saw was moving at that rate. When the real Sun was visible, however, the birds maintained a constant direction as it moved across the sky. In other words, they were able to compensate for the Sun's movement. This meant that some sort of biological clock was operating—and a very precise clock at that.

15. According to paragraph 5, how did the birds fly when the real Sun was visible?

    (A) They kept the direction of their flight constant.

    (B) They changed the direction of their flight at a rate of 15 degrees per hour.

    (C) They kept flying toward the Sun.

    (D) They flew in the same direction as the birds that were seeing the artificial Sun.

16. The experiment described in paragraph 5 caused Kramer to conclude that birds possess a biological clock because

   (A) when birds navigate they are able to compensate for the changing position of the Sun in the sky

   (B) birds' innate bearings keep them oriented in a direction that is within 15 degrees of the Sun's direction

   (C) birds' migration is triggered by natural environmental cues, such as the position of the Sun

   (D) birds shift their direction at a rate of 15 degrees per hour whether the Sun is visible or not

What about birds that migrate at night? Perhaps they navigate by the night sky. To test the idea, caged night-migrating birds were placed on the floor of a planetarium during their migratory period. A planetarium is essentially a theater with a domelike ceiling onto which a night sky can be projected for any night of the year. When the planetarium sky matched the sky outside, the birds fluttered in the direction of their normal migration. But when the dome was rotated, the birds changed their direction to match the artificial sky. The results clearly indicated that the birds were orienting according to the stars.

17. According to paragraph 6, how did the birds navigate in the planetarium's nighttime environment?

   (A) By waiting for the dome to stop rotating

   (B) By their position on the planetarium floor

   (C) By orienting themselves to the stars in the artificial night sky

   (D) By navigating randomly until they found the correct orientation

There is **accumulating** evidence indicating that birds navigate by using a wide variety of environmental cues. Other areas under investigation include magnetism, landmarks, coastlines, sonar, and even smells. The studies are complicated by the fact that the data are sometimes contradictory and the mechanisms apparently change from time to time. Furthermore, one sensory ability may back up another.

18. The word "**accumulating**" in the passage is closest in meaning to

   (A) new

   (B) increasing

   (C) convincing

   (D) extensive

So, in another set of experiments, Kramer put identical food boxes around the cage, with food in only one of the boxes. **(A)** The boxes were stationary, and the one containing food was always at the same point of the compass. **(B)** However, its position with respect to the surroundings could be changed by revolving either the inner cage containing the birds or the outer walls, which served as the background. **(C)** As long as the birds could see the Sun, no matter how their surroundings were altered, they went directly to the correct food box. **(D)** Whether the box appeared in front of the right wall or the left wall, they showed no signs of confusion. On overcast days, however, the birds were disoriented and had trouble locating their food box.

19. Look at the part of the passage that is displayed above. The letters **(A)**, **(B)**, **(C)**, and **(D)** indicate where the following sentence could be added.

    He arranged the feed boxes at various positions on a compass.

    Where would the sentence best fit?

    Ⓐ Choice A
    Ⓑ Choice B
    Ⓒ Choice C
    Ⓓ Choice D

20. **Directions:** An introductory sentence for a brief summary of the passage is provided below. Complete the summary by selecting the THREE answer choices that express the most important ideas in the passage. Some sentences do not belong in the summary because they express ideas that are not presented in the passage or are minor ideas in the passage. **This question is worth 2 points.**

Write your answer choices in the spaces where they belong. You can either write the letter of your answer choice or you can copy the sentence.

> **Gustave Kramer conducted important research related to the ability of birds to orient and navigate.**
>
> ●
>
> ●
>
> ●

Answer Choices

A Because caged birds become disoriented when the sky is overcast, Kramer hypothesized that birds orient themselves according to the Sun's position.

B In one set of experiments, Kramer placed the box containing food at the same point of the compass each time he put food boxes in the birds' environment.

C Kramer demonstrated that an internal biological clock allows birds to compensate for the Sun's movement.

D After several studies, Kramer surmised that an internal biological clock allows some species of birds to navigate at night.

E The role of environmental cues in birds' navigation is clear, for on overcast days, birds use objects besides the Sun to orient themselves.

F Kramer showed that night-migrating birds use the sky to navigate by the stars.

LISTENING

In this section, you will be able to demonstrate your ability to understand conversations and lectures in English.

In the actual test, the section is divided into two separately timed parts. You will hear each conversation or lecture only one time. A clock will indicate how much time remains. The clock will count down only while you are answering questions, not while you are listening. You may take up to 16.5 minutes to answer the questions.

In this practice test, there is no time limit for answering questions.

You may take notes while you listen. You may use your notes to help you answer the questions. Your notes will not be scored.

Answer the questions based on what is stated or implied by the speakers.

In some questions, you will see this icon: 🎧. This means that you will hear, but not see, part of the question.

Answer each question before moving on. Do not return to previous questions.

At the end of this practice test, you will find an answer key.

Directions: Listen to Track 51.

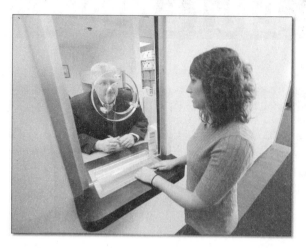

Directions: Now answer the questions.

1. What are the speakers mainly discussing?

   Ⓐ What the gym pass is used for
   Ⓑ How to try out for the swimming team
   Ⓒ The popularity of the new exercise classes at the gym
   Ⓓ The schedule of exercise classes at the gym

2. Why does the woman's initial excitement turn to disappointment?

   Ⓐ She is told that all swimming classes are full.
   Ⓑ She learns that she will have to pay extra for classes.
   Ⓒ She finds out that there are no swimming classes at her level.
   Ⓓ She thought all sports activities were supervised by coaches.

3. What does the man imply about people who play sports in the gym?

   Ⓐ They do not need an instructor to coach them.
   Ⓑ They do not usually take swimming classes.
   Ⓒ They must pay an extra fee to use the equipment.
   Ⓓ They do not need a gym pass.

4. Why does the woman make an appointment with the swimming instructor?

   Ⓐ To find out when the pool is available
   Ⓑ To apply for a job as assistant swim instructor
   Ⓒ To complain about the gym's policy
   Ⓓ To find out which swimming class she should take

5. *Listen again to part of the conversation by playing Track 52.* *Then answer the question.*

What does the man imply when he says this?

(A) He wants to change the subject.

(B) He wants to tell a story.

(C) He disagrees with the woman.

(D) He understands the woman's point.

Directions: Listen to Track 53.

Directions: Now answer the questions.

6. What is the talk mainly about?

    Ⓐ Various predators that threaten young birds
    Ⓑ Various patterns of growth in young birds
    Ⓒ One way that birds protect their young
    Ⓓ One way that birds provide food for their young

7. According to the lecture, what do birds usually do when putting on a distraction display?
    Select 2 answers.

    Ⓐ They imitate another kind of animal.
    Ⓑ They fly in circles around their nest.
    Ⓒ They cover their nest with their wings.
    Ⓓ They pretend they are sick or injured.

8. According to the lecture, when do birds put on their most conspicuous distraction displays?

    Ⓐ Just before they lay their eggs
    Ⓑ Immediately after they have laid their eggs
    Ⓒ Just before their young become independent
    Ⓓ Immediately after their young have left the nest

9. *Listen to Track 54 to answer the question.*

   Why does the professor say this?

   Ⓐ To introduce an explanation
   Ⓑ To express uncertainty
   Ⓒ To point out an error
   Ⓓ To emphasize a point that should be obvious

10. *Listen again to part of the lecture by playing Track 55.* *Then answer the question.*

    Why does the professor say this?

    Ⓐ To explain the behavior of the predator
    Ⓑ To emphasize that predators have excellent hunting skills
    Ⓒ To state the purpose of the birds' behavior
    Ⓓ To emphasize the risks involved in a distraction display

11. *Listen again to part of the lecture by playing Track 56.* *Then answer the question.*

    Why does the professor say this?

    Ⓐ To describe the behavior of an injured sandpiper
    Ⓑ To give an example of a well-performed broken-wing display
    Ⓒ To show why some sandpipers fail to distract predators
    Ⓓ To distinguish the sandpiper's display from another kind of display

Directions: Listen to Track 57.

Architecture

Cape Cod house

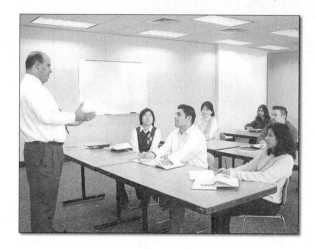

Directions: Now answer the questions.

12. What aspect of architecture in the United States is the lecture mainly about?

   Ⓐ The differences between rural and urban styles of housing

   Ⓑ The reasons for the popularity of a particular type of house

   Ⓒ The various styles of houses that are popular in New England

   Ⓓ The decorative details that are typical of houses built in New England

13. What is mentioned in the lecture as an application of the principle that "form follows function"?

   Ⓐ Smaller houses should have fewer rooms.

   Ⓑ A house's design should reflect the inhabitants' needs.

   Ⓒ The materials for a house should be selected before the house is designed.

   Ⓓ Houses in cold, harsh climates should be built with inexpensive materials.

14. Why does the woman refer to visiting her grandparents?

   Ⓐ To explain why she is interested in residential architecture

   Ⓑ To explain why she knows a lot about the history of Cape Cod

   Ⓒ To explain why she is familiar with Cape Cod houses

   Ⓓ To explain why she enjoys visiting rural New England

15. According to the lecture, what are two features of Cape Cod houses that were influenced by climate? *Select 2 answers.*

   Ａ The thickness of the walls

   Ｂ The slope of the roof

   Ｃ The size of the chimney

   Ｄ The simplicity of the exterior

16. According to the professor, what contributed to the attitude of conformity in rural New England communities during the 1600s and 1700s?

    (A) People depended on their neighbors for their own survival.
    (B) People living in rural areas often had moved there from cities.
    (C) People had to live very close to their neighbors.
    (D) People had limited access to information from outside their community.

17. *Listen again to part of the lecture by playing Track 58.* *Then answer the question.*

    Why does the professor say this?

    (A) To indicate that the student's answer is wrong
    (B) To determine whether the student has prepared for the class
    (C) To point out that housing styles across the United States are very similar
    (D) To ask about students' preferences in architectural styles

Directions: Listen to Track 59.

Directions: Now answer the questions.

18. Why does the professor want to see the student?

   Ⓐ To discuss the student's grade on a paper

   Ⓑ To invite the student to work on a committee

   Ⓒ To inform the student about a change in the class schedule

   Ⓓ To ask the student to become her research assistant

19. Why does the student say he is interested in doing what the professor asks?

   Ⓐ He thinks it may help him improve his research skills.

   Ⓑ He thinks it will enable him to get a better grade in the professor's class.

   Ⓒ He thinks it may help him get into graduate school.

   Ⓓ He thinks it will be good teaching practice for him.

20. What will the applicants talk about?

   Ⓐ An academic interest they have

   Ⓑ Reasons why they deserve to be hired

   Ⓒ Their educational background

   Ⓓ The classes they hope to teach

21. Why does the professor mention that one of the applicants will give a talk on a topic the student is particularly interested in?

   Ⓐ To see if the student would enjoy joining the applicant's research team

   Ⓑ To suggest that the student may not totally agree with what the applicant has to say

   Ⓒ To persuade the student to come to a talk on Friday

   Ⓓ To warn the student to focus on the applicant's teaching ability

22. *Listen again to part of the conversation by playing Track 60.* *Then answer the question.*

Why does the student say this?

   (A) He does not know of any job applicants.
   (B) He is not interested in learning about the hiring process.
   (C) He does not want to be responsible for any decisions that are made.
   (D) He does not understand why the professor has asked him the question.

Directions: Listen to Track 61.

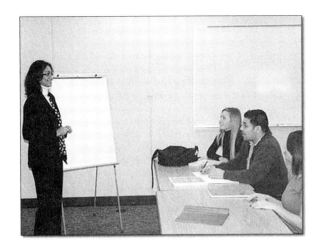

Directions: Now answer the questions.

23. What is the lecture mainly about?

   Ⓐ The effect of the decrease in temperatures on wetlands

   Ⓑ The use of computer models to analyze temperature patterns

   Ⓒ The theory that land development affected the climate of south Florida

   Ⓓ The importance of the citrus industry to the south Florida economy

24. Why does the professor mention the building of canals in the wetlands?

   Ⓐ To describe what the wetlands used to look like

   Ⓑ To emphasize that farmers need to transport their crops to other areas

   Ⓒ To explain how the wetlands were transformed into farmland

   Ⓓ To explain why people want to build farms there

25. What does the professor imply about major weather patterns such as El Niño?

   Ⓐ She does not believe they are the main cause of the changes in Florida's climate.

   Ⓑ She is certain that they have caused a worldwide decrease in the number of frosts.

   Ⓒ She believes they contributed to the increase of citrus production in Florida.

   Ⓓ She does not fully understand what causes them.

26. What point about bodies of water does the professor emphasize to the students?

   Ⓐ Bodies of water in Florida are slightly warmer now than they were 100 years ago.

   Ⓑ Bodies of water in south Florida are increasing in size.

   Ⓒ Bodies of water release heat back into the environment.

   Ⓓ Bodies of water are a source of moisture for crops.

27. What data from 100 years ago and today were entered into the computer model that the professor discusses?

 Ⓐ The average temperatures in south Florida
 Ⓑ The market prices of citrus fruit grown in south Florida
 Ⓒ The numbers of animal species in south Florida wetlands
 Ⓓ The landscape characteristics of south Florida

28. *Listen again to part of the lecture by playing Track 62.* *Then answer the question.*

 Why does the student say this?

 Ⓐ To remind the professor of her previous point
 Ⓑ To check if he understood the professor's point
 Ⓒ To express surprise at what the professor said
 Ⓓ To answer the professor's question about the farmers

SPEAKING

In this section, you will be able to demonstrate your ability to speak about a variety of topics.

In the actual test, the Speaking section will last approximately 16 minutes. You will answer four questions by speaking into the microphone. You may take notes while you listen. You may use your notes to help you answer the questions. Your notes will not be scored. For each question, you will have time to prepare before giving your response. You should answer the questions as completely as possible in the time allowed.

For this practice test, you may want to use a personal recording device to record and play back your responses.

For each question, play the audio track listed and follow the directions to complete the task.

At the end of this practice test, you will find important points for each question, sample responses, and comments on those responses by official raters.

1. You will now give your opinion about a familiar topic. After you hear the question, you should give yourself 15 seconds to prepare and 45 seconds to speak.

    Listen to Track 63.

    Some people think that children should be allowed to watch whatever television programs they choose to. Others think that parents should exercise control over the television programs their children watch. Which do you agree with? Explain why.

Preparation Time: 15 seconds
Response Time: 45 seconds

2. Now you will read a passage about a campus situation and then listen to a conversation about the same topic. You will then answer a question, using information from both the reading passage and the conversation. You should give yourself 30 seconds to prepare and 60 seconds to speak.

    Listen to Track 64.

Reading Time: 45 seconds

    Housing Renovations Planned

    Over the last ten years, the number of Central College students living on campus in dormitories has decreased by twenty percent. In an effort to counteract the trend, the college has announced a plan to renovate its on-campus housing. The renovations will take two years, and they will include improvements to the bathrooms, lighting, and heating in the dormitories. "A lot of people are moving off campus because the dorms aren't in great shape," explained the college president. "By renovating the dorms, we can make them more appealing than off-campus housing, and more students will choose to remain on campus."

Listen to Track 65.

The woman expresses her opinion about the college's plan. State her opinion and explain the reasons she gives for holding that opinion.

Preparation Time: 30 seconds
Response Time: 60 seconds

3. Now you will read a passage about an academic subject and then listen to a lecture on the same topic. You will then answer a question, using information from both the reading passage and the lecture. You should give yourself 30 seconds to prepare and 60 seconds to speak.

Listen to Track 66.

Reading Time: 45 seconds

Outsider Art

Outsider Art is a term used to describe art that is made by people who choose to live and work outside society. The artists who produce this kind of art—Outsider Artists—work in isolation from other artists and have little or no formal artistic training. Because they do not learn conventional artistic techniques from teachers or other artists, Outsider Artists must invent their own ways of doing things. As a result of the unconventional methods that Outsider Artists often use, their work can look strange and not at all like traditional art to the observer.

Listen to Track 67.

Explain why Henry Darger is considered an Outsider Artist.

Preparation Time: 30 seconds
Response Time: 60 seconds

4. Now you will listen to a lecture. You will then be asked to summarize the lecture. You should give yourself 20 seconds to prepare and 60 seconds to speak.

Listen to Track 68.

Using the points and examples from the lecture, explain what unity and contrast are and how they make interior design more effective.

Preparation Time: 20 seconds
Response Time: 60 seconds

WRITING

In this section, you will be able to demonstrate your ability to use writing to communicate in an academic environment. There will be two writing tasks.

At the end of this practice test, you will find topic notes for each question.

Turn the page to see the directions for the first writing task.

Writing Based on Reading and Listening

For this task, you will read a passage about an academic topic. Then you will listen to a lecture about the same topic. You may take notes while you listen.

In your response, provide a detailed summary of the lecture and explain how the lecture relates to the reading passage.

In the actual test, you will have 3 minutes to read the passage and 20 minutes to write your response. While you write, you will be able to see the reading passage. If you finish your response before time is up, you may go on to the second writing task.

Reading Time: 3 minutes

A recent study reveals that people, especially young people, are reading far less literature—novels, plays, and poems—than they used to. This is troubling because the trend has unfortunate effects for the reading public, for culture in general, and for the future of literature itself.

While there has been a decline in book reading generally, the decline has been especially sharp for literature. This is unfortunate because nothing else provides the intellectual stimulation that literature does. Literature encourages us to exercise our imaginations, empathize with others, and expand our understanding of language. So by reading less literature, the reading public is missing out on important benefits.

Unfortunately, missing out on the benefits of literature is not the only problem. What are people reading instead? Consider the prevalence of self-help books on lists of best sellers. These are usually superficial, poorly written, and intellectually undemanding. Additionally, instead of sitting down with a challenging novel, many persons are now more likely to turn on the television, watch a music video, or read a Web page. Clearly, diverting time previously spent in reading literature to trivial forms of entertainment has lowered the level of culture in general.

The trend of reading less literature is all the more regrettable because it is taking place during a period when good literature is being written. There are many talented writers today, but they lack an audience. This fact is bound to lead publishers to invest less in literature and so support fewer serious writers. Thus, the writing as well as the reading of literature is likely to decline because of the poor standards of today's readers.

Listen to Track 69.

Directions: You have 20 minutes to plan and write your response. Your response will be judged on the basis of the quality of your writing and on how well your response presents the points in the lecture and their relationship to the reading passage. Typically, an effective response will contain a minimum of 150 words.

Listen to Track 70.

> **Response Time: 20 minutes**

Question 1

Summarize the points made in the lecture, being sure to explain how they cast doubt on specific points made in the reading passage.

_____

_____

_____

_____

_____

_____

_____

_____

Writing for an Academic Discussion

For this task, you will read an online discussion. A professor has posted a question about a topic, and some classmates have responded with their ideas.

In the actual test, you will have 10 minutes to write a response that contributes to the discussion.

Question 2

Your professor is teaching a class on political science. Write a post responding to the professor's question.

In your response, you should do the following.

- Express and support your opinion.
- Make a contribution to the discussion in your own words.

An effective response will contain at least 100 words.

Dr. Achebe

Next week in class, we'll be looking at countries where voting in elections is mandatory. In some of these countries, failure to vote can result in fines and other penalties, though these are not always enforced. Today I'd like you to start thinking about this topic and share your opinion on the discussion board. Should governments require all their citizens to vote in elections? Why or why not?

Andrew

Requiring citizens to vote has potential merits. One benefit I can think of is that this requirement may change people's attitudes toward voting. People will feel more like their vote matters because their government really wants them to vote. Then, people will likely see voting as their civic duty and feel proud to vote.

Claire

I don't think that requiring citizens to vote in elections is a good idea. Some people don't watch the news and don't pay attention to politics, so we can't really expect them to make informed choices. They might vote for candidates without giving it much thought. It'd be better to encourage voluntary participation in the voting process through outreach efforts.

Response Time: 10 minutes

ANSWERS

Reading Section

1. D
2. C
3. B
4. B
5. A
6. D
7. D
8. B
9. D
10. B, C, E

11. D
12. B
13. C
14. B
15. A
16. A
17. C
18. B
19. A
20. A, C, F

Listening Section

1.	A	15.	B, D
2.	B	16.	A
3.	A	17.	A
4.	D	18.	B
5.	C	19.	C
6.	C	20.	A
7.	A, D	21.	D
8.	C	22.	D
9.	A	23.	C
10.	C	24.	C
11.	D	25.	A
12.	B	26.	C
13.	B	27.	D
14.	C	28.	A

Speaking Section

Prompts, Important Points, and Sample Responses with Rater Comments

Use the sample Independent and Integrated Speaking Rubrics in Appendix A to see how responses are scored. The raters who listen to your responses will analyze them in three general categories. These categories are Delivery, Language Use, and Topic Development. All three categories have equal importance.

This section includes important points that should be covered when answering each question. All of these points must be present in a response in order for it to receive the highest score in the Topic Development category. These important points are guides to the kind of information raters expect to hear in a high-level response.

This section also refers to sample responses, which can be found on the audio tracks. Some responses were scored at the highest level, while others were not. The responses are followed by comments from certified ETS raters.

1: Paired Choice

Prompt

Some people think that children should be allowed to watch whatever television programs they choose to. Others think that parents should exercise control over the television programs their children watch. Which do you agree with? Explain why.

Important Points

In this question, you need to choose the statement that you agree with and explain why you agree with it. In order to give an effective response, you should provide clear, specific reasons that support your opinion. You will not be scored on which statement you agree with, but rather on how effectively you are able to present and support your opinion.

A reason to support the first statement could be that learning to make good decisions is an important part of growing up and rather than restricting a child's viewing, a parent should focus on teaching the child to make good decisions. A reason to support the second statement might include an example of an inappropriate program that parents should not let their children watch and explain why watching that program might have a negative effect on a child.

High-Level Response:
Listen to Track 71. 🎧
Rater Comments

This speaker demonstrates good control in language use and accurately uses a variety of grammatical structures and effective vocabulary. Her pronunciation is clear throughout, and her use of intonation is appropriate. She chooses to develop the idea of parental responsibility toward children and explains why she thinks this is important. The response would have been even fuller if she had given an example of a program that is not suitable for young children and why.

Mid-Level Response:
Listen to Track 72. 🎧
Rater Comments

This speaker states his opinion clearly but does not develop his ideas fully with clear support. He does provide a reason for his opinion that children should be able to watch whatever they want: that they can tell real things apart from "*not real things.*" He then repeats the same basic idea in other words with imprecise language: "*I sure that a child view television with an enjoy and not with a real situation.*" The speaker does not demonstrate that he can use a variety of grammatical structures or that he has a wide range of vocabulary. Though an accent is evident, pronunciation is generally clear overall.

2: Fit and Explain
Prompt

The woman expresses her opinion about the college's plan. State her opinion and explain the reasons she gives for holding that opinion.

Important Points

To respond to this item, you should explain that the woman does not believe that the university's plan to renovate the dormitories in

order to get more students to live on campus will work. To explain the points she makes, you could say that she argues that the renovations will create noise or disturbances and that people will actually move off campus because of that in the short term. You should also point out her argument that in the long term students will likely remain in off-campus housing after the construction ends, since the university will have to raise the cost of housing to pay for the renovations.

High-Level Response:
Listen to Track 73. 🎧
Rater Comments

This speaker demonstrates a clear understanding of the information from both the reading and the conversation. He doesn't say until the end of his response that the woman disagrees with the plan and that she doesn't think it will work. However, this doesn't prevent the listener from following the logic of the response. Consider this sentence from his response: "*She saying the price of the dorm fee will be raised . . . and it will go back to the student, and therefore student will look for the off-campus apartment, which seems cheaper.*" The speaker makes some minor grammatical errors and mispronounces a few select words (*price, cheaper*), but he uses intonation well and is able to communicate the point effectively. Overall, this response is well developed and easy to understand.

Mid-Level Response:
Listen to Track 74. 🎧
Rater Comments

In this response, the speaker touches on most of the important points; however, she does not do so with the fluidity and clarity characteristic of a high-level response. Her vocabulary is limited, and she hesitates and repeats words and phrases frequently, which requires listener effort. For example, it is hard to follow when she says, "*and and after the construction, the man was saying that maybe it's good after the construction.*" She also does not explicitly explain that the noise from the renovations will cause students to move off campus, and that later on, they will not move back because the renovations will be paid for by raising the price of housing.

3: General/Specific

Prompt

Explain why Henry Darger is considered an Outsider Artist.

Important Points

In this question, you need to explain how Henry Darger fits the description of an Outsider Artist as described in the reading passage. Since Outsider Artists live and work outside of society, they produce art that is unusual and is made in ways that are different from those of other artists. Henry Darger fits this description because he lived and worked alone and taught himself to paint. Therefore his art looked different from other artists' work; for example, in one painting he used cut-out pictures of children from magazines, and his paintings also had more detail and were longer than paintings by most other artists.

High-Level Response:
Listen to Track 75. 🎧

Rater Comments

The speaker does a very good job of choosing details from the lecture that illustrate why Henry Darger is considered an Outsider Artist. He first describes characteristics of Outsider Artists, then describes how Darger matches these characteristics: *"He lived alone; he had no friends . . . he never showed those paintings to anybody; he never studied art. And his work is a unique work, and he has his own style."* Occasionally, the speaker uses the wrong vocabulary word, such as using "conversation" instead of "lecture," but these errors do not make his ideas hard to follow. His response is also fluent, and his pronunciation is almost always easy to understand.

Mid-Level Response:
Listen to Track 76. 🎧

Rater Comments

The speaker organizes her response well, giving two main reasons that Darger was considered an Outsider Artist. However, she does not quite show how living and working alone or lacking a formal art education made him an Outsider Artist—she just seems to be explaining why he is a modern artist.

Most of her pronunciation is clear, but sometimes it is difficult to understand certain phrases. She also makes a number of grammar mistakes: *"he was a man who were different," "his production was totally innovate," "that's why he has make a big difference."* Because of how often she makes these mistakes, the listener sometimes has to work harder to follow her ideas.

4: Summary

Prompt

Using the points and examples from the lecture, explain what unity and contrast are and how they make interior design more effective.

Important Points

In this question, your summary of the key ideas from the lecture should include the definitions of unity and contrast described by the professor. You should also describe how interior designers use unity and contrast, connecting the concepts to the specific examples mentioned. "Unity" is the repetition of similar elements, which creates a sense of order and comfort. For example, a designer might use similar colors throughout a room. "Contrast" is an occasional break in unity, which makes the design more interesting. For example, a designer might introduce a strikingly different color in one or two places. Contrast makes the design more interesting; however, too much contrast will make the room feel busy. Effective design creates a balance between unity and contrast. The order in which you present these ideas does not matter, as long as the response is logical and coherent.

High-Level Response:
Listen to Track 77. 🎧

Rater Comments

This is a complete and coherent response that presents the principles of unity and contrast, connects them clearly to the examples given, and explains why both are necessary for effective interior design. The speaker's logical organization of information and effective use of transitions make the response easy to follow (for example *"however, too much of unity is also boring . . . and therefore, comes into picture the second important aspect, which* is contrast"). Note that although the speaker makes occasional minor errors in grammar and usage, the meaning remains clear. The influence of the speaker's native language may be heard in the pronunciation and intonation, but he is still easy to understand. The speaker generally uses pauses and stress to communicate emphasis appropriately and make the response easier to follow, for example "*what it will bring is* [pause] *disruption.*"

Mid-Level Response:
Listen to Track 78. 🎧
Rater Comments

    This response describes unity and contrast and provides examples, but the explanation is not as full and clear as it could be. For example, the speaker describes unity as just using the same colors in a design, rather than similar elements in general, and does not mention the purpose of unity (order and comfort). At times, inaccurate words or phrases make it difficult to guess what the speaker means ("*You need contrasting thing to blend* [plant?] *the application*"). The speaker would also benefit from more careful pronunciation in general, as some sections are very difficult to understand, thus obscuring her ideas. Overall, the speaker does not communicate her ideas as clearly as the high-level speaker does.

Writing Section

Prompts, Topic Notes, and Sample Responses with Rater Comments

    Use the sample Integrated Writing and Writing for an Academic Discussion Rubrics in Appendix A to see how responses are scored.

    This section includes topic notes that are guides to the kind of information raters expect to read in a high-level response.

    This section also refers to sample responses. These responses were scored at the highest level. The responses are followed by comments from certified ETS raters.

Question 1
Prompt

    Summarize the points made in the lecture, being sure to explain how they cast doubt on the specific points made in the reading passage.

Topic Notes

    The reading discusses three bad effects of people reading less literature than they used to. The lecture shows why these effects are not so bad or are caused by something other than people choosing not to read so much literature.

    Responses with scores of 4 and 5 typically discuss all three points in the table with good accuracy and level of detail. There can be some blending of the ideas in the first two points.

Point made in the reading	Corresponding point from the lecture
The passage argues that reading less literature means that readers are missing out on ways to stimulate their imagination and help with their mental development.	The lecturer points out that there are other forms of writing that are of high quality and just as intellectually stimulating as literature.
The passage argues that many of the kinds of reading that people currently spend time on instead of literature are just trivial entertainment and lead to lower cultural standards.	The lecturer argues that people spend time on culturally valuable activities such as listening to good music or watching good movies. The definition of culture is changing.
The passage says that another bad effect of the decline in reading literature is that talented writers of literature are not being supported.	The lecturer argues that maybe there is less readership of literature because the writers of literature nowadays are making their books/works too hard to understand.

Sample Response

   The lecturer discusses the points made in the text but reaches a different conclusion in each case. For one thing, she states that yes, people are reading less literature then they were in earlier times but this does not equal an imediate decline of culture. On the contrary, in her opinion our culture is simply evolving and changing. Although literature is one of the most obvious elements of culture, there are also lots of other forms of artistic expression in our everchanging culture, e.g. music. And those elements are not less valuable and less creative then literature and they appeal to more modern concerns than literature.

   Also the lecturer disputes the text that says we are going to lose interesting writers of literature. She says that today literature is not interesting enough for the reader! In the lecturers opinion this is mainly due to the fact that modern literature is often written with the intention of beeing difficult to understand, which does not make it very attractive for the modern reader.

   And finally just because people are not reading literature anymore this does not mean they are not reading at all and losing their imagination and empathy; instead there are many other valuable types of books which people are reading, e.g. science textbooks and political analyzis. These books can stimulate readers and provide satisfaction and learning.

Rater Comments

   This response earns a score of 5. The response clearly conveys the key ideas contained in the three points from the lecture. Notice that the points are not presented in the order they are discussed in the reading and lecture, but the way that this writer has presented them is coherent and accurate. Grammatical errors such as "then" instead of "than" in the first paragraph and a missing possessive apostrophe with "lecturers" in the second paragraph are few and minor. Grammatical variety and complexity are clearly present.

Question 2

Prompt

Refer to page 141 to review the Writing for an Academic Discussion question.

Topic Notes

   To earn a top score, you should develop a response that contributes to the discussion about the idea of requiring citizens to vote in elections. An effective response will contain at least 100 words.

   One discussion participant argues that requiring citizens to vote could be advantageous as it will lead people to have a positive attitude toward voting; the other argues that the major disadvantage of making voting obligatory is that it can result in random or ill-informed voting and that encouraging citizens to vote through outreach efforts is a better solution. You might seize on the ideas already stated and develop them in greater detail or introduce entirely new ideas. You may argue, for example, that obligatory voting could lead to more democracy since every citizen's voice would be heard and their opinions would be accounted for.

You should make sure that your ideas are well-supported by reasons and examples and are expressed clearly. Since your response represents an online post, it does not need to be organized into separate paragraphs. However, your ideas need to be well-connected, coherent, and clear. Your response is scored using the Writing for an Academic Discussion rubric (see Appendix A).

Sample Response

In my opinion, people should not be forced to vote. I am a bit of a cynic. I believe that all candidates are the same. It does not make much of a difference which political party you vote for. Traditionally, whoever comes to power works to advance their own interests. Making my vote would be absurd, an exercise in futility. A better idea would be to hold political parties accountable for their actions. There has to be some sort of accountability for candidates who make promises to get elected but never follow through. There have to be laws that prohibit lying to the public to get into office.

Rater Comments

This writer has composed a relevant and very clearly expressed contribution to the online discussion, demonstrating consistent facility in the use of language. The writer clearly explains that requiring people to vote is "absurd" and "an exercise in futility." The writer goes on to provide an alternative course of action that would be more fruitful, which is "to hold political parties accountable for their actions." So rather than forcing people to vote, it is better to have "laws that prohibit lying to the public to get into office." Given the writer's effective use of a variety of syntactic structures and precise word choices, with just a few slipups that can be expected from a competent writer writing under timed conditions (e.g., "Making my vote"), this response should be seen as a high-level response.

TOEFL iBT® Test 4

READING

In this section, you will be able to demonstrate your ability to understand academic passages in English. You will read and answer questions about **two passages**.

In the actual test, you will have 36 minutes total to read both passages and answer the questions. A clock will indicate how much time remains.

Some passages may include one or more notes explaining words or phrases. The words or phrases are marked with footnote numbers, and the notes explaining them appear at the end of the passage.

Most questions are worth 1 point, but the last question for each passage is worth 2 points.

You may review and revise your answers in this section as long as time remains.

At the end of this practice test, you will find an answer key.

Directions: Read the passage. Then answer the questions. You have 18 minutes on average to answer the questions.

THE CHACO PHENOMENON

A truly remarkable transformation in settlement patterns occurred in the San Juan basin in northwestern New Mexico in the late tenth and early eleventh centuries, with small household farmsteads giving way to aggregated communities centered on communal masonry buildings that are now called "great houses." These structures are found throughout the basin but are concentrated in Chaco Canyon, where several examples contained hundreds of rooms and reached four stories in height. The largest great house is Pueblo Bonito, with over 600 rooms covering two acres. The entire episode of great house construction in Chaco, the Bonito phase (900–1140 c.e), was obviously a time of immense cooperative effort. At least 200,000 wooden beams averaging 5 meters long and 20 centimeters in diameter were brought to the canyon from distances between 40 and 100 kilometers away to build a dozen great houses, signifying a huge labor investment and a complex production process. The bulk of construction took place in the eleventh century, but by 1140 c.e it had ceased abruptly, after which there was a rapid decline in use of the great houses and apparent abandonment of the canyon in the thirteenth century.

For more than a century, archaeologists have struggled to understand the circumstances surrounding the rise and collapse of Chacoan society—dubbed the Chaco Phenomenon. In particular, research has focused on determining why such an apparently inhospitable place as Chaco, which today is extremely arid and has very short growing seasons, should have favored the concentration of labor that must have been required for such massive construction projects over brief periods of time. Until the 1970s, it was widely assumed that Chaco had been a forested oasis that attracted farmers who initially flourished but eventually fell victim to their own success and exuberance, as they denuded the canyon of trees and vegetation to build large great houses. In the 1980s this reconstruction was largely dismissed in response to evidence that there had never been a forest in Chaco and that canyon soils had poor agricultural potential. As scientific interpretations about Chaco changed, the focus of explanatory models changed from the attractiveness of the canyon for farmers to the position of the canyon within a regional network of dispersed agricultural communities.

The adoption of a regional perspective in explaining the Chaco Phenomenon was based in part on the discovery of formal trails connecting many of the great houses in Chaco, as well as linking the canyon to smaller great houses located throughout the San Juan basin; the latter are referred to as Chaco "outliers." These trails are densest around the concentration of great houses in the center, and the canyon itself is roughly at the center of the basin. Consequently, the canyon occupies the geographical and social center of the network formed by the connecting trails. The current consensus view is that religion provides the fundamental explanation for this centrifugal pattern.

Archaeologists now describe Chaco during the Bonito phase as a location of high devotional expression and the pilgrimage center of a sacred landscape. These descriptions emphasize aspects of the archaeological record presumed to be associated with ritual activity, including caches of turquoise beads and pendants, unusual ceramic vessels and wooden objects, several rooms with multiple human burials, and especially the large number of kivas (multipurpose rooms used for religious, political, and social functions) found in great houses. Most of these indicators occur only at Pueblo Bonito, but archaeologists generally assume that all the great houses had a similar ritual function. In fact, some scholars have suggested that the great houses were temples rather than residences.

However, new geological field studies in Chaco have produced results that may require a significant reassessment of the assumption that the canyon was not a favorable agricultural setting. It appears that during the first half of the eleventh century, during the extraordinary boom in construction, a large volume of water and suspended sediment flowed into the canyon. A large natural lake may have existed at the western end of Chaco, near the biggest concentration of great houses. The presence of large quantities of water and, equally important, a source of sediment that replenished agricultural fields, presumably made the canyon an extremely attractive place for newly arriving people from the northern San Juan River basin.

Directions: Now answer the questions.

PARAGRAPH 1

A truly remarkable transformation in settlement patterns occurred in the San Juan basin in northwestern New Mexico in the late tenth and early eleventh centuries, with small household farmsteads giving way to aggregated communities centered on communal masonry buildings that are now called "great houses." These structures are found throughout the basin but are concentrated in Chaco Canyon, where several examples contained hundreds of rooms and reached four stories in height. The largest great house is Pueblo Bonito, with over 600 rooms covering two acres. The entire episode of great house construction in Chaco, the Bonito phase (900–1140 C.E), was obviously a time of immense cooperative effort. At least 200,000 wooden beams averaging 5 meters long and 20 centimeters in diameter were brought to the canyon from distances between 40 and 100 kilometers away to build a dozen great houses, **signifying** a huge labor investment and a complex production process. The bulk of construction took place in the eleventh century, but by 1140 C.E it had ceased abruptly, after which there was a rapid decline in use of the great houses and apparent abandonment of the canyon in the thirteenth century.

1. The word "**signifying**" in the passage is closest in meaning to

   A) creating
   B) indicating
   C) initiating
   D) requiring

2. According to paragraph 1, all of the following provide evidence that the Bonito phase was a time of immense cooperative effort EXCEPT

   A) the large amounts of material needed
   B) the size of the Pueblo Bonito complex
   C) the unusual materials used in construction
   D) the distance the materials needed to be transported

PARAGRAPH 2

For more than a century, archaeologists have struggled to understand the circumstances surrounding the rise and collapse of Chacoan society—dubbed the Chaco Phenomenon. **In particular, research has focused on determining why such an apparently inhospitable place as Chaco, which today is extremely arid and has very short growing seasons, should have favored the concentration of labor that must have been required for such massive construction projects over brief periods of time.** Until the 1970s, it was widely assumed that Chaco had been a forested oasis that attracted farmers who initially flourished but eventually fell victim to their own success and exuberance, as they denuded the canyon of trees and vegetation to build large great houses. In the 1980s this reconstruction was largely dismissed in response to evidence that there had never been a forest in Chaco and that canyon soils had poor agricultural potential. As scientific interpretations about Chaco changed, the focus of explanatory models changed from the attractiveness of the canyon for farmers to the position of the canyon within a regional network of dispersed agricultural communities.

3. Which of the sentences below best expresses the essential information in the highlighted sentence in the passage? Incorrect choices change the meaning in important ways or leave out essential information.

   (A) Researchers have tried to establish why an area as dry as Chaco was the site of such large construction efforts.
   (B) Researchers have tried to establish whether the concentration of massive construction projects in a brief period of time made Chaco the dry area that it is today.
   (C) Researchers have established that Chaco's brief growing season required a concentration of labor to produce large quantities of food in a short period of time.
   (D) Researchers have established that the hot, dry climate of Chaco forced workers to complete construction on large buildings in short periods of time.

4. It can be inferred from paragraph 2 that the pre-1970s theory about the Chaco Phenomenon
   (A) was based on the widespread farm and tool remains found by archaeologists on the site
   (B) was largely reinforced by findings in the 1980s
   (C) was not supported by substantial evidence
   (D) was so strong that it went unchallenged for many decades

5. According to paragraph 2, why did scientists change their view about the cause of the collapse of Chacoan society?
   (A) They found evidence that Chaco had always lacked trees and good soil.
   (B) They discovered that Chaco Canyon was much drier than they had previously believed.
   (C) They learned that the population was not large enough to supply the laborers needed to build the great houses.
   (D) They found evidence that the farming economy was excessively concentrated in the central canyon.

PARAGRAPH 4

Archaeologists now describe Chaco during the Bonito phase as a location of high devotional expression and the pilgrimage center of a sacred landscape. These descriptions emphasize aspects of the archaeological record presumed to be associated with ritual activity, including caches of turquoise beads and pendants, unusual ceramic vessels and wooden objects, several rooms with multiple human burials, and especially the large number of kivas (multipurpose rooms used for religious, political, and social functions) found in great houses. Most of these indicators occur only at Pueblo Bonito, but archaeologists generally assume that all the great houses had a similar ritual **function**. In fact, some scholars have suggested that the great houses were temples rather than residences.

6.   The word "**function**" in the passage is closest in meaning to

    (A) center

    (B) practice

    (C) design

    (D) purpose

7.   Which of the following is presented in paragraph 4 as support for the current view of the nature of Chaco during the Bonito phase?

    (A) Evidence that kivas served as temporary houses for pilgrims

    (B) Evidence that outlier communities were centers of trade for jewelry and other products

    (C) Evidence of turquoise beads and pendants in the homes of wealthy residents

    (D) Evidence of objects and rooms associated with religious ceremonies

PARAGRAPH 5

However, new geological field studies in Chaco have produced results that may require a significant reassessment of the assumption that the canyon was not a favorable agricultural setting. It appears that during the first half of the eleventh century, during the extraordinary boom in construction, a large volume of water and suspended sediment flowed into the canyon. **A large natural lake may have existed at the western end of Chaco, near the biggest concentration of great houses.** The presence of large quantities of water and, equally important, a source of sediment that replenished agricultural fields, presumably made the canyon an extremely attractive place for newly arriving people from the northern San Juan River basin.

8.   Why does the author state that "**A large natural lake may have existed at the western end of Chaco, near the biggest concentration of great houses**"?

    (A) To suggest that geological studies are better than archaeological studies in identifying the historical uses of land

    (B) To demonstrate that large construction projects require a large population of workers

    (C) To support the idea that Chaco may have been favorable to agriculture during the Bonito phase

    (D) To show that the Chacoan people preferred to build their homes near water

P
A
R
A
G
R
A
P
H
S

2
&
3

For more than a century, archaeologists have struggled to understand the circumstances surrounding the rise and collapse of Chacoan society—dubbed the Chaco Phenomenon. In particular, research has focused on determining why such an apparently inhospitable place as Chaco, which today is extremely arid and has very short growing seasons, should have favored the concentration of labor that must have been required for such massive construction projects over brief periods of time. Until the 1970s, it was widely assumed that Chaco had been a forested oasis that attracted farmers who initially flourished but eventually fell victim to their own success and exuberance, as they denuded the canyon of trees and vegetation to build large great houses. In the 1980s this reconstruction was largely dismissed in response to evidence that there had never been a forest in Chaco, and that canyon soils had poor agricultural potential. As scientific interpretations about Chaco changed, the focus of explanatory models changed from the attractiveness of the canyon for farmers to the position of the canyon within a regional network of dispersed agricultural communities.

(A) The adoption of a regional perspective in explaining the Chaco Phenomenon was based in part on the discovery of formal trails connecting many of the great houses in Chaco, as well as linking the canyon to smaller great houses located throughout the San Juan basin; the latter are referred to as Chaco "outliers." **(B)** These trails are densest around the concentration of great houses in the center, and the canyon itself is roughly at the center of the basin. **(C)** Consequently, the canyon occupies the geographical and social center of the network formed by the connecting trails. **(D)** The current consensus view is that religion provides the fundamental explanation for this centrifugal pattern.

9. Look at the part of the passage that is displayed above. The letters **(A)**, **(B)**, **(C)**, and **(D)** indicate where the following sentence could be added.

   Scholars have attempted to find a reason for this weblike arrangement of great houses around a central canyon.

   Where would the sentence best fit?
   Ⓐ Choice A
   Ⓑ Choice B
   Ⓒ Choice C
   Ⓓ Choice D

10. **Directions:** An introductory sentence for a brief summary of the passage is provided below. Complete the summary by selecting the THREE answer choices that express the most important ideas in the passage. Some sentences do not belong in the summary because they express ideas that are not presented in the passage or are minor ideas in the passage. **This question is worth 2 points.**

Write your answer choices in the spaces where they belong. You can either write the letter of your answer choice or you can copy the sentence.

> **The population of the Chaco Canyon in New Mexico changed significantly between the tenth and eleventh centuries, as evidenced by the remains of its great houses.**
>
> ●
>
> ●
>
> ●

Answer Choices

A. Before the 1970s, scholars believed that the fall of Chacoan society was caused by farmers' cutting down all the trees to build their great houses.

B. Archaeological findings indicate that Chaco Canyon was completely abandoned by the end of the thirteenth century.

C. After discovering trails connecting Chaco to surrounding communities, scholars came to believe that there were many forested oases to support those communities.

D. Researchers' findings in the 1980s revealed that Chaco Canyon had been a fertile agricultural area, which caused the population near the center of the canyon to increase steadily during the Bonito phase.

E. Archaeological evidence has led current scholars to believe that Chaco was a religious center during the Bonito phase.

F. Recent geological studies indicating the presence of water in Chaco Canyon in the eleventh century may alter scholars' belief that the area was not favorable for farming.

Directions: Read the passage. Then answer the questions. You have 18 minutes on average to answer the questions.

TRANSITION TO SOUND IN FILM

The shift from silent to sound film at the end of the 1920s marks, so far, the most important transformation in motion picture history. Despite all the highly visible technological developments in theatrical and home delivery of the moving image that have occurred over the decades since then, no single innovation has come close to being regarded as a similar kind of watershed. In nearly every language, however the words are phrased, the most basic division in cinema history lies between films that are mute and films that speak.

Yet this most fundamental standard of historical periodization conceals a host of paradoxes. Nearly every movie theater, however modest, had a piano or organ to provide musical accompaniment to silent pictures. In many instances, spectators in the era before recorded sound experienced elaborate aural presentations alongside movies' visual images, from the Japanese *benshi* (narrators) crafting multivoiced dialogue narratives to original musical compositions performed by symphony-size orchestras in Europe and the United States. In Berlin, for the premiere performance outside the Soviet Union of *The Battleship Potemkin*, film director Sergei Eisenstein worked with Austrian composer Edmund Meisel (1894–1930) on a musical score matching sound to image; the Berlin screenings with live music helped to bring the film its wide international fame.

Beyond that, the triumph of recorded sound has overshadowed the rich diversity of technological and aesthetic experiments with the visual image that were going forward simultaneously in the 1920s. New color processes, larger or differently shaped screen sizes, multiple-screen projections, even television, were among the developments invented or tried out during the period, sometimes with startling success. The high costs of converting to sound and the early limitations of sound technology were among the factors that suppressed innovations or retarded advancement in these other areas. The introduction of new screen formats was put off for a quarter century, and color, though utilized over the next two decades for special productions, also did not become a norm until the 1950s.

Though it may be difficult to imagine from a later perspective, a strain of critical opinion in the 1920s predicted that sound film would be a technical novelty that would soon fade from sight, just as had many previous attempts, dating well back before the First World War, to link images with recorded sound. These critics were making a common assumption—that the technological inadequacies of earlier efforts (poor synchronization, weak sound amplification, fragile sound recordings) would invariably occur again. To be sure, their evaluation of the technical flaws in 1920s sound experiments was not so far off the mark, yet they neglected to take into account important new forces in the motion picture field that, in a sense, would not take no for an answer.

These forces were the rapidly expanding electronics and telecommunications companies that were developing and linking telephone and wireless technologies in the 1920s. In the United States, they included such firms as American Telephone and Telegraph, General Electric, and Westinghouse. They were interested in all forms of sound technology and all potential avenues for commercial exploitation. Their competition and collaboration were creating the broadcasting industry in the United States, beginning with the introduction of commercial radio programming in the early 1920s. With financial assets considerably greater than those in the motion picture industry, and perhaps a wider vision of the relationships among entertainment and communications media, they revitalized research into recording sound for motion pictures.

In 1929 the United States motion picture industry released more than 300 sound films—a rough figure, since a number were silent films with music tracks, or films prepared in dual versions, to take account of the many cinemas not yet wired for sound. At the production level, in the United States the conversion was virtually complete by 1930. In Europe it took a little longer, mainly because there were more small producers for whom the costs of sound were prohibitive, and in other parts of the world problems with rights or access to equipment delayed the shift to sound production for a few more years (though cinemas in major cities may have been wired in order to play foreign sound films). The triumph of sound cinema was swift, complete, and enormously popular.

Directions: Now answer the questions.

P A R A G R A P H 2

Yet this most fundamental standard of historical periodization conceals a host of **paradoxes**. Nearly every movie theater, however modest, had a piano or organ to provide musical accompaniment to silent pictures. In many instances, spectators in the era before recorded sound experienced elaborate aural presentations alongside movies' visual images, from the **Japanese benshi** (narrators) crafting multivoiced dialogue narratives to **original musical compositions** performed by symphony-size orchestras in Europe and the United States. In Berlin, for the premiere performance outside the Soviet Union of *The Battleship Potemkin*, film director Sergei Eisenstein worked with Austrian composer Edmund Meisel (1894–1930) on a musical score matching sound to image; the Berlin screenings with live music helped to bring the film its wide international fame.

11. The word "**paradoxes**" in the passage is closest in meaning to

   Ⓐ difficulties
   Ⓑ accomplishments
   Ⓒ parallels
   Ⓓ contradictions

12. Why does the author mention "**Japanese benshi**" and "**original musical compositions**"?

   Ⓐ To suggest that audiences preferred other forms of entertainment to film before the transition to sound in the 1920s
   Ⓑ To provide examples of some of the first sounds that were recorded for film
   Ⓒ To indicate some ways in which sound accompanied film before the innovation of sound films in the late 1920s
   Ⓓ To show how the use of sound in films changed during different historical periods

PARAGRAPH 3

Beyond that, the triumph of recorded sound has overshadowed the rich diversity of technological and aesthetic experiments with the visual image that were going forward simultaneously in the 1920s. New color processes, larger or differently shaped screen sizes, multiple-screen projections, even television, were among the developments invented or tried out during the period, sometimes with startling success. The high costs of converting to sound and the early limitations of sound technology were among the factors that suppressed innovations or retarded advancement in these other areas. The introduction of new screen formats was put off for a quarter century, and color, though utilized over the next two decades for special productions, also did not become a norm until the 1950s.

13. According to paragraph 3, which of the following is NOT true of the technological and aesthetic experiments of the 1920s?

Ⓐ Because the costs of introducing recorded sound were low, it was the only innovation that was put to use in the 1920s.

Ⓑ The introduction of recorded sound prevented the development of other technological innovations in the 1920s.

Ⓒ The new technological and aesthetic developments of the 1920s included the use of color, new screen formats, and television.

Ⓓ Many of the innovations developed in the 1920s were not widely introduced until as late as the 1950s.

PARAGRAPH 4

Though it may be difficult to imagine from a later perspective, a strain of critical opinion in the 1920s predicted that sound film would be a technical novelty that would soon fade from sight, just as had many previous attempts, dating well back before the First World War, to link images with recorded sound. These critics were making a common assumption—that the technological inadequacies of earlier efforts (poor synchronization, weak sound amplification, fragile sound recordings) would invariably occur again. To be sure, their evaluation of the technical flaws in 1920s sound experiments was not so far off the mark, yet they **neglected** to take into account important new forces in the motion picture field that, in a sense, would not take no for an answer.

14. Which of the sentences below best expresses the essential information in the highlighted sentence in the passage? Incorrect choices change the meaning in important ways or leave out essential information.

Ⓐ It was difficult for some critics in the 1920s to imagine why the idea of sound film had faded from sight well before the First World War.

Ⓑ As surprising as it seems today, some critics in the 1920s believed that the new attempts at sound films would fade just as quickly as the attempts made before the First World War.

Ⓒ Though some early critics thought that sound film would fade, its popularity during the First World War proved that it was not simply a technical novelty.

Ⓓ Although some critics predicted well before the First World War that sound film would be an important technical innovation, it was not attempted until the 1920s.

15. The word "**neglected**" in the passage is closest in meaning to

Ⓐ failed

Ⓑ needed

Ⓒ started

Ⓓ expected

16. According to paragraph 4, which of the following is true about the technical problems of early sound films?

Ⓐ Linking images with recorded sound was a larger obstacle than weak sound amplification or fragile sound recordings.

Ⓑ Sound films in the 1920s were unable to solve the technical flaws found in sound films before the First World War.

Ⓒ Technical inadequacies occurred less frequently in early sound films than critics suggested.

Ⓓ Critics assumed that it would be impossible to overcome the technical difficulties experienced with earlier sound films.

PARAGRAPH 5

These forces were the rapidly expanding electronics and telecommunications companies that were developing and linking telephone and wireless technologies in the 1920s. In the United States, they included such firms as American Telephone and Telegraph, General Electric, and Westinghouse. They were interested in all forms of sound technology and all potential avenues for commercial exploitation. Their competition and collaboration were creating the broadcasting industry in the United States, beginning with the introduction of commercial radio programming in the early 1920s. With financial assets considerably greater than those in the motion picture industry, and perhaps a wider vision of the relationships among entertainment and communications media, they revitalized research into recording sound for motion pictures.

17. In paragraph 5, commercial radio programming is best described as the result of

Ⓐ a financially successful development that enabled large telecommunications firms to weaken their competition

Ⓑ the desire of electronics and telecommunications companies to make sound technology profitable

Ⓒ a major development in the broadcasting industry that occurred before the 1920s

Ⓓ the cooperation between telecommunications companies and the motion picture industry

PARAGRAPH 6

In 1929 the United States motion picture industry released more than 300 sound films—a rough figure, since a number were silent films with music tracks, or films prepared in dual versions, to take account of the many cinemas not yet wired for sound. At the production level, in the United States the conversion was virtually complete by 1930. In Europe it took a little longer, mainly because there were more small producers for whom the costs of sound were prohibitive, and in other parts of the world problems with rights or access to equipment delayed the shift to sound production for a few more years (though cinemas in major cities may have been wired in order to play foreign sound films). The triumph of sound cinema was swift, complete, and enormously popular.

18. According to paragraph 6, which of the following accounts for the delay in the conversion to sound films in Europe?

   Ⓐ European producers often lacked knowledge about the necessary equipment for the transition to sound films.

   Ⓑ Smaller European producers were often unable to afford to add sound to their films.

   Ⓒ It was often difficult to wire older cinemas in the major cities to play sound films.

   Ⓓ Smaller European producers believed that silent films with music accompaniment were aesthetically superior to sound films.

PARAGRAPHS 5 & 6

These forces were the rapidly expanding electronics and telecommunications companies that were developing and linking telephone and wireless technologies in the 1920s. In the United States, they included such firms as American Telephone and Telegraph, General Electric, and Westinghouse. They were interested in all forms of sound technology and all potential avenues for commercial exploitation. Their competition and collaboration were creating the broadcasting industry in the United States, beginning with the introduction of commercial radio programming in the early 1920s. **(A)** With financial assets considerably greater than those in the motion picture industry, and perhaps a wider vision of the relationships among entertainment and communications media, they revitalized research into recording sound for motion pictures.

   (B) In 1929 the United States motion picture industry released more than 300 sound films—a rough figure, since a number were silent films with music tracks, or films prepared in dual versions, to take account of the many cinemas not yet wired for sound. **(C)** At the production level, in the United States the conversion was virtually complete by 1930. **(D)** In Europe it took a little longer, mainly because there were more small producers for whom the costs of sound were prohibitive, and in other parts of the world problems with rights or access to equipment delayed the shift to sound production for a few more years (though cinemas in major cities may have been wired in order to play foreign sound films). The triumph of sound cinema was swift, complete, and enormously popular.

19. Look at the part of the passage that is displayed above. The letters **(A)**, **(B)**, **(C)**, and **(D)** indicate where the following sentence could be added.

When this research resulted in the development of vastly improved sound techniques, film studios became convinced of the importance of converting to sound.

Where would the sentence best fit?

   Ⓐ Choice A

   Ⓑ Choice B

   Ⓒ Choice C

   Ⓓ Choice D

20. **Directions:** An introductory sentence for a brief summary of the passage is provided below. Complete the summary by selecting the THREE answer choices that express the most important ideas in the passage. Some sentences do not belong in the summary because they express ideas that are not presented in the passage or are minor ideas in the passage. **This question is worth 2 points.**

Write your answer choices in the spaces where they belong. You can either write the letter of your answer choice or you can copy the sentence.

> **The transition from silent to sound films was the most important development in film history.**
>
> ●
>
> ●
>
> ●

Answer Choices

A Although music and speech had frequently accompanied film presentations before the 1920s, there was a strong desire to add sound to the films themselves.

B Japanese filmmakers had developed the technology for creating sound films before directors in Europe and the United States began experimenting with sound.

C Because of intense interest in developing and introducing sound in film, the general use of other technological innovations being developed in the 1920s was delayed.

D Before the First World War, film directors showed little interest in linking images with recorded sound.

E The rapid progress in sound technology made possible by the involvement of telecommunications companies transformed the motion picture industry.

F The arrival of sound film technology in the United States forced smaller producers in the motion picture industry out of business.

LISTENING

In this section, you will be able to demonstrate your ability to understand conversations and lectures in English.

In the actual test, the section is divided into two separately timed parts. You will hear each conversation or lecture only one time. A clock will indicate how much time remains. The clock will count down only while you are answering questions, not while you are listening. You may take up to 16.5 minutes to answer the questions.

In this practice test, there is no time limit for answering questions.

You may take notes while you listen. You may use your notes to help you answer the questions. Your notes will not be scored.

Answer the questions based on what is stated or implied by the speakers.

In some questions, you will see this icon: 🎧. This means that you will hear, but not see, part of the question.

Answer each question before moving on. Do not return to previous questions.

At the end of this practice test, you will find an answer key.

Directions: Listen to Track 79.

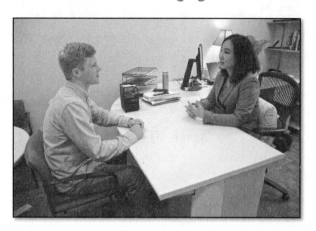

Directions: Now answer the questions.

1. Why does the professor ask the man to come to her office?

    Ⓐ To check on the man's progress on a paper he is writing
    Ⓑ To show the man techniques for organizing his time
    Ⓒ To encourage the man to revise a paper he wrote
    Ⓓ To clarify her comments on a paper the man wrote

2. Why does the man hesitate before agreeing to the professor's request?

    Ⓐ He is not sure his effort would be successful.
    Ⓑ He feels overwhelmed by all his schoolwork.
    Ⓒ He is unclear about what the professor wants him to do.
    Ⓓ He does not like to work on more than one assignment at a time.

3. What is the professor's main criticism of the man's paper?

    Ⓐ It included unnecessary information.
    Ⓑ It did not include enough examples to illustrate the main point.
    Ⓒ The main point was expressed too abstractly.
    Ⓓ The paper ignored a key historical fact.

4. Why does the professor suggest that the student change the introduction of his paper?

    Ⓐ To make it less repetitive
    Ⓑ To more clearly state the man's point of view
    Ⓒ To correct spelling and grammar mistakes
    Ⓓ To reflect changes made elsewhere in the paper

5. *Listen again to part of the conversation by playing Track 80.* *Then answer the question.*

    What does the professor mean when she says this?

    Ⓐ She understands the student's problem.
    Ⓑ She wants the student to explain his comment.
    Ⓒ She did not hear what the student said.
    Ⓓ She does not accept the student's excuse.

Directions: Listen to Track 81.

Biology

chromosome

Directions: Now answer the questions.

6. What does the professor mainly discuss?

   Ⓐ How genes control human development
   Ⓑ Why various types of human cells divide at different rates
   Ⓒ How human chromosomes differ from one another
   Ⓓ Why most human cells cannot keep dividing successfully

7. The professor discusses research about the percentage of a chromosome's DNA that contains genetic information. How did she feel about this research?

   Ⓐ She doubted its accuracy.
   Ⓑ She was surprised by its conclusion.
   Ⓒ She was concerned about its implications.
   Ⓓ She thought it was unnecessary.

8. What does the professor say about the DNA in a telomere?

   (A) It causes a cell to begin dividing.
   (B) It separates one gene from another.
   (C) It is genetically meaningless.
   (D) It has no function.

9. Why does the professor mention shoelaces?

   (A) To point out that chromosomes are arranged in pairs
   (B) To describe the coiled shape of a chromosome
   (C) To illustrate how chromosomes are protected from damage
   (D) To explain how chromosomes are joined before dividing

10. What does the professor imply about the length of the telomeres on a cell's chromosomes?

   (A) Longer telomeres allow the cell to divide more times.
   (B) Longer telomeres contain more genetic information.
   (C) Shorter telomeres are wound into tighter coils.
   (D) Shorter telomeres are less likely to break.

11. According to the professor, how is the chemical telomerase related to the telomere?

   (A) It resembles the telomere in structure.
   (B) It helps repair broken telomeres.
   (C) It is produced at the end of the telomere.
   (D) It prevents telomeres from becoming too long.

Directions: Listen to Track 82.

Directions: Now answer the questions.

12. What is the lecture mainly about?

   Ⓐ Two competing theories of business management

   Ⓑ Tools that business managers can use to improve the efficiency of their employees

   Ⓒ A method for businesses to learn about the needs of their customers

   Ⓓ A way that business managers can better relate to their employees

13. According to the discussion, what is a potential drawback of MBWA?

   Ⓐ MBWA provides information about the opinions of a small number of people.

   Ⓑ MBWA can provide conflicting information.

   Ⓒ Customers often are reluctant to share their opinions.

   Ⓓ Customers may be annoyed about being observed while they shop.

14. What does the professor say about the relationship between MBWA and market research?

   Ⓐ MBWA is a refined version of a market research technique.

   Ⓑ Market research information is more valuable than information from MBWA.

   Ⓒ Information provided by MBWA complements information collected from market research.

   Ⓓ Business managers should replace market research with MBWA.

15. Why does the professor mention Dalton's soup and Elkin jeans?

   Ⓐ To illustrate that the success of MBWA often depends on the product involved

   Ⓑ To give examples of two companies that were resistant to trying MBWA

   Ⓒ To contrast a successful use of MBWA with an unsuccessful use

   Ⓓ To give examples of how the technique of MBWA is used in practice

16. Why does the professor discuss the mayor of Baltimore?

Ⓐ To explain the origins of the method of MBWA

Ⓑ To demonstrate that MBWA can be useful outside the business world

Ⓒ To provide an example of how MBWA can sometimes fail

Ⓓ To give an example where market research and MBWA provide similar types of information

17. *Listen to Track 83 to answer the question.*

    What does the professor imply when she says this?

    Ⓐ It is surprising that Dalton's tried to use MBWA.

    Ⓑ It is surprising that MBWA was successful for Dalton's.

    Ⓒ She does not have a high opinion of the quality of Dalton's soups.

    Ⓓ Dalton's positive experience with MBWA led many other companies to try MBWA.

Directions: Listen to Track 84.

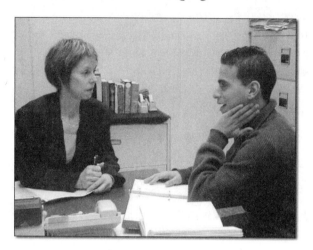

Directions: Now answer the questions.

18. What is the student's problem?

    Ⓐ He missed the tuition due date.

    Ⓑ He has not been paid.

    Ⓒ His bank lost his paycheck.

    Ⓓ His tuition payment got lost.

19. What happened at the payroll department?

    Ⓐ A new computer system was installed.

    Ⓑ Information was entered into the computer system incorrectly.

    Ⓒ Some employee information got lost.

    Ⓓ Paychecks were distributed for the wrong amount.

20. What does the woman imply about the people who work in the payroll office?

    Ⓐ They did not realize they had a problem.

    Ⓑ They are rather disorganized.

    Ⓒ They had tried to contact the man several times.

    Ⓓ They prefer to process checks manually.

21. What will the student probably need to do to get paid?

    Ⓐ Talk to the person who hired him

    Ⓑ Go to the payroll department

    Ⓒ Call the director of the payroll department

    Ⓓ Resubmit the payroll paperwork

22. How does the student's attitude change during the conversation?

    Ⓐ From annoyed to appreciative

    Ⓑ From frustrated to excited

    Ⓒ From surprised to frustrated

    Ⓓ From appreciative to surprised

Directions: Listen to Track 85.

Architecture

duct

Directions: Now answer the questions.

23. What is the main purpose of the lecture?

 Ⓐ To identify the problems associated with reducing energy demands in new buildings

 Ⓑ To explain how traditionally designed buildings can be renovated to become more energy efficient

 Ⓒ To describe new energy requirements for office buildings in the United States

 Ⓓ To present an example of an energy-efficient approach to designing new buildings

24. What point does the professor intend to make when he brings up the shape of the facility's buildings?

 Ⓐ The shape was chosen to maximize the availability of light throughout the buildings.

 Ⓑ The shape allows the buildings to have a smaller footprint than traditional office buildings have.

 Ⓒ The shape allows the buildings to have thinner exterior walls than traditional office buildings have.

 Ⓓ The shape was necessary in order to allow the greatest number of solar panels.

25. What is one student's reaction when she hears that the facility's design calls for many windows?

　　Ⓐ She thinks that having many small windows is a less attractive design than having a few wide windows.

　　Ⓑ She is impressed that the windows can generate electricity from sunlight.

　　Ⓒ She questions whether the windows will function reliably.

　　Ⓓ She is surprised because she thinks the windows will waste energy.

26. According to the professor, what determines the temperature of the barriers in the facility's basements?

　　Ⓐ The amount of heat generated by the facility's solar panels

　　Ⓑ The amount of heat transferred from the facility's windows

　　Ⓒ The temperature of air drawn in from other locations

　　Ⓓ The temperature of the surrounding soil

27. Why does one of the students mention a castle?

　　Ⓐ To confirm his understanding of the concept of thermal mass

　　Ⓑ To find out whether the buildings' concrete has better thermal properties than stone has

　　Ⓒ To suggest that there are alternatives to the design being discussed

　　Ⓓ To imply that there could be drawbacks to relying on thermal mass to heat or cool a building

28. *Listen to Track 86 to answer the question.*

　　Why does the professor say this?

　　Ⓐ Insulated windows were not considered because of the number of windows in the design.

　　Ⓑ A technology that is better than insulated windows was used in the facility.

　　Ⓒ New industry standards for multiple-layered windows are being established based on this facility.

　　Ⓓ Architects used multiple layers of glass as the standard window for this facility.

SPEAKING

In this section, you will be able to demonstrate your ability to speak about a variety of topics.

In the actual test, the Speaking section will last approximately 16 minutes. You will answer four questions by speaking into the microphone. You may take notes while you listen. You may use your notes to help you answer the questions. Your notes will not be scored. For each question, you will have time to prepare before giving your response. You should answer the questions as completely as possible in the time allowed.

For this practice test, you may want to use a personal recording device to record and play back your responses.

For each question, play the audio track listed and follow the directions to complete the task.

At the end of this practice test, you will find important points for each question, sample responses, and comments on those responses by official raters.

1. You will now give your opinion about a familiar topic. After you hear the question, you should give yourself 15 seconds to prepare and 45 seconds to speak.

   Listen to Track 87.

   > Some people believe it's essential for a person's education to learn to play a musical instrument. Others don't believe music education is important. Which view do you agree with? Explain why.
   >
   > | Preparation Time: 15 seconds |
   > | --- |
   > | Response Time: 45 seconds |

2. Now you will read a passage about a campus situation and then listen to a conversation about the same topic. You will then answer a question, using information from both the reading passage and the conversation. You should give yourself 30 seconds to prepare and 60 seconds to speak.

   Listen to Track 88.

Reading Time: 45 seconds

   > **College Radio Station to Undergo Major Changes?**
   >
   > The university is considering making major changes to the college radio station. Changes would include an expansion of the station's broadcasting range, which would allow the radio's programming to reach nearby towns. One goal of the plan is to attract more students to apply to its communications program. Another goal is to provide the university with an extra source of revenue. University officials expect the enhanced radio station to significantly increase the number of listeners, which will in turn encourage businesses to place commercials on the radio.

Listen to Track 89.

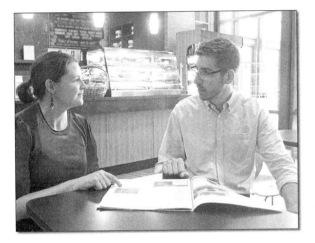

The woman supports the proposal described in the article. Explain why she thinks it will achieve the university's goals.

Preparation Time: 30 seconds
Response Time: 60 seconds

3. Now you will read a passage about an academic subject and then listen to a lecture on the same topic. You will then answer a question, using information from both the reading passage and the lecture. You should give yourself 30 seconds to prepare and 60 seconds to speak.

Listen to Track 90.

Reading Time: 50 seconds

Subliminal Perception

Humans are constantly perceiving visual and auditory stimuli. Sometimes our perception of these stimuli occurs consciously; we are aware of a stimulus and know that we are perceiving it. But our perception of a stimulus can also occur without our awareness: an image might appear and disappear before our eyes too quickly for us to notice that we saw it, or a sound might be too faint for us to realize that we heard it. This phenomenon—the perception of a stimulus just below the threshold of conscious awareness—is called subliminal perception. Experiments have shown that subliminally perceived stimuli can influence people's thoughts and attitudes.

Listen to Track 91.

Describe what subliminal perception is and explain how the experiment discussed by the professor illustrates this phenomenon.

Preparation Time: 30 seconds
Response Time: 60 seconds

4. Now you will listen to a lecture. You will then be asked to summarize the lecture. You should give yourself 20 seconds to prepare and 60 seconds to speak.

Listen to Track 92.

Using the examples from the lecture, explain how industrialism influenced both nineteenth-century and twentieth-century photographers.

Preparation Time: 20 seconds
Response Time: 60 seconds

WRITING

In this section, you will be able to demonstrate your ability to use writing to communicate in an academic environment. There will be two writing tasks.

At the end of this practice test, you will find topic notes for each question.

Turn the page to see the directions for the first writing task.

Writing Based on Reading and Listening

For this task, you will read a passage about an academic topic. Then you will listen to a lecture about the same topic. You may take notes while you listen.

In your response, provide a detailed summary of the lecture and explain how the lecture relates to the reading passage.

In the actual test, you will have 3 minutes to read the passage and 20 minutes to write your response. While you write, you will be able to see the reading passage. If you finish your response before time is up, you may go on to the second writing task.

> **Reading Time: 3 minutes**

Jane Austen (1775–1817) is one of the most famous of all English novelists, and today her novels are more popular than ever, with several recently adapted as Hollywood movies. But we do not have many records of what she looked like. For a long time, the only accepted image of Austen was an amateur sketch of an adult Austen made by her sister Cassandra. However, recently a professionally painted, full-length portrait of a teenage girl owned by a member of the Austen family has come up for sale. Although the professional painting is not titled *Jane Austen*, there are good reasons to believe she is the subject.

First, in 1882, several decades after Austen's death, Austen's family gave permission to use the portrait as an illustration in an edition of her letters. Austen's family clearly recognized it as a portrait of the author. So, for over a century now, the Austen family itself has endorsed the claim that the girl in the portrait is Jane Austen.

Second, the face in the portrait clearly resembles the one in Cassandra's sketch, which we know depicts Austen. Though somewhat amateurish, the sketch communicates definite details about Austen's face. Even though the Cassandra sketch is of an adult Jane Austen, the features are still similar to those of the teenage girl in the painting. The eyebrows, nose, mouth, and overall shape of the face are very much like those in the full-length portrait.

Third, although the painting is unsigned and undated, there is evidence that it was painted when Austen was a teenager. The style links it to Ozias Humphrey, a society portrait painter who was the kind of professional the wealthy Austen family would hire. Humphrey was active in the late 1780s and early 1790s, exactly the period when Jane Austen was the age of the girl in the painting.

Listen to Track 93.

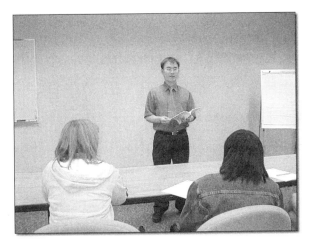

Directions: You have 20 minutes to plan and write your response. Your response will be judged on the basis of the quality of your writing and on how well your response presents the points in the lecture and their relationship to the reading passage. Typically, an effective response will contain a minimum of 150 words.

Listen to Track 94.

Response Time: 20 minutes

Question 1

Summarize the points made in the lecture, being sure to explain how they respond to the specific arguments made in the reading passage.

_____

_____

_____

_____

_____

_____

_____

_____

Writing for an Academic Discussion

For this task, you will read an online discussion. A professor has posted a question about a topic, and some classmates have responded with their ideas.

In the actual test, you will have 10 minutes to write a response that contributes to the discussion.

Question 2

Your professor is teaching a class on business management. Write a post responding to the professor's question.

In your response, you should do the following.

- Express and support your opinion.
- Make a contribution to the discussion in your own words.

An effective response will contain at least 100 words.

Dr. Diaz

In today's fast-paced world, speed is valued. We praise workers who work at a fast pace and make decisions quickly. People who take a lot of time when carrying out tasks or making decisions are often subject to criticism. However, some people believe that taking one's time when working or making decisions is important. Do you agree that taking one's time on work tasks is a good quality for a person to have? Why or why not?

Paul

I disagree. People who have been assigned a task need to meet whatever deadline has been given to them. If they delay completing their work, it has a negative impact on their colleagues. So many projects are collaborative, and one person being late puts pressure on all the other people who have their own deadlines to meet.

Claire

Sure, some tasks need to be completed immediately, but when an important business decision needs to be made, it should not be hurried. Take hiring new employees, for example. That needs to be done properly. I appreciate a hiring manager who does a thorough job evaluating candidates.

Response Time: 10 minutes

ANSWERS

Reading Section

1. B
2. C
3. A
4. C
5. A
6. D
7. D
8. C
9. D
10. A, E, F

11. D
12. C
13. A
14. B
15. A
16. D
17. B
18. B
19. B
20. A, C, E

Listening Section

1. C
2. B
3. A
4. D
5. A
6. D
7. B
8. C
9. C
10. A
11. B
12. C
13. A
14. C

15. D
16. B
17. A
18. B
19. C
20. B
21. D
22. A
23. D
24. A
25. D
26. C
27. A
28. B

Speaking Section

Prompts, Important Points, and Sample Responses with Rater Comments

Use the sample Independent and Integrated Speaking Rubrics in Appendix A to see how responses are scored. The raters who listen to your responses will analyze them in three general categories. These categories are Delivery, Language Use, and Topic Development. All three categories have equal importance.

This section includes important points that should be covered when answering each question. All of these points must be present in a response in order for it to receive the highest score in the Topic Development category. These important points are guides to the kind of information raters expect to hear in a high-level response.

This section also refers to sample responses, which can be found on the audio tracks. Some responses were scored at the highest level, while others were not. The responses are followed by comments from certified ETS raters.

1: Paired Choice

Prompt

Some people believe it's essential for a person's education to learn to play a musical instrument. Others don't believe music education is important. Which view do you agree with? Explain why.

Important Points

When answering this question, you should take a clear stance and explain whether you think that music education or playing a musical instrument is important. You should provide at least one reason to support your point of view, and you should explain that reason in detail. It is acceptable to list several reasons for agreeing or disagreeing with the importance of music education, but you should not simply make a list of reasons without providing any support or explanation for them.

High-Level Response:
Listen to Track 95. 🎧
Rater Comments

In this response, the speaker takes an interesting stance by disagreeing with both statements, though he expresses a clear opinion and gives support for that opinion. He believes that music education is important but not essential. He is able to give reasons for his point of view and support for these reasons. He speaks about people who *"have gone through life successfully without having to learn a musical instrument."* But he also mentions that learning a musical instrument can help with other skills, such as *"logical thinking and math skills,"* and he references studies that have proven this point. He has some minor hesitations in his speech, but he is able to correct himself easily, and he is very easy to understand.

Mid-Level Response:
Listen to Track 96. 🎧
Rater Comments

In this response, the speaker agrees that learning to play a musical instrument is essential. The general content of this response is very close to that of the high-level response, but this speaker does not express her ideas as clearly. She is able to list several reasons for her opinion, but her explanations are sometimes not well developed and therefore are not clear (*"It's very helpful to develop their brain also because they use in the tip of the fingers, for example, keyboard instrument"*). Her pronunciation is mostly clear and easy to understand, but her speech is not always smooth (she pauses frequently and uses words like *"um"*). Her word choice is sometimes inaccurate (*"develop their emotional feeling"*), and she makes small grammatical errors, but she mostly communicates her point of view successfully.

2: Fit and Explain

Prompt

The woman supports the proposal described in the article. Explain why she thinks it will achieve the university's goals.

Important Points

In your answer to this prompt, you should explain that the woman thinks the proposal to expand the student radio station will attract more students to the communications program and allow the university to make money. She thinks that more students will be attracted to the communications program because the proposed changes would allow the radio station to reach a larger audience, which will enable students to get real-life work experience and get better jobs when they graduate. She also thinks that the changes to the radio station will allow the university to make extra money by adding commercials. The extra money made from commercials can be used to offer more scholarships or to help fund other projects in the program. Note that it is not necessary to explain the technical aspects of expanding the broadcasting range of the radio station, as long as it's clear that the changes will allow the station to reach a larger audience.

High-Level Response:
Listen to Track 97.
Rater Comments

The speaker clearly explains why the woman thinks the plan will benefit the school. Both goals (improving job prospects for students and generating money through commercials) are addressed with an appropriate level of detail. The response is well organized and makes logical connections between the plan and its effects (*"the staff will have . . . a better chance of getting a job, because it'll promote interacting with people that are not only students, but people who live in nearby towns."*) The idea of expanding the radio station is implied rather than directly stated (*"right now it is only limited to campus and campus students"*), but this is acceptable for this particular item since the prompt does not ask the speaker to describe the plan. Although the speaker occasionally pauses to think, he speaks for long, fluid stretches between pauses, using appropriate intonation to express meaning. He uses precise vocabulary and complex structures accurately throughout.

Mid-Level Response:
Listen to Track 98.
Rater Comments

Although the speaker addresses all of the points and is understandable, vagueness and simple language keep this response in the middle range. For example, when the speaker says, *"more program would provide for opportunity for more students to have a real experience of what that is,"* the listener has to guess what *"that"* refers to. The speaker also tends to repeat things instead of elaborating on them. For example, after the sentence quoted above, he adds, *"and then they would have – get more jobs after they finish it because they get experience of doing it"* instead of adding details like the fact that the station's wider range would allow students to work with a different type of audience. Sometimes the speaker's sentence structure limits his ability to express himself and make connections between pieces of information. For example, instead of *"they also get more money out of it because of the commercials,"* it would be better to say something like, *"the radio station would also be able to earn more money because their wider audience would allow them to attract more commercials."*

3: General/Specific
Prompt

Describe what subliminal perception is and explain how the experiment discussed by the professor illustrates this phenomenon.

Important Points

In this question, you should describe what subliminal perception is, then discuss the specific information from the experiment and explain how it is related to the general idea of subliminal perception. Subliminal perception is the idea that people perceive an image or other stimulus even if they are not aware that they have experienced it. These subliminal perceptions can influence people's thoughts and actions. The professor describes an experiment in which people were subliminally exposed to different photos (an angry or a happy boy) and then shown a second photo of a boy with a neutral expression. Those who had seen the angry boy described the neutral boy negatively, whereas those who had seen the happy boy described the neutral boy positively. This experiment shows that because of subliminal perception, people were influenced by a photo they were not aware of seeing.

High-Level Response:
Listen to Track 99. 🎧
Rater Comments

The speaker gives a full response. She gives a brief definition of subliminal perception, then describes the experiment in more detail, with good accuracy. She also briefly connects the specific experiment to the general idea of subliminal perception. Although she has a prominent accent, her pronunciation is clear and easy to understand. The response also progresses naturally from idea to idea, making it easier for the listener to follow. Occasional imprecise use of vocabulary or structure (for example, *"the group that have noticed the boy angry"*) does not affect meaning.

Mid-Level Response:
Listen to Track 100. 🎧
Rater Comments

Overall, the speaker's pronunciation is good. There is some hesitation at times in the response, but not to the extent that it creates unnecessary effort for the listener. The content at the beginning and middle of the response is good in general, but the speaker is unable to control more difficult structures, resulting in unclear language and confusion (*"One teacher was shown with in order to the people during the experiment to watch it just a little amount of time"*). Also, although she attempts to summarize the results and connect the experiment to the general idea, she does not describe <u>how</u> the people in the different groups reacted differently (i.e., that one group described the boy negatively and the other group described the boy positively), which is a major omission of the content.

4: Summary
Prompt

Using the examples from the lecture, explain how industrialism influenced both nineteenth-century and twentieth-century photographers.

Important Points

A response to this task should mention that industrialism influenced nineteenth-century and twentieth-century photographers in different ways. On the one hand, nineteenth-century photographers reacted against industrialism by taking pictures that emphasized peaceful nature scenes or rural activities. You should mention how the photograph of the farmworkers that the professor describes is an example of this. Then you should address the point that twentieth-century photographers celebrated or glorified machines and technology. Again, you should mention the professor's example of the automobile factory and include some details about how it glorifies machinery.

High-Level Response:
Listen to Track 101. 🎧
Rater Comments

This is an example of a high-level response. The response is clear and well-paced; while pronunciation is somewhat influenced by the speaker's native language, intelligibility is high, and the response is easy to follow. The response is not perfect (for example, the speaker says that the handheld cart in the first photo was used for *"plowing through clay"* instead of gathering hay); however, this minor error does not detract from the response's overall ability to coherently communicate the ideas from the lecture.

Mid-Level Response:
Listen to Track 102. 🎧
Rater Comments

This is an example of a mid-level response. Though it is generally intelligible and coherent, it does not have the same high level of fluency and efficiency as the high-level response. In the delivery dimension, minor multiple errors in pronunciation and word stress require some listener effort (e.g., *"photographers"*). The response also exhibits language-use limitations, including minor but multiple errors in word choice (e.g., *"nineteenth photographers," "photographies"* instead of "photographs," etc.), which also require some listener effort to process. The pace of the response is somewhat slow as well; while in and of itself this is not a fault, the slower pacing could be responsible for the response being somewhat incomplete as the first example of the farmworkers is omitted and the second example of the automobile factory is mentioned but time runs out before any detail about how the machines were glorified can be included (e.g., sunlight shining onto the machines, the machines sparkling and gleaming, etc.).

Writing Section

Prompts, Topic Notes, and Sample Responses with Rater Comments

Use the sample Integrated Writing and Writing for an Academic Discussion Rubrics in Appendix A to see how responses are scored.

This section includes topic notes that are guides to the kind of information raters expect to read in a high-level response.

This section also refers to sample responses. These responses were scored at the highest level. The responses are followed by comments from certified ETS raters.

Question 1

Prompt

Summarize the points made in the lecture, being sure to explain how they respond to the specific arguments made in the reading passage.

Topic Notes

The reading discusses a painting that has been identified as depicting a teenaged Jane Austen, but the lecturer presents three reasons that cast doubt on the reading's conclusions.

Responses with scores of 4 and 5 typically discuss all three points in the table with good accuracy and level of detail.

Point made in the reading	Corresponding point from the lecture
Jane Austen's family members authorized the portrait for use in the 1882 edition of her letters.	Although Jane Austen's relatives did authorize the portrait in question for use with an edition of her letters, so much time had passed since Jane died that none of them would have actually seen Jane as a teenager.
There is a strong resemblance between Cassandra's sketch of Jane and the portrait.	The portrait could actually be of one of the many female relatives (for example, Mary Ann Campion) who may have resembled Jane and who were teenagers at the time the portrait was painted.
Although we don't know who painted the portrait, its style is like that of a painter who was active at the same time the Austen family might have hired him to paint a teenaged Jane.	A date stamped on the canvas indicates that the canvas was sold by William Legg, who didn't begin selling canvas until Jane was older than the girl in the portrait.

Sample Response

The lecture casts doubt and questions the evidence presented in the reading passage regarding a painting allegedly of Jane Austen.

First, about the family's recognition of the painting as that of Jane's as a teenager. The lecturer points out that in 1882, when the Austen family authorized the use of the painting as a portrait of Jane in the publication of her letters, Jane had been dead for 70 years. Hence, the family members who claimed this portrait to be of Jane's probably have never seen her, and don't necessarily know how she looked.

While the reading passage presents the resemblance of the face features to prove that the teenager in the portrait is indeed Jane, the lecturer sees otherwise: the teenager in the portrait could have been any cousin or niece of Jane. The lecturer claims that there was much resemblance between the Austen family members; specifically he names Mary, one of Jane's distant cousins.

Third, according to the passage the portrait was attributed to Humphrey. However, the lecture presents other evidence relating to the date of the portrait based on the stamp on the canvas itself. According to the stamp it was sold by William Legg, who didn't sell canvas in London when Jane was a teenager. He only began selling canvas in London when Jane was 27 years old.

Rater Comments

This response earns a score of 5. It is a well-organized response that successfully explains the opposing relationship between the reading and the lecture. The three main points from the lecture are clearly identified, and the writer has provided relevant details for each of those main points. One detail about the second point is presented with a minor inaccuracy—Mary Ann Campion is described by the lecturer as Jane Austen's niece, not her cousin—but overall the writer's coverage of this point is sufficient to achieve the highest score. The very few language errors in the response do not interfere with the clear presentation of the essential content from the reading and lecture.

Question 2

Prompt

Refer to page 189 to review the Writing for an Academic Discussion question.

Topic Notes

To earn a top score, you should develop a response that contributes to the discussion about the idea that taking one's time on work tasks is a good quality for an employee. An effective response will contain at least 100 words.

One discussion participant argues against that idea, pointing out that effective collaboration requires everyone to meet their deadlines. The other discussion participant mostly agrees that it is a good quality, pointing out that decision-making—especially hiring decisions—should not be hurried. You might expand on the ideas already stated by the discussion participants or introduce entirely new ideas. You may support the first discussion participant's view and describe in more detail the negative impact on a collaborative team when one or more members are late with a task. You may support the other discussion participant's view and describe other kinds of decisions or tasks in which thoroughness is more important than deadlines. Your own contribution might go somewhere between the two views, explaining, for example, that the best quality a worker can have is the ability to distinguish between situations or tasks in which meeting deadlines is essential versus situations in which a high level of excellence is needed even if deadlines are missed.

You should make sure that your ideas are well-supported by reasons and examples and are expressed clearly. Since your response represents an online post, it does not need to be organized into separate paragraphs. However, your ideas need to be well-connected, coherent, and clear. Your response is scored using the Writing for an Academic Discussion rubric (see Appendix A).

Sample Response

I believe once a task is picked up, be it in any field, it has to be completed with perfection. Of course maintaining deadlines are important, and hence the speed should be maintained as well. But if any task takes longer due to some unforseen issues, the task should not be hurried up just for the sake of meeting the deadline. In such cases, the issues and problems should be discussed with a manager and appropriate action should be taken. It can happen that a task is completed speedily just to meet the deadline, but since it was not completed perfectly, it later led to additional tasks to correct the problems, which is inefficient. To conclude, speed is important, but at the same time perfection in completing the task should also be given equal importance.

Rater Comments

This is a high-level response. It makes a relevant contribution to the discussion by supporting the idea that speed and perfection are equally important but that perfection should not be unnecessarily sacrificed for speed, since imperfect work often leads to additional tasks to correct it. The writer uses a variety of grammatical structures and idiomatic vocabulary effectively, such as "once a task is picked up, be it in any field" and "it can happen that a task is completed speedily just to meet the deadline." The response contains some errors (e.g., the misspelling of "unforeseen" and the verb error in "maintaining deadlines are important"), but they are minor and expected from even proficient writers who are writing under timed writing conditions.

TOEFL iBT® Test 5

READING

In this section, you will be able to demonstrate your ability to understand academic passages in English. You will read and answer questions about **two passages**.

In the actual test, you will have 36 minutes total to read both passages and answer the questions. A clock will indicate how much time remains.

Some passages may include one or more notes explaining words or phrases. The words or phrases are marked with footnote numbers, and the notes explaining them appear at the end of the passage.

Most questions are worth 1 point, but the last question for each passage is worth 2 points.

You may review and revise your answers in this section as long as time remains.

At the end of this practice test, you will find an answer key.

Directions: Read the passage. Then answer the questions. You have 18 minutes on average to answer the questions.

STEEL AND THE UNITED STATES INDUSTRIAL ECONOMY

The period from the early 1890s to the early 1940s can be thought of as the high point of the factory-based industrial economy in the United States. Metals and machines—the mechanical arts—were the economy's technological engine. Just as the Internet provides the common technology platform on which a growing share of economic activity is based today, this period's core technology system was steel, a strong alloy of iron and carbon. Most of the major new processes and products of the era (e.g., steel processing, mechanical harvesters, machine tools, mechanical mining drills, and transcontinental railroads) were based on breakthroughs in metallurgy that produced metals with qualities that allowed them to be shaped and molded to tolerances unknown in the past. Hardened steel enabled machine tools to cut metal parts to precise tolerances, which increased the use of standardized and interchangeable parts. That in turn enabled the development of assembly-line production. The centrality of iron and steel to industry in this period is why books on the American economy written as late as 1957 would usually begin with a chapter on the iron and steel industry, since (in one commentator's words) "they serve a vital position in civilization."

Steel enjoyed rapid declines in price and improvements because of the introduction of the Bessemer converter (a large pear-shaped container in which air is blown through molten iron to remove impurities and create steel) in the mid-1870s. In 1873 steel was selling for $100 a ton. By 1885 it had fallen to $20 a ton, and by the mid-1890s it was down to $12. The rapid decline in the prices and the dramatic improvements in quality (e.g., hardness and resistance to corrosion) meant that steel could be economically useful in a host of new applications. Between 1870 and the early 1900s, steel overtook iron in production, rising from virtually no production in 1870 to almost 40 million tons in 1915. These developments were at the heart of the mechanical revolution, with cheap steel underpinning the development of automobiles, bicycles, sewing machines, typewriters, machine tools of every description, harvesters, steel girder–based skyscrapers, elevators, and a host of other innovations.

Consider steel's role in the transformation of railroading, what used to be known as the "iron horse." Before steel, railroads had grown, but limitations in metallurgy and machining meant that they were slower, smaller, and less powerful. Cheap steel made more durable tracks, more powerful locomotives, and better brakes all possible. New steel technology enabled coal cars to carry up to 100 tons by 1920, up from 10 tons in 1870. Organizational changes complemented technological ones. In 1871, 23 different track gauges (the distance between the two rails) were in use. By 1886 the nation used just one. And by 1900 virtually every state was part of a national railroad network. Rail miles grew from about 32,000 in 1860 to about 180,000 in the mid-1890s. A national rail network was critical to the support of a factory-based manufacturing economy. Factories were successful because they were able to operate efficiently on a large scale. But they needed to find ways to get their output to distant markets, and the railroad was that way. Railroads thus helped foster a manufacturing economy, which in turn led to greater demands for rail. This self-reinforcing cycle meant that railroad employment increased significantly, from 750,000 in 1890 to 2.1 million in 1920—a number not achieved since. Regions producing steel (like Pittsburgh) or using steel (like Cleveland) boomed with rapidly expanding populations. For example, Cleveland's prosperity was based on making metal products (ships, bridges, houses, conveyors, pumps, compressors, and bicycles). By 1880 Cleveland boasted 23 metal firms capitalized at between $200,000 and $1 million each.

While other innovations, such as the telephone, electricity, chemical processing, and the automobile, emerged in this period, they did not become truly national, widely adopted industries until after the Second World War (1939–1945), when an economy of mass production developed. From 1880 to 1904 the telephone infrastructure spread from New York and a few northeastern cities to virtually the whole nonrural nation. However, it was not until the economic period of mass production in the 1950s that it would be possible to speak of truly universal telephone service penetration. One indicator of this is that telegraph traffic grew steadily until the 1940s, when telephone costs finally fell enough to make it a more competitive long-distance alternative.

Directions: Now answer the questions.

PARAGRAPH 1

The period from the early 1890s to the early 1940s can be thought of as the high point of the factory-based industrial economy in the United States. Metals and machines—the mechanical arts—were the economy's technological engine. Just as the Internet provides the common technology platform on which a growing share of economic activity is based today, this period's core technology system was steel, a strong alloy of iron and carbon. Most of the major new processes and products of the era (e.g., steel processing, mechanical harvesters, machine tools, mechanical mining drills, and transcontinental railroads) were based on breakthroughs in metallurgy that produced metals with qualities that allowed them to be shaped and molded to tolerances unknown in the past. Hardened steel enabled machine tools to cut metal parts to precise tolerances, which increased the use of standardized and interchangeable parts. That in turn enabled the development of assembly-line production. The centrality of iron and steel to industry in this period is why books on the American economy written as late as 1957 would usually begin with a chapter on the iron and steel industry, since (in one commentator's words) "they serve a vital position in civilization."

1. According to paragraph 1, which of the following was true of hardened steel?

  (A) It was cut to precise tolerances.
  (B) It was the metal used for standardized and interchangeable parts.
  (C) It was used to cut metal.
  (D) It was used in assembly-line production.

Steel enjoyed rapid declines in price and improvements because of the introduction of the Bessemer converter (a large pear-shaped container in which air is blown through molten iron to remove impurities and create steel) in the mid-1870s. In 1873, steel was selling for $100 a ton. By 1885 it had fallen to $20 a ton, and by the mid-1890s it was down to $12. The rapid decline in the prices and the dramatic improvements in quality (e.g., hardness and **resistance to corrosion**) meant that steel could be economically useful in a host of new applications. Between 1870 and the early 1900s, steel overtook iron in production, rising from virtually no production in 1870 to almost 40 million tons in 1915. These developments were at the heart of the mechanical revolution, with cheap steel underpinning the development of automobiles, bicycles, sewing machines, typewriters, machine tools of every description, harvesters, steel girder-based skyscrapers, elevators, and a host of other innovations.

2. To say that steel has the quality of "**resistance to corrosion**" means that steel

    (A) removes corrosion

    (B) does not easily become corroded

    (C) interrupts corrosion

    (D) is not weakened when it corrodes

3. Paragraph 2 supports which of the following about the Bessemer converter?

    (A) It was used to make automobiles, sewing machines, harvesters, and elevators.

    (B) It was first used in iron production but its later use in steel production allowed steel to eventually overtake iron in production between 1870 and the early 1890s.

    (C) It contributed to the production of high-quality steel, which made the mechanical revolution possible.

    (D) It experienced a rapid decline in price from its introduction in the mid-1870s until the mid-1890s.

Consider steel's role in the transformation of railroading, what used to be known as the "iron horse." Before steel, railroads had grown, but limitations in metallurgy and machining meant that they were slower, smaller, and less powerful. Cheap steel made more durable tracks, more powerful locomotives, and better brakes all possible. New steel technology enabled coal cars to carry up to 100 tons by 1920, up from 10 tons in 1870. Organizational changes complemented technological ones. In 1871, 23 different track gauges (the distance between the two rails) were in use. By 1886 the nation used just one. And by 1900 virtually every state was part of a national railroad network. Rail miles grew from about 32,000 in 1860 to about 180,000 in the mid-1890s. A national rail network was **critical to the support of a factory-based manufacturing economy**. Factories were successful because they were able to operate efficiently on a large scale. But they needed to find ways to get their output to distant markets, and the railroad was that way. Railroads thus helped foster a manufacturing economy, which in turn led to greater demands for rail. This **self-reinforcing** cycle meant that railroad employment increased significantly, from 750,000 in 1890 to 2.1 million in 1920—a number not achieved since. Regions producing steel (like Pittsburgh) or using steel (like Cleveland) boomed with rapidly expanding populations. For example, Cleveland's prosperity was based on making metal products (ships, bridges, houses, conveyors, pumps, compressors, and bicycles). By 1880 Cleveland boasted 23 metal firms capitalized at between $200,000 and $1 million each.

4. Which of the following is mentioned in paragraph 3 as the reason that a rail network was **"critical to the support of a factory-based manufacturing economy"**?

    (A) It delivered steel to the factories.
    (B) It made it easier for factories to get access to raw materials used for manufacturing.
    (C) It provided convenient transportation for people who worked in factories.
    (D) It allowed factories to get their products to markets.

5. The word "**self-reinforcing**" in the passage is closest in meaning to

    (A) self-sufficient
    (B) self-contained
    (C) self-reproducing
    (D) self-strengthening

6. According to paragraph 3, all of the following were true of Cleveland EXCEPT:

    (A) The number of its inhabitants increased greatly.
    (B) It became rich producing steel.
    (C) It made a variety of metal products.
    (D) It had numerous well-capitalized businesses.

PARAGRAPH 4

While other innovations, such as the telephone, electricity, chemical processing, and the automobile, emerged in this period, they did not become truly national, widely adopted industries until after the Second World War (1939–1945), when an economy of mass production developed. From 1880 to 1904 the telephone infrastructure spread from New York and a few northeastern cities to virtually the whole nonrural nation. However, it was not until the economic period of mass production in the 1950s that it would be possible to speak of truly universal telephone service penetration. One indicator of this is that **telegraph traffic grew steadily until the 1940s**, when telephone costs finally fell enough to make it a more competitive long-distance alternative.

7. The author provides the information that "**telegraph traffic grew steadily until the 1940s**" in order to

    (A) support the claim that the telephone did not dominate communications until the 1950s
    (B) explain how competition finally drove down telephone costs in rural regions
    (C) argue that the telegraph was one of the most widely adopted industries before the postwar mass production economy
    (D) provide evidence that telecommunications were nearly as important in the previous century as they are today

8. According to paragraph 4, what was true about the innovations that emerged during the industrial era?

    (A) They became nationally available due to the development of mass production.
    (B) Their spread throughout the nation was interrupted by the Second World War.
    (C) They required expensive infrastructure to become available throughout the nation.
    (D) They made New York and a few other northeastern cities very popular.

P
A
R
A
G
R
A
P
H

3

Consider steel's role in the transformation of railroading, what used to be known as the "iron horse." **(A)** Before steel, railroads had grown, but limitations in metallurgy and machining meant that they were slower, smaller, and less powerful. **(B)** Cheap steel made more durable tracks, more powerful locomotives, and better brakes all possible. **(C)** New steel technology enabled coal cars to carry up to 100 tons by 1920, up from 10 tons in 1870. **(D)** Organizational changes complemented technological ones. In 1871, 23 different track gauges (the distance between the two rails) were in use. By 1886 the nation used just one. And by 1900 virtually every state was part of a national railroad network. Rail miles grew from about 32,000 in 1860 to about 180,000 in the mid-1890s. A national rail network was critical to the support of a factory-based manufacturing economy. Factories were successful because they were able to operate efficiently on a large scale. But they needed to find ways to get their output to distant markets, and the railroad was that way. Railroads thus helped foster a manufacturing economy, which in turn led to greater demands for rail. This self-reinforcing cycle meant that railroad employment increased significantly, from 750,000 in 1890 to 2.1 million in 1920—a number not achieved since. Regions producing steel (like Pittsburgh) or using steel (like Cleveland) boomed with rapidly expanding populations. For example, Cleveland's prosperity was based on making metal products (ships, bridges, houses, conveyors, pumps, compressors, and bicycles). By 1880 Cleveland boasted 23 metal firms capitalized at between $200,000 and $1 million each.

9. Look at the part of the passage that is displayed above. The letters **(A)**, **(B)**, **(C)**, and **(D)** indicate where the following sentence could be added.

   That all changed once it became possible to improve steel's quality more economically.

   Where would the sentence best fit?

   Ⓐ Choice A
   Ⓑ Choice B
   Ⓒ Choice C
   Ⓓ Choice D

10. **Directions:** An introductory sentence for a brief summary of the passage is provided below. Complete the summary by selecting the THREE answer choices that express the most important ideas in the passage. Some sentences do not belong in the summary because they express ideas that are not presented in the passage or are minor ideas in the passage. **This question is worth 2 points.**

> **From the early 1890s to the early 1940s, the United States economy was powered by metals and machines.**
>
> ●
>
> ●
>
> ●

Answer Choices

A Steel was the main technology of the age, allowing for standardized parts, assembly lines, machine tools, and a host of products from sewing machines to skyscrapers.

B Because the price of steel tended to fluctuate, industries continued to use iron in new products and applications until the price of steel stabilized in the early 1900s.

C The railroads, which saw many improvements as steel replaced iron, were essential to the factory-based economy.

D Organizational changes complemented technological ones as alliances were made between companies that produced steel and those that used steel to make products.

E Other important innovations of this period, including the telephone, electricity, and the automobile, did not become truly universal until the 1950s.

F Industrial regions like Pittsburgh and Cleveland flourished, while rural areas, which often did not even have telephones, suffered from decline and economic neglect.

Directions: Read the passage. Then answer the questions. You have 18 minutes on average to answer the questions.

METHODS OF STUDYING INFANT PERCEPTION

In the study of perceptual abilities of infants, a number of techniques are used to determine infants' responses to various stimuli. Because they cannot verbalize or fill out questionnaires, indirect techniques of naturalistic observation are used as the primary means of determining what infants can see, hear, feel, and so forth. Each of these methods compares an infant's state prior to the introduction of a stimulus with its state during or immediately following the stimulus. The difference between the two measures provides the researcher with an indication of the level and duration of the response to the stimulus. For example, if a uniformly moving pattern of some sort is passed across the visual field of a neonate (newborn), repetitive following movements of the eye occur. The occurrence of these eye movements provides evidence that the moving pattern is perceived at some level by the newborn. Similarly, changes in the infant's general level of motor activity—turning the head, blinking the eyes, crying, and so forth—have been used by researchers as visual indicators of the infant's perceptual abilities.

Such techniques, however, have limitations. First, the observation may be unreliable in that two or more observers may not agree that the particular response occurred, or to what degree it occurred. Second, responses are difficult to quantify. Often the rapid and diffuse movements of the infant make it difficult to get an accurate record of the number of responses. The third, and most potent, limitation is that it is not possible to be certain that the infant's response was due to the stimulus presented or to a change from no stimulus to a stimulus. The infant may be responding to aspects of the stimulus different than those identified by the investigator. Therefore, when observational assessment is used as a technique for studying infant perceptual abilities, care must be taken not to overgeneralize from the data or to rely on one or two studies as conclusive evidence of a particular perceptual ability of the infant.

Observational assessment techniques have become much more sophisticated, reducing the limitations just presented. Film analysis of the infant's responses, heart and respiration rate monitors, and nonnutritive sucking devices are used as effective tools in understanding infant perception. Film analysis permits researchers to carefully study the infant's responses over and over and in slow motion. Precise measurements can be made of the length and frequency of the infant's attention between two stimuli. Heart and respiration monitors provide the investigator with the number of heartbeats or breaths taken when a new stimulus is presented. Numerical increases are used as quantifiable indicators of heightened interest in the new stimulus. Increases in nonnutritive sucking were first used as an assessment measure by researchers in 1969. They devised an apparatus that connected a baby's pacifier[1] to a counting device. As stimuli were presented, changes in the infant's sucking behavior were recorded. Increases in the number of sucks were used as an indicator of the infant's attention to or preference for a given visual display.

Two additional techniques of studying infant perception have come into vogue. The first is the habituation-dishabituation technique, in which a single stimulus is presented repeatedly to the infant until there is a measurable decline (habituation) in whatever attending behavior is being observed. At that point a new stimulus is presented, and any recovery (dishabituation) in responsiveness is recorded. If the infant fails to dishabituate and continues to show habituation with the new stimulus, it is assumed that the baby is unable to perceive the new stimulus as different. The habituation-dishabituation paradigm has been used most extensively with studies of auditory and olfactory perception in infants. The second technique relies on evoked potentials, which are electrical brain responses that may be related to a particular stimulus because of where they originate. Changes in the electrical pattern of the brain indicate that the stimulus is getting through to the infant's central nervous system and eliciting some form of response.

Each of the preceding techniques provides the researcher with evidence that the infant can detect or discriminate between stimuli. With these sophisticated observational assessment and electrophysiological measures, we know that the neonate of only a few days is far more perceptive than previously suspected. However, these measures are only "indirect" indicators of the infant's perceptual abilities.

¹**pacifier:** a small plastic device for babies to suck or bite on

Directions: Now answer the questions.

P A R A G R A P H 1

In the study of perceptual abilities of infants, a number of techniques are used to determine infants' responses to various stimuli. Because they cannot verbalize or fill out questionnaires, indirect techniques of naturalistic observation are used as the primary means of determining what infants can see, hear, feel, and so forth. Each of these methods compares an infant's state prior to the introduction of a stimulus with its state during or immediately following the stimulus. The difference between the two measures provides the researcher with an indication of the level and duration of the response to the stimulus. For example, if a uniformly moving pattern of some sort is passed across the visual field of a neonate (newborn), **repetitive following movements of the eye** occur. The occurrence of these eye movements provides evidence that the moving pattern is perceived at some level by the newborn. Similarly, changes in the infant's general level of motor activity—turning the head, blinking the eyes, crying, and so forth—have been used by researchers as visual indicators of the infant's perceptual abilities.

11. Why does the author mention "**repetitive following movements of the eye**"?

Ⓐ To identify a response that indicates a neonate's perception of a stimulus
Ⓑ To explain why a neonate is capable of responding to stimuli only through repetitive movements
Ⓒ To argue that motor activity in a neonate may be random and unrelated to stimuli
Ⓓ To emphasize that responses to stimuli vary in infants according to age

P A R A G R A P H 2

Such techniques, however, have limitations. First, the observation may be unreliable in that two or more observers may not agree that the particular response occurred, or to what degree it occurred. Second, responses are difficult to quantify. Often the rapid and diffuse movements of the infant make it difficult to get an accurate record of the number of responses. The third, and most potent, limitation is that it is not possible to be certain that the infant's response was due to the stimulus presented or to a change from no stimulus to a stimulus. The infant may be responding to aspects of the stimulus different than those identified by the investigator. **Therefore, when observational assessment is used as a technique for studying infant perceptual abilities, care must be taken not to overgeneralize from the data or to rely on one or two studies as conclusive evidence of a particular perceptual ability of the infant.**

12. Which of the following is NOT mentioned in paragraph 2 as a problem in using the technique of direct observation?

    Ⓐ It is impossible to be certain of the actual cause of an infant's response.

    Ⓑ Infants' responses, which occur quickly and diffusely, are often difficult to measure.

    Ⓒ Infants do not respond well to stimuli presented in an unnatural laboratory setting.

    Ⓓ It may be difficult for observers to agree on the presence or the degree of a response.

13. Which of the sentences below best expresses the essential information in the highlighted sentence in the passage? Incorrect choices change the meaning in important ways or leave out essential information.

    Ⓐ Researchers using observational assessment techniques on infants must not overgeneralize and must base their conclusions on data from many studies.

    Ⓑ On the basis of the data from one or two studies, it seems that some infants develop a particular perceptual ability not observed in others.

    Ⓒ To use data from one or two studies on infants' perceptual abilities, it is necessary to use techniques that will provide conclusive evidence.

    Ⓓ When researchers fail to make generalizations from their studies, their observed data is often inconclusive.

PARAGRAPH 3

Observational assessment techniques have become much more sophisticated, reducing the limitations just presented. Film analysis of the infant's responses, heart and respiration rate monitors, and nonnutritive sucking devices are used as effective tools in understanding infant perception. Film analysis permits researchers to carefully study the infant's responses over and over and in slow motion. Precise measurements can be made of the length and frequency of the infant's attention between two stimuli. Heart and respiration monitors provide the investigator with the number of heartbeats or breaths taken when a new stimulus is presented. Numerical increases are used as **quantifiable** indicators of heightened interest in the new stimulus. Increases in nonnutritive sucking were first used as an assessment measure by researchers in 1969. They devised an apparatus that connected a baby's pacifier to a counting device. As stimuli were presented, changes in the infant's sucking behavior were recorded. Increases in the number of sucks were used as an indicator of the infant's attention to or preference for a given visual display.

14. What is the author's primary purpose in paragraph 3 ?

    Ⓐ To explain why researchers must conduct more than one type of study when they are attempting to understand infant perception

    Ⓑ To describe new techniques for observing infant perception that overcome problems identified in the previous paragraph

    Ⓒ To present and evaluate the conclusions of various studies on infant perception

    Ⓓ To point out the strengths and weaknesses of three new methods for quantifying an infant's reaction to stimuli

15. The word "**quantifiable**" in the passage is closest in meaning to

   (A) visual
   (B) permanent
   (C) meaningful
   (D) measurable

16. Paragraph 3 mentions all of the following as indications of an infant's heightened interest in a new stimulus EXCEPT an increase in

   (A) sucking behavior
   (B) heart rate
   (C) the number of breaths taken
   (D) eye movements

PARAGRAPH 4

Two additional techniques of studying infant perception have come into vogue. The first is the habituation-dishabituation technique, in which a single stimulus is presented repeatedly to the infant until there is a measurable decline (habituation) in whatever attending behavior is being observed. At that point a new stimulus is presented, and any recovery (dishabituation) in responsiveness is recorded. If the infant fails to dishabituate and continues to show habituation with the new stimulus, it is assumed that the baby is unable to perceive the new stimulus as different. The habituation-dishabituation paradigm has been used most extensively with studies of auditory and olfactory perception in infants. The second technique relies on evoked potentials, which are electrical brain responses that may be related to a particular stimulus because of where they originate. Changes in the electrical pattern of the brain indicate that the stimulus is getting through to the infant's central nervous system and eliciting some form of response.

17. According to paragraph 4, which of the following leads to the conclusion that infants are able to differentiate between stimuli in a habituation-dishabituation study?

   (A) Dishabituation occurs with the introduction of a new stimulus.
   (B) Electrical responses in the infant's brain decline with each new stimulus.
   (C) Habituation is continued with the introduction of a new stimulus.
   (D) The infant displays little change in electrical brain responses.

PARAGRAPH 5

Each of the preceding techniques provides the researcher with evidence that the infant can detect or discriminate between stimuli. With these sophisticated observational assessment and electrophysiological measures, we know that the neonate of only a few days is far more perceptive than previously suspected. However, these measures are only "indirect" indicators of the infant's perceptual abilities.

18. Paragraph 5 indicates that researchers who used the techniques described in the passage discovered that

(A) infants find it difficult to perceive some types of stimuli

(B) neonates of only a few days cannot yet discriminate between stimuli

(C) observational assessment is less useful for studying infant perception than researchers previously believed

(D) a neonate is able to perceive stimuli better than researchers once thought

P A R A G R A P H 3

Observational assessment techniques have become much more sophisticated, reducing the limitations just presented. Film analysis of the infant's responses, heart and respiration rate monitors, and nonnutritive sucking devices are used as effective tools in understanding infant perception. **(A)** Film analysis permits researchers to carefully study the infant's responses over and over and in slow motion. **(B)** Precise measurements can be made of the length and frequency of the infant's attention between two stimuli. **(C)** Heart and respiration monitors provide the investigator with the number of heartbeats or breaths taken when a new stimulus is presented. **(D)** Numerical increases are used as quantifiable indicators of heightened interest in the new stimulus. Increases in nonnutritive sucking were first used as an assessment measure by researchers in 1969. They devised an apparatus that connected a baby's pacifier to a counting device. As stimuli were presented, changes in the infant's sucking behavior were recorded. Increases in the number of sucks were used as an indicator of the infant's attention to or preference for a given visual display.

19. Look at the part of the passage that is displayed above. The letters **(A)**, **(B)**, **(C)**, and **(D)** indicate where the following sentence could be added.

The repetition allows researchers to observe the infant's behavior until they reach agreement about the presence and the degree of the infant's response.

Where would the sentence best fit?

(A) Choice A

(B) Choice B

(C) Choice C

(D) Choice D

20. **Directions:** An introductory sentence for a brief summary of the passage is provided below. Complete the summary by selecting the THREE answer choices that express the most important ideas in the passage. Some sentences do not belong in the summary because they express ideas that are not presented in the passage or are minor ideas in the passage. **This question is worth 2 points.**

Write your answer choices in the spaces where they belong. You can either write the letter of your answer choice or you can copy the sentence.

> **Researchers use a number of techniques to determine how infants respond to changes in their environment.**

- ●

- ●

- ●

Answer Choices

A. Data from observational methods must be confirmed through multiple studies.

B. Visual indicators such as turning the head, blinking the eyes, or crying remain the best evidence of an infant's perceptual abilities.

C. New techniques for studying infant perception have improved the accuracy with which researchers observe and quantify infant responses.

D. Pacifiers are commonly used in studies to calm an infant who has been presented with excessive stimuli.

E. Indirect observation is most accurate when researchers use it to test auditory and olfactory perception in neonates.

F. Sophisticated techniques that have aided new discoveries about perception in the neonate continue to be indirect measures.

LISTENING

In this section, you will be able to demonstrate your ability to understand conversations and lectures in English.

In the actual test, the section is divided into two separately timed parts. You will hear each conversation or lecture only one time. A clock will indicate how much time remains. The clock will count down only while you are answering questions, not while you are listening. You may take up to 16.5 minutes to answer the questions.

In this practice test, there is no time limit for answering questions.

You may take notes while you listen. You may use your notes to help you answer the questions. Your notes will not be scored.

Answer the questions based on what is stated or implied by the speakers.

In some questions, you will see this icon: 🎧 . This means that you will hear, but not see, part of the question.

Answer each question before moving on. Do not return to previous questions.

At the end of this practice test, you will find an answer key.

Directions: Listen to Track 103.

Directions: Now answer the questions.

1. Why does the student go to see the professor?

   Ⓐ To report on the research he has done
   Ⓑ To ask for permission to observe a class
   Ⓒ To get help understanding an assignment
   Ⓓ To ask about a question on a recent test

2. According to the professor, what should the student do after completing the first observation?

   Ⓐ Look for another child to observe
   Ⓑ Research the child's developmental stage
   Ⓒ Report his progress to the class
   Ⓓ Submit the notes he took during the observation

3. Why does the student mention a child playing with a toy car?

   Ⓐ To identify a behavior that would show a child's imagination developing
   Ⓑ To identify a behavior that might illustrate egocentric thinking
   Ⓒ To give an example of a behavior he has observed
   Ⓓ To give an example of a behavior he would not need to describe

4. Why should the student contact the education department secretary?

   Ⓐ Her child attends a school run by the university.
   Ⓑ She has a list of families that might be able to help the man.
   Ⓒ She can contact students who have worked on a similar project.
   Ⓓ She will explain how to observe a class without disturbing it.

5. *Listen again to part of the conversation by playing Track 104.* *Then answer the question.*

What does the professor mean when she says this?

(A) The man's paper has a strong introduction.
(B) The man has already started his research project.
(C) The assignment cannot be submitted late.
(D) The man does not fully understand the assignment.

Directions: Listen to Track 105.

City Planning

pedestrian malls

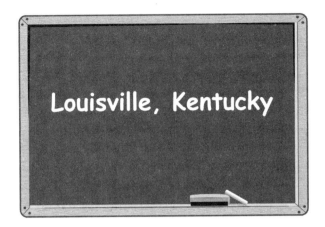

Directions: Now answer the questions.

6. What is the main topic of the lecture?

    (A) How the first pedestrian mall was developed
    (B) How pedestrian malls have affected business in America
    (C) Key considerations in creating a pedestrian mall
    (D) Ways that cities can better use pedestrian malls

7. According to the professor, what is the basic reason for building pedestrian malls in the city center?

    (A) To increase retail activity in the area
    (B) To reduce the noise made by automobile traffic
    (C) To increase shopping conveniences for city residents
    (D) To encourage people to move from the suburbs back into the city center

8. What are two aspects of location that need to be considered when planning a pedestrian mall? *Select 2 answers.*

    [A] The proximity to the customer base
    [B] The number of nearby tourist sites
    [C] The variety of restaurants in the area
    [D] The access to public transportation

9. Why does the professor explain the design of a pedestrian mall?

    (A) To illustrate its importance to the success of a pedestrian mall
    (B) To explain why pedestrian malls are so appealing to shoppers
    (C) To point out how a pedestrian mall looks different from other malls
    (D) To show how the design is more important than the location

10. Why does the professor mention the Louisville, Kentucky, pedestrian mall?

    Ⓐ To discuss her favorite pedestrian mall to visit

    Ⓑ To illustrate how a pedestrian mall can overcome financial difficulties

    Ⓒ To give an example of a typical American pedestrian mall

    Ⓓ To show how poor planning can affect the success of a pedestrian mall

11. *Listen to Track 106 to answer the question.*

    What does the professor mean when she says this?

    Ⓐ Art is of little importance in designing a pedestrian mall.

    Ⓑ There should be a wide variety of art on display in pedestrian malls.

    Ⓒ Art is a key feature in the designing of a pedestrian mall.

    Ⓓ Most pedestrian mall designers do not like art as much as she does.

Directions: Listen to Track 107.

Ecology

Directions: Now answer the questions.

12. What is the class mainly discussing?

    Ⓐ How beavers select the ecosystems where they live

    Ⓑ How ecosystems differ from one another

    Ⓒ The impact of human activities on an ecosystem

    Ⓓ The role of one species in an ecosystem

13. Why does the professor interrupt the student when he first mentions European settlement in North America?

    Ⓐ She had already mentioned that point.

    Ⓑ She thinks the information he gave is unrelated to the topic.

    Ⓒ She prefers to present the information in the lecture in a specific order.

    Ⓓ She questions the accuracy of his point.

14. What does the professor say about still water and swiftly flowing water?

    Ⓐ Beavers cannot adapt to living near swiftly flowing water.

    Ⓑ Still water and swiftly flowing water support similar ecosystems.

    Ⓒ Still water supports more life than swiftly flowing water.

    Ⓓ Wetland areas include large quantities of swiftly flowing water.

15. According to the professor, what was the impact of the extensive hunting of beavers in North America?

    Ⓐ It led to a decrease in the number of wetlands.

    Ⓑ It led to a decrease in the number of swiftly flowing streams.

    Ⓒ It led to an increase in the number of other animal species in the wetlands.

    Ⓓ It led to an increase in the amount of groundwater.

16. *Listen again to part of the lecture by playing Track 108.* *Then answer the question.*

Why does the professor say this?

Ⓐ To point out that some terms have different meanings in other fields
Ⓑ To indicate that she is not going to explain the term
Ⓒ To defend a point she made earlier about ecosystems
Ⓓ To clarify a term used in biology

17. *Listen to Track 109 to answer the question.*

What does the professor imply when she says this?

Ⓐ Beaver dams would cause floods in many areas where people now live.
Ⓑ Beaver dams would cause most of the water supply to be inaccessible.
Ⓒ Large areas of land would become unusable by humans.
Ⓓ More groundwater would be available for human consumption.

Directions: Listen to Track 110.

Directions: Now answer the questions.

18. Why does the man go to see the woman?

   Ⓐ To pick up some informational flyers about music scholarships
   Ⓑ To find out whether he still has time to apply for a certain music scholarship
   Ⓒ To find out whether he can become a music major
   Ⓓ To get information on what types of financial aid are available for music students

19. What can be inferred from the conversation when the woman tells the man about the materials needed to apply for the Atwood Music Scholarship?

   Ⓐ The woman is less familiar with the application process for the Atwood Scholarship than with the process for other scholarships.
   Ⓑ The woman thinks some of the materials required should not be relevant for obtaining a music scholarship.
   Ⓒ The man might not be able to obtain all the materials he needs before the application deadline.
   Ⓓ The man's experience makes him highly qualified for the Atwood Scholarship.

20. What does the woman tell the man about submitting his materials for the Atwood Scholarship?

   Ⓐ Some materials can be submitted after the initial application deadline.
   Ⓑ The man should bring all the materials to her.
   Ⓒ The man must submit five copies of each document he submits.
   Ⓓ The materials should be sent directly to the Atwood selection committee.

21. What does the woman indicate about the audition recording the man must submit?
    Select 3 answers.

    A Recordings of the man's concert pieces might not meet the requirements for the audition recording.

    B The audition recording will be evaluated by the five people on the selection committee.

    C The audition recording should be ten minutes in length.

    D The man can select whatever saxophone solos he likes for the audition recording.

    E The woman does not know the specific details about what should be included in the audition recording.

22. What can be inferred when the woman mentions the Gorman Music Fund? *Select 2 answers.*

    A The man can apply for both the Gorman Fund and the Atwood Scholarship.

    B The Gorman Fund provides scholarship money for more than one student each year.

    C The Gorman Fund provides a larger amount of money than the Atwood Scholarship.

    D The information about the Gorman Fund that is on the university Web site will be updated soon.

Directions: Listen to Track 111.

Poetry

chanson

Directions: Now answer the questions.

23. What is the main purpose of the talk?

   Ⓐ To investigate the information known about the troubadours
   Ⓑ To explain the role of patriotic poetry during medieval times
   Ⓒ To explain why opinions about knights changed during the medieval period
   Ⓓ To compare two different types of medieval poems

24. According to the professor, who was the intended audience for chanson poetry?
   Select 2 answers.

   Ⓐ Lords
   Ⓑ Ladies
   Ⓒ Knights
   Ⓓ Troubadours

25. According to the professor, what is true about the hero in chanson poetry and the hero in romance poetry? *Put a check (✓) in the correct boxes.*

	Chanson Hero	Romance Hero
Is admired for loyalty to country		
Engages in conflict for adventure		
Is willing to face extreme dangers to protect a lord		
Is concerned with individual improvement		

26. Why does the professor mention that romance poems often included biographical sketches?

    Ⓐ To emphasize the similarities between chanson authors and romance authors
    Ⓑ To explain why the social status of troubadours is known today
    Ⓒ To point out why the biographical sketches are reliable sources of information
    Ⓓ To provide evidence that many troubadours were also historians

27. What does the professor say about the political climate during the time troubadours were writing poetry?

    Ⓐ It enabled chanson poetry to gain wide popularity over romance poetry.
    Ⓑ It gave the troubadours time to devote themselves to writing poetry.
    Ⓒ It inspired troubadours to write poetry that described their lord's deeds.
    Ⓓ It made it difficult for troubadours to travel safely within their country.

28. *Listen again to part of the lecture by playing Track 112.* 🎧 *Then answer the question.*

    Why does the professor say this?

    Ⓐ To indicate that he understands why the student may be confused
    Ⓑ To emphasize that the student has asked a very important question
    Ⓒ To remind the student that she may know the answer to her own question
    Ⓓ To invite other members of the class to answer the question

SPEAKING

In this section, you will be able to demonstrate your ability to speak about a variety of topics.

In the actual test, the Speaking section will last approximately 16 minutes. You will answer four questions by speaking into the microphone. You may take notes while you listen. You may use your notes to help you answer the questions. Your notes will not be scored. For each question, you will have time to prepare before giving your response. You should answer the questions as completely as possible in the time allowed.

For this practice test, you may want to use a personal recording device to record and play back your responses.

For each question, play the audio track listed and follow the directions to complete the task.

At the end of this practice test, you will find important points for each question, sample responses, and comments on those responses by official raters.

1. You will now give your opinion about a familiar topic. After you hear the question, you should give yourself 15 seconds to prepare and 45 seconds to speak.

Listen to Track 113.

> When looking for information for a research project, some students prefer to get their information mainly from the Internet. Others prefer to mainly use printed materials such as books and academic journals. Which do you prefer, and why?
>
> | **Preparation Time: 15 seconds** |
> | --- |
> | **Response Time: 45 seconds** |

2. Now you will read a passage about a campus situation and then listen to a conversation about the same topic. You will then answer a question, using information from both the reading passage and the conversation. You should give yourself 30 seconds to prepare and 60 seconds to speak.

Listen to Track 114.

Reading Time: 45 seconds

New Stadium

A university official announced plans to spend $2 million to build a new athletic stadium, commenting that a new stadium would help the university achieve its goal of attracting more top students. The official also said that, additionally, building a new stadium would allow the university to strengthen its relationship with the town, since a new and larger stadium would have the space to seat not only students, parents, and alumni, but members of the local community as well.

Listen to Track 115.

The woman expresses her opinion about the university's plan. State her opinion and explain the reasons she gives for holding that opinion.

Preparation Time: 30 seconds
Response Time: 60 seconds

3. Now you will read a passage about an academic subject and then listen to a lecture on the same topic. You will then answer a question, using information from both the reading passage and the lecture. You should give yourself 30 seconds to prepare and 60 seconds to speak.

Listen to Track 116.

Reading Time: 50 seconds

Perceptual Constancy

How an object affects our senses depends in part on external conditions, and these conditions are always changing. An object viewed from one angle presents a different shape to our eye than when viewed from another angle; similarly, as the distance from which we view an object changes, the object will appear larger or smaller. In spite of this, even as conditions change and we see objects differently, we still recognize that they remain the same. This is what is known as perceptual constancy. If not for perceptual constancy, we might have difficulty recognizing familiar objects if we viewed them in a new and different context.

Listen to Track 117.

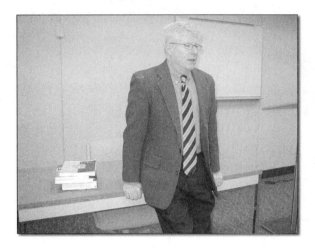

Explain what is meant by perceptual constancy, using the examples provided by the professor.

| **Preparation Time: 30 seconds** |
| **Response Time: 60 seconds** |

4. Now you will listen to a lecture. You will then be asked to summarize the lecture. You should give yourself 20 seconds to prepare and 60 seconds to speak.

Listen to Track 118.

Using the examples of the leafy sea dragon and the cuttlefish, describe two kinds of camouflage and the benefits they provide.

| **Preparation Time: 20 seconds** |
| **Response Time: 60 seconds** |

WRITING

In this section, you will be able to demonstrate your ability to use writing to communicate in an academic environment. There will be two writing tasks.

At the end of this practice test, you will find topic notes for each question.

Turn the page to see the directions for the first writing task.

Writing Based on Reading and Listening

For this task, you will read a passage about an academic topic. Then you will listen to a lecture about the same topic. You may take notes while you listen.

In your response, provide a detailed summary of the lecture and explain how the lecture relates to the reading passage.

In the actual test, you will have 3 minutes to read the passage and 20 minutes to write your response. While you write, you will be able to see the reading passage. If you finish your response before time is up, you may go on to the second writing task.

Reading Time: 3 minutes

Private collectors have been selling and buying fossils, the petrified remains of ancient organisms, ever since the eighteenth century. In recent years, however, the sale of fossils, particularly of dinosaurs and other large vertebrates, has grown into a big business. Rare and important fossils are now being sold to private ownership for millions of dollars. This is an unfortunate development for both scientists and the general public.

The public suffers because fossils that would otherwise be donated to museums where everyone can see them are sold to private collectors who do not allow the public to view their collections. Making it harder for the public to see fossils can lead to a decline in public interest in fossils, which would be a pity.

More importantly, scientists are likely to lose access to some of the most important fossils and thereby miss out on potentially crucial discoveries about extinct life-forms. Wealthy fossil buyers with a desire to own the rarest and most important fossils can spend virtually limitless amounts of money to acquire them. Scientists and the museums and universities they work for often cannot compete successfully for fossils against millionaire fossil buyers.

Moreover, commercial fossil collectors often destroy valuable scientific evidence associated with the fossils they unearth. Most commercial fossil collectors are untrained or uninterested in carrying out the careful fieldwork and documentation that reveal the most about animal life in the past. For example, scientists have learned about the biology of nest-building dinosaurs called oviraptors by carefully observing the exact position of oviraptor fossils in the ground and the presence of other fossils in the immediate surroundings. Commercial fossil collectors typically pay no attention to how fossils lie in the ground or to the smaller fossils that may surround bigger ones.

Listen to Track 119.

Directions: You have 20 minutes to plan and write your response. Your response will be judged on the basis of the quality of your writing and on how well your response presents the points in the lecture and their relationship to the reading passage. Typically, an effective response will contain a minimum of 150 words.

Listen to Track 120.

Response Time: 20 minutes

Question 1

Summarize the points made in the lecture, being sure to explain how they oppose specific points made in the reading passage.

_____

_____

_____

_____

_____

_____

_____

_____

_____

Writing for an Academic Discussion

For this task, you will read an online discussion. A professor has posted a question about a topic, and some classmates have responded with their ideas.

In the actual test, you will have 10 minutes to write a response that contributes to the discussion.

Question 2

Your professor is teaching a class on urban development. Write a post responding to the professor's question.

In your response, you should do the following.

- Express and support your opinion.
- Make a contribution to the discussion in your own words.

An effective response will contain at least 100 words.

Dr. Achebe

Abandoned railroad lines can be a problem for cities. The disused tracks can become dangerous as they deteriorate, and they are unattractive as they become overgrown with weeds. To solve this problem and make these areas useful to the public, some cities have converted abandoned railroad lines into parks, gardens, or trails. Do you believe that city governments should fund this type of project? Why or why not?

Kelly

Cities often lack enough parks for their residents, so I believe that it would be good for city governments to spend money to repurpose abandoned railroad tracks as parks. Even though these areas may be long and narrow, they can be made into beautiful parks that could extend through several neighborhoods.

Andrew

A lack of sufficient housing is a bigger problem for many cities than a lack of parks. The areas taken up by unused railroad tracks should be devoted to affordable housing. This solution could be even more cost-effective than having the city build parks or gardens because the cost of constructing the housing might be covered by the developers.

Response Time: 10 minutes

ANSWERS

Reading Section

1.	C	11.	A
2.	B	12.	C
3.	C	13.	A
4.	D	14.	B
5.	D	15.	D
6.	B	16.	D
7.	A	17.	A
8.	A	18.	D
9.	B	19.	B
10.	A, C, E	20.	A, C, F

Listening Section

1.	C	21.	A, B, E
2.	B	22.	A, C
3.	A	23.	D
4.	B	24.	A, C
5.	D		
6.	C		
7.	A		
8.	A, D		
9.	A		
10.	D		
11.	A		
12.	D		
13.	C		
14.	C		
15.	A		
16.	D		
17.	D		
18.	B		
19.	C		
20.	D		

25.

	Chanson Hero	Romance Hero
Is admired for loyalty to country	X	
Engages in conflict for adventure		X
Is willing to face extreme dangers to protect the lord	X	
Is concerned with individual improvement		X

26. B

27. B

28. C

Speaking Section

Prompts, Important Points, and Sample Responses with Rater Comments

Use the sample Independent and Integrated Speaking Rubrics in Appendix A to see how responses are scored. The raters who listen to your responses will analyze them in three general categories. These categories are Delivery, Language Use, and Topic Development. All three categories have equal importance.

This section includes important points that should be covered when answering each question. All of these points must be present in a response in order for it to receive the highest score in the Topic Development category. These important points are guides to the kind of information raters expect to hear in a high-level response.

This section also refers to sample responses, which can be found on the audio tracks. Some responses were scored at the highest level, while others were not. The responses are followed by comments from certified ETS raters.

1: Paired Choice

Prompt

When looking for information for a research project, some students prefer to get their information mainly from the Internet. Others prefer to mainly use printed materials such as books and academic journals. Which do you prefer, and why?

Important Points

Speakers should both state their preference and provide support for their choice, such as preferring the Internet because it allows for faster research, or preferring printed materials because they are more reliable sources. There are many ways to successfully support a choice. Speakers may provide one overarching reason and elaborate on it or provide several different reasons. They may provide concrete examples or general logic. It is also acceptable for speakers to say they find both Internet and printed materials useful in doing research, but speakers would need to clearly explain why and under what circumstances each type of source is appropriate, and this would be difficult for many speakers to do in the time given. In all cases, the listener should be able to easily follow why the speaker holds that opinion.

High-Level Response:
Listen to Track 121.

Rater Comments

The speaker clearly states his preference (using the Internet to find information for a research project) and why he prefers it ("*because you have a wider range of information from the Internet*"). He then goes on to elaborate on his reasons, explaining why printed materials are not as convenient ("*if you need a particular type of information you want to go and search for a particular journal*") and comparing them to the Internet. Although he does not give specific examples, his reasons are full and clear. The lack of examples is acceptable, since this particular prompt did not ask for them. A noticeable accent and occasional mispronunciations do not prevent the listener from easily understanding the response.

Mid-Level Response:
Listen to Track 122.

Rater Comments

The speaker states her preference ("*I prefer to research some information from the Internet*") and provides some support for her choice ("*... it is easier and faster method to access some informations ...*"). However, beyond that initial statement, only a moderate amount of relevant support is provided. The speaker has some language limitations that prevent her from providing full support: she speaks slowly and with hesitation and does not successfully use a wide variety of vocabulary or grammatical structures. Also, it is not immediately clear how the speaker's final point about exchanging opinions with others is relevant to the question. For example, she says, "*I can not only save my time, but also exchange opinions with others easily.*" It is not obvious what exchanging opinions with others has to do with getting information for a research project, and the speaker does not explain the connection.

2: Fit and Explain

Prompt

The woman expresses her opinion about the university's plan. State her opinion and explain the reasons she gives for holding that opinion.

Important Points

In this question, you should use the reading and listening passages to describe the university's plan (to spend money to build a new stadium), state the woman's opinion about the plan, and explain the reasons why the woman disagrees with the plan. The woman disagrees with the idea that a new stadium will attract top students because she thinks that other facilities in the university are in poor condition—including the science labs, the library, and the student center—and that money should be spent on them before a new stadium. She also disagrees that a new stadium would attract people from the local community because she thinks people don't come because the teams always lose and a larger stadium wouldn't change that.

High-Level Response:
Listen to Track 123. 🎧

Rater Comments

The speaker gives a full response. He organizes the response well, devoting equal time to the woman's two reasons and covering most of the material in the important points above. Note that providing every detail of the plan or the woman's reasons is not a requirement for full credit; when discussing the poor facilities, for example, the speaker simply says *"like the library, and other places."* His vocabulary and language use is precise and appropriate throughout for the most part, though there are a few minor errors that do not interfere with comprehension. Pronunciation is good overall, but there is some evident hesitation throughout. The response could be more fluid, but it is not choppy to the point that it creates listener effort.

Mid-Level Response:
Listen to Track 124. 🎧

Rater Comments

The speaker does address all of the main points, but they are not developed fully. For one, he does not clearly state at the beginning what the plan is (to build a new stadium); this is important for the listener to understand the response fully. He also leaves out other important information, such as the condition of the other facilities he mentions, which is again important in order to understand the woman's opinion. He does include a transition (*"second, she says . . ."*) before discussing her second reason, which helps organization. Though the response is understandable, the language is often imprecise and demonstrates a limited range of vocabulary and grammatical structures (for example, *"Only new stadium cannot invite top students"*). The speech is generally intelligible, but pronunciation problems, mainly with individual sounds, and hesitations when searching for language do create some listener effort.

3: General/Specific

Prompt

Explain what is meant by perceptual constancy, using the examples provided by the professor.

Important Points

This task asks you to explain how the examples given by the professor in the lecture illustrate the concept of perceptual constancy from the reading. There are different ways you can organize your response. You might begin by explaining that *perceptual constancy* is the idea that even though objects appear different depending on external conditions, we are able to recognize that they are the same objects. Or you might choose to begin with the examples and conclude with a summary of the theory of *perceptual constancy*. Either approach is acceptable, but you should be sure to include both examples in your response (a plate may look round or oval depending on the angle from which we look at it, but we still recognize it as a plate; and the professor may appear smaller when viewed from the back of the room [instead of the front], but we still understand that the professor is the same person, and that he has not gotten smaller).

High-Level Response:
Listen to Track 125. 🎧
Rater Comments

This speaker's pronunciation is very clear, and her response is well organized and easy for the listener to follow. She explains the examples from the lecture first and defines the concept later. This is a different but effective approach to answering the prompt. Her word choice and expression are not always perfect. For example, when defining the concept of perceptual constancy she says, *"we know by distance or angle ... it doesn't look the same."* This is a somewhat vague statement. She could have used a clearer and more complex sentence like, *"Even though an object looks different when viewed from a different angle or distance, we know it is the same object."* Nevertheless, her delivery is fluid, and she is able to construct long, clear phrases in the explanation of the examples *"... a professor in a front row, he looks bigger than you see the professor in the back row, but ... without even thinking, you know that it's the same professor, and the same guy who's lecturing."*

Mid-Level Response:
Listen to Track 126. 🎧
Rater Comments

This speaker covers most of the information required of the task, but his response is not as clear or efficient as that of the high-level speaker. His word choice is imprecise and at times causes difficulty for the listener. For instance, he says, *"... perceptual constancy means you may remain same ideas when looking at something from different aspects."* The phrase *"You may remain same ideas"* is not grammatically correct and the use of the term "ideas" is rather vague in meaning. The speaker could have more accurately expressed the idea as "continue to recognize an object." Also, he uses the word *"aspect"* instead of "angle" or "perspective," which is confusing for the listener. The speaker's pronunciation is relatively clear, but he repeats words and phrases often, which is at times distracting and requires some effort from the listener to follow his

response. Overall, there is some evidence that he understood the reading and lecture, but limitations in grammar and vocabulary prevent him from expressing some of the ideas clearly.

4: Summary

Prompt

Using the examples of the leafy sea dragon and the cuttlefish, describe two kinds of camouflage and the benefits they provide.

Important Points

When answering this question, you should provide a summary of the lecture in order to describe the two different kinds of camouflage the professor talks about and how the types of camouflage protect the animals that use them. You should explain that some sea animals have permanent camouflage (like their colors and shapes) that blend in with their specific environment, and describe the example of the leafy sea dragon, which is green and looks like the leaves it is surrounded by. You should also explain that other animals have camouflage that changes colors to match whatever environment the animals are in, so that they can move around and still be protected. For example, the cuttlefish can turn brown when it is swimming over the sea floor, and green when it is swimming near plants.

High-Level Response:
Listen to Track 127. 🎧
Rater Comments

This speaker provides a full, complete summary of the lecture. He describes the two types of camouflage, the examples of the sea creatures that use the types of camouflage and how the camouflage benefits them, as well as how the types of camouflage differ from each other. He makes use of complex structures, such as *"the cuttlefish is different from the sea dragon in that it doesn't have ..."* and makes only minor errors. His pronunciation and delivery in general are very clear. While the speaker could benefit from increased attention to the stress at the sentence level and using intonation more for emphasis, overall, the response is complete and highly intelligible.

Mid-Level Response:

Listen to Track 128. 🎧

Rater Comments

This speaker provides a mostly complete response. It contains a description of what camouflage is and why it is useful, as well as explanations of the two sea creatures and how they use camouflage. The speaker could have provided a stronger response, however, if he had provided more information about the differences between the two types of camouflage

(he mentioned that cuttlefish can change their color and shape, but didn't contrast this with the sea dragon's permanent camouflage). His hesitation between words and within words is at times distracting, but overall his message is clear. The speaker would likely benefit from working on agreement (between subjects and verbs and between modifiers and nouns) and more advanced vocabulary (to avoid confusing phrases such as *two different method* and *they shape any type any colors*).

Writing Section

Prompts, Topic Notes, and Sample Responses with Rater Comments

Use the sample Integrated Writing and Writing for an Academic Discussion Rubrics in Appendix A to see how responses are scored.

This section includes topic notes that are guides to the kind of information raters expect to read in a high-level response.

This section also refers to sample responses. These responses were scored at the highest level. The responses are followed by comments from certified ETS raters.

Question 1

Prompt

Summarize the points made in the lecture, being sure to explain how they oppose specific points made in the reading passage.

Topic Notes

The reading discusses reasons why collecting and selling fossils for commercial purposes (for profit only), which now happens much more frequently than it did in the past, is a bad practice. The lecturer explains that these reasons are not convincing, and that the benefits from having more commercial operations collect fossils these days are worth the drawbacks.

Point Made in the Reading	Corresponding Point from the Lecture
When fossils are sold to private collectors, it means that museums will have fewer of them, and in turn the general public will have fewer chances to see them.	The general public will have more chances to see them; commercial fossil collecting is making more fossils available, so many more public institutions can now buy them.
It will also mean that scientists will lose opportunities to make discoveries from studying fossils, since they won't have access to really important ones.	Even if important fossils are sold to private collectors, scientists would still see the fossils because they have to be identified first by scientists.
Because most commercial fossil collectors are untrained, they will destroy important scientific evidence that scientists could have obtained had they been the ones to collect the fossils.	Even if some damage is done, it is better than having fossils go undiscovered, which was more likely to have been the case when only scientists were doing the collecting.

Responses with scores of 4 and 5 typically discuss all three points in the table with good accuracy and level of detail.

Sample Response

Unlike the passage, which focuses on the negative sides of fossil trade, the lecture focuses on the benefits of having a fossil market.

First of all, the passage mentions that the fossils will be less exposed to the public's eye if they are owned by collectors, because they will not be donated to public museums. However, the professor argues that by letting all institutions to have the opportunity to purchase fossils, even the lower level public institutions such as libraries can purchase the fossils for display, which can be viewed by many people.

Secondly, the professor opposes to the passage's opinion that the scientists would miss out on the important information given by fossils possessed by wealthy collectors. The professor brings up a point that all fossils need to be scientifically identified and carefully investigated by certified scientists before going into the market.

Lastly, although it may be true that the collectors may damage the fossils, it is better to have them find it and damage it than to never find the fossils. There are not many fossil searching activities going on, and without the help of the collectors, many of the fossils probably would not have even been found. Taking that into consideration, it is certainly better to have some information from the fossils than to have none at all.

Rater Comments

This response earns a score of 5. It is a well-organized response that successfully explains the opposing relationship between the reading and the lecture. The three main points from the lecture are clearly identified, and the writer has provided relevant details or explanations for each of those main points. The writer's expression "There are not many fossil searching activities going on . . ." in the third point is somewhat vague, since the idea conveyed by the lecturer is actually that there are currently not that many fossil collecting efforts specifically by universities and scientific institutions. So the writer's idea here does not correspond to what the lecture is implying, which is that nowadays, because commercial operations started increasing their fossil hunting activities in recent years, between the large number of commercial operations and the limited activity of universities and scientific institutions, there is quite a lot of fossil searching activity going on. However, the lecturer's main idea, that without the commercial collectors, many fossils would go undiscovered, is conveyed. Overall, content from the lecture points is presented precisely, and the very few language errors in the response do not interfere with meaning.

Question 2

Prompt

Refer to page 237 to review the Writing for an Academic Discussion question.

Topic Notes

To earn a top score, you should develop a response that contributes to the discussion about the topic of whether city governments should fund projects to convert abandoned railroad lines into green spaces. An effective response will contain at least 100 words.

One discussion participant agrees with the proposed idea because there are often not enough parks in cities; the other argues in favor of devoting unused railroad tracks to housing because this solution addresses a bigger problem of insufficient housing and is potentially cheaper. You might expand on the ideas already stated by the discussion participants or introduce entirely new ideas. You may argue, for example, that the city government should consider the city's existing issues, needs, and available resources along with other factors, such as the potential for revenue generation or local business promotion. You might advocate for a balanced approach to address both housing and park needs while considering funding, environmental benefits, and community building.

You should make sure that your ideas are well-supported by reasons and examples and are expressed clearly. Since your response represents an online post, it does not need to be organized into separate paragraphs. However, your ideas need to be well-connected, coherent, and clear. Your response is scored using the Writing for an Academic Discussion rubric (see Appendix A).

Sample Response

An important question to consider is whether this project can bring revenue for the city. So while repurposing the railroads to parks is a great idea, this project needs to also address some of the existing issues the city faces. If the railroads can be remodelled in a way that can generate revenue, while keeping the city green, and possibly address some of the existing issues the city has, such as shortage of housing or shortage of food supplies, through this project, it would be beneficial for everyone. The city can convert the railroads into vegetable gardens, generate revenue and make it a source of food supply for the city and thus promote local businesses. The city could also divide up the land into small plots and lease it to local vendors for small businesses as well. The city could also start a moving railroad restaurent that can attract people and generate revenue. With any solution that we identify, we should consider how it can solve an existing problem and bring additional value.

Rater Comments

This writer has composed a very clearly expressed contribution to the online discussion, demonstrating consistent facility in the use of language. The writer presents relevant and well-elaborated ideas, considering various aspects such as existing city issues, revenue generation, and local business promotion and creative solutions like vegetable gardens and a railroad restaurant. The writer emphasizes the importance of identifying solutions that solve issues and bring value to the city and its residents. The writer demonstrates a good command of the language and effectively uses a variety of syntactic structures and sophisticated word choices, with just a few slipups that can be expected from a competent writer working under timed conditions: "bring revenue for the city," "repurposing the railroads to parks," and "restaurent."

Appendix A

Speaking and Writing Scoring Rubrics

This section contains all the rubrics (scoring guidance) used by raters to score your Speaking and Writing section responses. There are two different rubrics used to score the Speaking section and two different rubrics used to score the Writing section.

Speaking question 1, Paired Choice, is scored using the Independent Speaking Rubric, while the next three questions—Fit and Explain, General/Specific, and Summary— are scored using the Integrated Speaking Rubric. Writing question 1 is scored using the Integrated Writing Rubric, while question 2 is scored using the Writing for an Academic Discussion Rubric.

The chart below shows the main features of your responses that must be considered when assigning a score.

Section	Question	Rubric	Main features considered when scoring
Speaking	1	Independent Speaking	**Delivery** • How clear is your speech? Good responses are fluid and clear, have good pronunciation, a natural pace, and natural-sounding intonation patterns. • Even at the highest level, there may be some minor problems; however, they do not cause difficulty for the listener. **Language use** • How effectively do you use grammar and vocabulary to convey ideas? In a good response, there is control of both basic and more complex language structures, and appropriate vocabulary is used. • Even at the highest level, some minor or systematic errors may be noticeable; however, they do not obscure meaning. **Topic development** • How fully do you answer the question, and how coherently do you present your ideas? In a good response, the relationships between ideas are clear and easy to follow, as is the progression from one idea to the next. Good responses generally use all or most of the time allotted.

Section	Question	Rubric	Main features considered when scoring
Speaking	2, 3, 4	Integrated Speaking	**Delivery** • How clear is your speech? Good responses are fluid and clear, have good pronunciation, a natural pace, and natural-sounding intonation patterns. • Even at the highest level, there may be some minor problems; however, they do not cause difficulty for the listener. **Language use** • How effectively do you use grammar and vocabulary to convey ideas? In a good response, there is control of both basic and more complex language structures, and appropriate vocabulary is used. • Even at the highest level, some minor or systematic errors may be noticeable; however, they do not obscure meaning. **Topic development** • How fully do you answer the question, and how coherently do you present your ideas? Are you able to synthesize and summarize the information that was presented? In a good response, the relationships between ideas are clear and easy to follow, as is the progression from one idea to the next. Good responses generally use all or most of the time allotted. • Even at the highest level, a response may have minor inaccuracies about details or minor omissions of relevant details.
Writing	1	Integrated Writing	**Quality of the writing** • A good response is well organized. Use of grammar and vocabulary is appropriate and precise. **Completeness and accuracy of the content** • In a good response, important information from the lecture has been successfully selected, and it is coherently and accurately presented in relation to relevant information from the reading. • Even at the highest level, a response may have occasional language errors; however, they do not result in inaccurate or imprecise presentation of content or connections.
Writing	2	Writing for an Academic Discussion	**Quality of the writing** • A good response is a relevant and very clearly expressed contribution to the online discussion, and it demonstrates consistent facility in the use of language. • Even at the highest level, a response may have minor lexical or grammatical errors; however, they do not interfere with meaning.

TOEFL iBT® Speaking Scoring Rubric—Independent Task

Score	General Description	Delivery	Language Use	Topic Development
4	The response fulfills the demands of the task, with at most minor lapses in completeness. It is highly intelligible and exhibits sustained, coherent discourse. A response at this level is characterized by all of the following:	Generally well-paced flow (fluid expression). Speech is clear. It may include minor lapses, or minor difficulties with pronunciation or intonation patterns, which do not affect overall intelligibility.	The response demonstrates effective use of grammar and vocabulary. It exhibits a fairly high degree of automaticity with good control of basic and complex structures (as appropriate). Some minor (or systematic) errors are noticeable but do not obscure meaning.	Response is sustained and sufficient to the task. It is generally well developed and coherent; relationships between ideas are clear (or clear progression of ideas).
3	The response addresses the task appropriately, but may fall short of being fully developed. It is generally intelligible and coherent, with some fluidity of expression, though it exhibits some noticeable lapses in the expression of ideas. A response at this level is characterized by at least two of the following:	Speech is generally clear, with some fluidity of expression, though minor difficulties with pronunciation, intonation, or pacing are noticeable and may require listener effort at times (though overall intelligibility is not significantly affected).	The response demonstrates fairly automatic and effective use of grammar and vocabulary, and fairly coherent expression of relevant ideas. Response may exhibit some imprecise or inaccurate use of vocabulary or grammatical structures or be somewhat limited in the range of structures used. This may affect overall fluency, but it does not seriously interfere with the communication of the message.	Response is mostly coherent and sustained and conveys relevant ideas/information. Overall development is somewhat limited, usually lacks elaboration or specificity. Relationships between ideas may at times not be immediately clear.

TOEFL iBT® Speaking Scoring Rubric—Independent Task, *continued*

Score	General Description	Delivery	Language Use	Topic Development
2	The response addresses the task, but development of the topic is limited. It contains intelligible speech, although problems with delivery and/or overall coherence occur; meaning may be obscured in places. A response at this level is characterized by at least two of the following:	Speech is basically intelligible, though listener effort is needed because of unclear articulation, awkward intonation, or choppy rhythm/pace; meaning may be obscured in places.	The response demonstrates limited range and control of grammar and vocabulary. These limitations often prevent full expression of ideas. For the most part, only basic sentence structures are used successfully and spoken with fluidity. Structures and vocabulary may express mainly simple (short) and/or general propositions, with simple or unclear connections made among them (serial listing, conjunction, juxtaposition).	The response is connected to the task, though the number of ideas presented or the development of ideas is limited. Mostly basic ideas are expressed with limited elaboration (details and support). At times relevant substance may be vaguely expressed or repetitious. Connections of ideas may be unclear.
1	The response is very limited in content and/or coherence or is only minimally connected to the task, or speech is largely unintelligible. A response at this level is characterized by at least two of the following:	Consistent pronunciation, stress, and intonation difficulties cause considerable listener effort; delivery is choppy, fragmented, or telegraphic; frequent pauses and hesitations.	Range and control of grammar and vocabulary severely limits (or prevents) expression of ideas and connections among ideas. Some low-level responses may rely heavily on practiced or formulaic expressions.	Limited relevant content is expressed. The response generally lacks substance beyond expression of very basic ideas. Speaker may be unable to sustain speech to complete the task and may rely heavily on repetition of the prompt.
0	Speaker makes no attempt to respond OR response is unrelated to the topic.			

TOEFL iBT® Speaking Scoring Rubric—Integrated Tasks

Score	General Description	Delivery	Language Use	Topic Development
4	**The response fulfills the demands of the task, with at most minor lapses in completeness. It is highly intelligible and exhibits sustained, coherent discourse. A response at this level is characterized by all of the following:**	Speech is generally clear, fluid and sustained. It may include minor lapses or minor difficulties with pronunciation or intonation. Pace may vary at times as speaker attempts to recall information. Overall intelligibility remains high.	The response demonstrates good control of basic and complex grammatical structures that allow for coherent, efficient (automatic) expression of relevant ideas. Contains generally effective word choice. Though some minor (or systematic) errors or imprecise use may be noticeable, they do not require listener effort (or obscure meaning).	The response presents a clear progression of ideas and conveys the relevant information required by the task. It includes appropriate detail, though it may have minor errors or minor omissions.
3	**The response addresses the task appropriately, but may fall short of being fully developed. It is generally intelligible and coherent, with some fluidity of expression, though it exhibits some noticeable lapses in the expression of ideas. A response at this level is characterized by at least two of the following:**	Speech is generally clear, with some fluidity of expression, but it exhibits minor difficulties with pronunciation, intonation or pacing and may require some listener effort at times. Overall intelligibility remains good, however.	The response demonstrates fairly automatic and effective use of grammar and vocabulary, and fairly coherent expression of relevant ideas. Response may exhibit some imprecise or inaccurate use of vocabulary or grammatical structures or be somewhat limited in the range of structures used. Such limitations do not seriously interfere with the communication of the message.	The response is sustained and conveys relevant information required by the task. However, it exhibits some incompleteness, inaccuracy, lack of specificity with respect to content, or choppiness in the progression of ideas.

TOEFL iBT® Speaking Scoring Rubric—Integrated Tasks, *continued*

Score	General Description	Delivery	Language Use	Topic Development
2	The response is connected to the task, though it may be missing some relevant information or contain inaccuracies. It contains some intelligible speech, but at times problems with intelligibility and/or overall coherence may obscure meaning. A response at this level is characterized by at least two of the following:	Speech is clear at times, though it exhibits problems with pronunciation, intonation or pacing and so may require significant listener effort. Speech may not be sustained at a consistent level throughout. Problems with intelligibility may obscure meaning in places (but not throughout).	The response is limited in the range and control of vocabulary and grammar demonstrated (some complex structures may be used, but typically contain errors). This results in limited or vague expression of relevant ideas and imprecise or inaccurate connections. Automaticity of expression may only be evident at the phrasal level.	The response conveys some relevant information but is clearly incomplete or inaccurate. It is incomplete if it omits key ideas, makes vague reference to key ideas, or demonstrates limited development of important information. An inaccurate response demonstrates misunderstanding of key ideas from the stimulus. Typically, ideas expressed may not be well connected or cohesive so that familiarity with the stimulus is necessary in order to follow what is being discussed.
1	The response is very limited in content or coherence or is only minimally connected to the task. Speech may be largely unintelligible. A response at this level is characterized by at least two of the following:	Consistent pronunciation and intonation problems cause considerable listener effort and frequently obscure meaning. Delivery is choppy, fragmented, or telegraphic. Speech contains frequent pauses and hesitations.	Range and control of grammar and vocabulary severely limit (or prevent) expression of ideas and connections among ideas. Some very low-level responses may rely on isolated words or short utterances to communicate ideas.	The response fails to provide much relevant content. Ideas that are expressed are often inaccurate, limited to vague utterances, or repetitions (including repetition of prompt).
0	Speaker makes no attempt to respond OR response is unrelated to the topic.			

TOEFL iBT® Writing Scoring Rubric—Integrated Tasks

Score	Task Description
5	A response at this level successfully selects the important information from the lecture and coherently and accurately presents this information in relation to the relevant information presented in the reading. The response is well organized, and occasional language errors that are present do not result in inaccurate or imprecise presentation of content or connections.
4	A response at this level is generally good in selecting the important information from the lecture and in coherently and accurately presenting this information in relation to the relevant information in the reading, but it may have minor omission, inaccuracy, vagueness, or imprecision of some content from the lecture or in connection to points made in the reading. A response is also scored at this level if it has more frequent or noticeable minor language errors, as long as such usage and grammatical structures do not result in anything more than an occasional lapse of clarity or in the connection of ideas.
3	A response at this level contains some important information from the lecture and conveys some relevant connection to the reading, but it is marked by one or more of the following: • Although the overall response is definitely oriented to the task, it conveys only vague, global, unclear, or somewhat imprecise connection of the points made in the lecture to points made in the reading. • The response may omit one major key point made in the lecture. • Some key points made in the lecture or the reading, or connections between the two, may be incomplete, inaccurate, or imprecise. • Errors of usage and/or grammar may be more frequent or may result in noticeably vague expressions or obscured meanings in conveying ideas and connections.
2	A response at this level contains some relevant information from the lecture but is marked by significant language difficulties or by significant omission or inaccuracy of important ideas from the lecture or in the connections between the lecture and the reading; a response at this level is marked by one or more of the following: • The response significantly misrepresents or completely omits the overall connection between the lecture and the reading. • The response significantly omits or significantly misrepresents important points made in the lecture. • The response contains language errors or expressions that largely obscure connections or meaning at key junctures, or that would likely obscure understanding of key ideas for a reader not already familiar with the reading and the lecture.
1	A response at this level is marked by one or more of the following: • The response provides little or no meaningful or relevant coherent content from the lecture. • The language level of the response is so low that it is difficult to derive meaning.
0	A response at this level merely copies sentences from the reading, rejects the topic or is otherwise not connected to the topic, is written in a foreign language, consists of keystroke characters, or is blank.

TOEFL iBT® Writing Scoring Rubric—Writing for an Academic Discussion

Score	Description
5	**A fully successful response** The response is a relevant and very clearly expressed contribution to the online discussion, and it demonstrates consistent facility in the use of language. A typical response displays the following: • Relevant and well-elaborated explanations, exemplifications, and/or details • Effective use of a variety of syntactic structures and precise, idiomatic word choice • Almost no lexical or grammatical errors other than those expected from a competent writer writing under timed conditions (e.g., common typos or common misspellings or substitutions like there/their)
4	**A generally successful response** The response is a relevant contribution to the online discussion, and facility in the use of language allows the writer's ideas to be easily understood. A typical response displays the following: • Relevant and adequately elaborated explanations, exemplifications, and/or details • A variety of syntactic structures and appropriate word choice • Few lexical or grammatical errors
3	**A partially successful response** The response is a mostly relevant and mostly understandable contribution to the online discussion, and there is some facility in the use of language. A typical response displays the following: • Elaboration in which part of an explanation, example, or detail may be missing, unclear, or irrelevant • Some variety in syntactic structures and a range of vocabulary • Some noticeable lexical and grammatical errors in sentence structure, word form, or use of idiomatic language
2	**A mostly unsuccessful response** The response reflects an attempt to contribute to the online discussion, but limitations in the use of language may make ideas hard to follow. A typical response displays the following: • Ideas that may be poorly elaborated or only partially relevant • A limited range of syntactic structures and vocabulary • An accumulation of errors in sentence structure, word forms, or use
1	**An unsuccessful response** The response reflects an ineffective attempt to contribute to the online discussion, and limitations in the use of language may prevent the expression of ideas. A typical response may display the following: • Words and phrases that indicate an attempt to address the task but with few or no coherent ideas • Severely limited range of syntactic structures and vocabulary • Serious and frequent errors in the use of language • Minimal original language; any coherent language is mostly borrowed from the stimulus
0	**The response is blank, rejects the topic, is not in English, is entirely copied from the prompt, is entirely unconnected to the prompt, or consists of arbitrary keystrokes.**

Appendix B

Audio Track Transcripts

TRACK 1 TRANSCRIPT

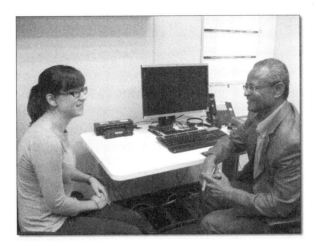

Narrator

Listen to a conversation between a student and her professor.

Professor

Before we get started, I . . . I just wanted to say I'm glad you chose food science for your major course of study.

Female student

Yeah, it seems like a great industry to get involved with. I mean, with a four-year degree in food science, I'll always be able to find a job.

Professor

You're absolutely right. Eh, before entering academia, I worked as a scientist for several food manufacturers and for the U.S. Food and Drug Administration. I even worked on a commercial fishing boat in *Alaska* a couple of summers while I was an undergraduate. We'd, we'd bring in the day's catch to a floating processor boat, where the fish got cleaned, packaged, and frozen—right at sea.

Female student

That's amazing. As a matter of fact, I'm sort of interested in food packaging.

Professor

Well, for that, you'll need a strong background in physics, math, and chemistry.

Female student

Those are my best subjects—for a long time I was leaning toward getting my degree in engineering.

Professor

Well, then you shouldn't have a, a problem. And fortunately, at this university, the Department of Food Science offers a program in food packaging. Elsewhere, you might have to hammer courses together on your own.

Female student

I guess I lucked out, then! Um, so since my appointment today's to discuss my, my term paper topic . . . I wanted to ask, could I write about food packaging? I realize we're supposed to research food-borne bacteria, but food packaging must play a role in all of that, right?

Professor

Absolutely. Maybe you should do some preliminary research on that . . .

Female student

I have! That's the problem. I'm overwhelmed!

Professor

Well, in your reading, did anything interest you in particular, I, I mean something you'd like to investigate?

Female student

Well, I was surprised about the different types of packaging used for milk. Y'know, clear plastic bottles, opaque bottles, cardboard containers . . .

Professor

True! In fact, the type of packaging has something to do with the way milk's treated against bacteria.

Female student

Yeah, and I read a study that showed how *light* can give milk a funny flavor and decrease its nutritional value. And yet, most milk bottles are clear. What's up with that?

Professor

Well, consumers like being able to visually examine the color of the milk. That might be *one* reason that opaque bottles haven't really caught on. But that study . . . I'm sure there're more studies on the subject . . . uh, you shouldn't base your paper on, on only one study.

Female student

Maybe I should write about those opaque plastic bottles . . . find out if there's any *scientific* reasons they aren't used more widely. Maybe opaque bottles aren't as good at keeping bacteria from *growing* in milk after the bottle's been opened or something. But where to begin researching this, I don't . . .

Professor

Y'know, there's a dairy not far from here, in Chelsea. It was one of the first dairies to bottle milk in *opaque* plastic, but now they're using *clear* plastic again . . . And they're always very supportive of the university and our students, so if you wanted . . .

Female student

Hmm . . . Yeah, I like that idea.

TRACK 2 TRANSCRIPT

Narrator

Listen again to part of the conversation. Then answer the question.

Professor

Maybe you should do some preliminary research on that . . .

Female student

I have! That's the problem. I'm overwhelmed!

Narrator

What does the woman mean when she says this:

Female student

I'm overwhelmed!

TRACK 3 TRANSCRIPT

Environmental Science

Narrator

Listen to part of a lecture in an environmental science class.

Professor

So, since we're on the topic of global climate change and its effects . . . in Alaska, in the northern *arctic* part of Alaska, over the last, oh . . . 30 years or so, temperatures have increased about half a degree Celsius per decade. And, scientists have noticed that there's been a change in surface vegetation during this time—shrubs are increasing in the tundra.

Tundra is flat land, with very little vegetation. Just a few species of plants grow there because the temperature's very cold and there's not much precipitation. And because of the cold temperatures, the tundra has two layers. The top layer, which is called the active layer, is frozen in the winter and spring, but thaws in the summer. Beneath this active layer is a second layer called permafrost, which is frozen all year-round and is impermeable to water.

Female student

So, because of the permafrost, none of the plants that grow there can have deep roots, can they?

Professor

No, and that's one of the reasons that shrubs survive in the arctic. Shrubs are little bushes; they're not tall, and being low to the ground protects them from the cold and wind. And their roots don't grow very deep, so the permafrost doesn't interfere with their growth. OK? Now, since the temperatures have been increasing in arctic Alaska, the growth of shrubs has increased. And this has presented climate scientists with a puzzle.

Male student

Um, I'm sorry, when you say the growth of shrubs has increased . . . um, do you mean that the shrubs are *bigger*, or that there are *more* shrubs?

Professor

Good question. And the answer is "both." The *size* of the shrubs has increased *and* shrub cover has spread to what was previously shrub-free tundra.

OK. So, what's the puzzle—warmer temperatures *should* lead to increased vegetation growth, right? Well, the connection's not so simple. The temperature increase has occurred during the winter and spring—not during the summer. But, the increase in shrubs has occurred in the *summer*. So, how can increased temperatures in the winter and spring result in increased shrub growth in the summer? Well, it may be biological processes that occur in the soil in the winter that cause increased shrub growth in the summer. And, here's how: there are microbes, microscopic organisms that live in the soil.

These microbes enable the soil to have more nitrogen, which plants need to live, and they remain quite active during the winter. There are two reasons for this. First, they live in the active layer which, remember, contains water that doesn't penetrate the permafrost. Second, most of the precipitation in the arctic is in the form of snow. And the snow which blankets the ground in the winter actually has an insulating effect on the soil beneath it . . . and it allows the temperature of the soil to remain warm enough for microbes to remain active.

So there's been increased nutrient production in the winter, and that's what's responsible for the growth of shrubs in the summer and their spread to new areas of the tundra. Areas with more nutrients are the areas with the largest increase in shrubs.

Female student

But what about runoff in the spring, when the snow finally melts? Won't the nutrients get washed away? Spring thaw always washes away soil, doesn't it?

Professor

Well, much of the soil is usually still frozen during peak runoff. And the nutrients are deep down in the active layer anyway—not high up, near the surface, which is the part of the active layer most affected by runoff. But, as I was about to say, there's more to the story. The tundra is windy, and as snow is blown across the tundra it's caught by shrubs . . . and deep snowdrifts often form around shrubs. And we've already mentioned the insulating effects of snow . . . So that extra warmth means even more microbial activity, which means even more food for the shrubs, which means even more shrubs—and more snow around them, etc. It's a circle, a loop. And because of this loop, which is promoted by warmer temperatures in the winter and spring . . . well, it looks like the tundra may be turning into shrubland.

Female student

But will it be long-term? I mean, maybe the shrubs will be abundant for a few years, and then it'll change back to tundra.

Professor

Well, shrub expansion has occurred in other environments, like semiarid grassland and tallgrass prairies. And shrub expansion in *these* environments does seem to persist . . . almost to the point of causing a shift. Once it's established, shrubland thrives. Particularly in the arctic, because arctic shrubs are good at taking advantage of increased nutrients in the soil—better than other arctic plants.

TRACK 4 TRANSCRIPT

Narrator
What does the professor imply when she says this:

Professor
So what's the puzzle? Warmer temperatures *should* lead to increased vegetation growth, right?

TRACK 5 TRANSCRIPT

Narrator
Listen to a conversation between a student and a library employee.

Student
Excuse me. Can you help me with something?

Librarian
I'll do my best. What do you need?

Student
Well, I received a letter in my mailbox saying that I'm supposed to return a book that I checked out back in January—uh, it's called *Modern Social Problems*—but because I'm writing my senior thesis, I'm supposed to be able to keep the book all semester.

Librarian
So you signed up for extended borrowing privileges?

Student
Yeah.

Librarian
But we're still asking you to bring the book back?

Student
Uh-huh.

Librarian

Well, let me take a look and see what the computer says. The title was *Modern Social Problems*?

Student

Yeah.

Librarian

OK . . . Oh, I see. It's been recalled. You can keep it all semester as long as no one else requests it. But someone else has . . . it looks like one of the professors in the sociology department has requested it, so you have to bring it back even though you've got extended borrowing privileges. You can check out the book again when it's returned in a couple of weeks.

Student

But I really need this book right now.

Librarian

Do you need all of it, or is there a certain section or chapter you're working with?

Student

I guess there's one particular chapter I've been using lately for a section of my thesis. Why?

Librarian

Well, you can photocopy up to one chapter of the book. Why don't you do that for the chapter you're working on right now—and by the time you need the rest of the book, maybe it'll have been returned. We can even do the photocopying for you, because of the circumstances.

Student

Oh, well, that would be great.

Librarian

I see you've got some books there. Is that the one you were asked to return?

Student

Uh, no. I left it in my dorm room. These are books I need to check out today. Um, is it OK if I bring that one by in a couple of days?

Librarian

Uh, actually, you need to return it today, that is, if you want to check out those books today. That's our policy.

Student

Oh, I didn't know that.

Librarian

Yeah, not a lot of people realize that. In fact, every semester we get a few students who've had their borrowing privileges suspended completely because they haven't returned books. They're allowed to use books only in the library; they're not allowed to check anything out because of unreturned books.

Student

That's not good. I guess I should head back down to the dorm right now then.

Librarian

But before you go, what you should do is fill out a form requesting the book back in two weeks. You don't want to waste any time getting it back.

Student

Thanks a lot! Now I don't feel quite so bad about having to return the book.

TRACK 6 TRANSCRIPT

Narrator

Listen again to part of the conversation. Then answer the question.

Librarian

So you signed up for extended borrowing privileges?

Student

Yeah.

Librarian

But we're still asking you to bring the book back?

Narrator

Why does the woman say this:

Librarian

But we're still asking you to bring the book back?

TRACK 7 TRANSCRIPT

Geology

Narrator

Listen to part of a lecture in a geology class.

Professor

So, continuing our discussion of desert lakes, now I want to focus on what is known as the Empty Quarter.

The Empty Quarter is a huge area of sand that covers about a quarter of the Arabian Peninsula. Today it's pretty desolate . . . barren and *extremely* hot. But, there've been times in the past when monsoon rains soaked the Empty Quarter and turned it from a desert into grassland that was dotted with lakes and home to various animals. There were actually two periods of rain and lake formation . . . the first one began about 37,000 years ago. And the second one dates from about 10,000 years ago.

Male student

Excuse me, professor, but I'm confused. Why would lakes form in the desert? It's just sand, after all.

Professor

Good question. We know from modern-day desert lakes . . . like Lake Eyre in South Australia . . . that under the right conditions, lakes **do** form in the desert. But the Empty Quarter lakes disappeared thousands of years ago. They left behind their beds, or basins, as *limestone formations* that we can still see today. They look like low-lying white or gray buttes . . . long, narrow hills with flat tops . . . barely a meter high. A recent study of some of the formations presents some new theories about the area's past. Keep in mind, though, that this study only looked at nineteen formations . . . and about a thousand have been documented, so there's a lot more work to be done.

According to this study, two factors were important for lake formation in the Empty Quarter. Um, first, the rains that fell there were torrential. So it would have been impossible for all the water to soak into the ground. Second, as you know, sand dunes contain other types of particles besides sand . . . including clay and silt. Now, when the rain fell, water ran down the sides of the dunes, carrying clay and silt particles with it. And wherever these particles settled, they formed a pan . . . a layer that water couldn't penetrate. Once this pan formed, further runoff collected and formed a lake.

Now the older lakes . . . about half the formations, the ones that started forming 37,000 years ago, the limestone formations we see . . . they're up to a kilometer long but only a few meters wide . . . and they're scattered along the desert floor, in valleys between the dunes. So the theory is the lakes formed there . . . on the desert floor . . . in these long, narrow valleys. And we know, because of what we know about similar ancient desert lakes, we know that the lakes didn't last very long . . . from a few months to a few years on average.

As for the more recent lakes, the ones from 10,000 years ago . . . Well, they seem to have been smaller and so may have dried up more quickly . . . Another difference, very important today for distinguishing between older lake beds and newer ones . . . is the location of the limestone formations: the more *recent* beds are high up in the dunes.

Why these differences? Well, there are some ideas about that and they have to do with the shapes of the sand dunes when the lakes were formed. 37,000 years ago the dunes were probably nicely rounded at the top . . . so the water just ran right down their sides to the desert floor. But there were thousands of years of wind between the two rainy periods . . . reshaping the dunes. So, during the second rainy period, the dunes were kind of . . . chopped up at the top . . . full of hollows and ridges. And these hollows would have captured the rain right there on the top.

Now, in a grassland and lake ecosystem, we'd expect to find fossils from a variety of animals. And numerous fossils have been found, at least at these particular sites. But . . . where did these animals come from? Well, the theory that has been suggested is that they migrated in from nearby habitats where they were already living. Then, as the lakes dried up, they died out.

The study makes a couple of interesting points about the fossils . . . which I hope will be looked at in future studies. At older lake sites, there's fossil remains from hippopotamuses, water buffalo . . . uh, animals that spend much of their lives standing *in* water . . . and also, fossils of cattle. However, at the sites of the more recent lakes, there's only cattle fossils . . . additional evidence for geologists that these lakes were probably smaller, shallower . . . because cattle only use water for drinking, so they survive on much less.

Interestingly, there are clam and snail shells, but no fossils of fish. We're not sure why. Uh, maybe there was a problem with the water . . . maybe it was too salty. That's certainly true of other desert lakes.

TRACK 8 TRANSCRIPT

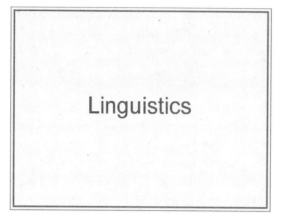

Narrator

Listen to part of a lecture in a linguistics class. The professor has been discussing animal communication systems.

Professor

OK, so last time we covered the dances honeybees do to indicate where food can be found, and the calls and songs of different types of birds . . . Today I'd like to look at-at some communication systems found in *mammals*—uh, particularly in *primates* such as, uh, orangutans, chimpanzees, gorillas . . . um, yes, Thomas?

Male student

Excuse me, professor, but . . . when you talk about *gorilla* language, do you mean, like, those experiments where humans taught them *sign* language, or-or a language like . . .

Professor

OK, OK, wait-wait-wait just a minute—now, who in this class heard me use the word "language"? No one, I hope—what we're talking about here are systems of *communication*, alright?

Male student

Oh, sorry, communication, right . . . uh, but could you maybe, like, clarify what the *difference* is?

Professor

Of course, that's a fair question . . . OK, well, to start with, let's make it clear that *language* is a *type* of communication, *not* the other way around. OK, so *all* communication systems, language included, have certain features in common. For example, the *signals* used to communicate—from the bees' dance movements to the words and sentences found in human language—all these signals convey *meaning*. And all communication systems serve a *purpose*—a, uh, *pragmatic function* of some sort—warning of danger, perhaps, or offering other needed information.

But there are several features peculiar to human language, that have, for the most part, never been found in the communication system of any other species. For one thing, *learnability*: Animals, uh, animals have instinctive communication systems; um, when a dog, a puppy gets to a certain age, it's able to bark. It barks without having to learn how from other dogs. It just . . . barks. But much of human language has to be learned, from other humans. What else makes human language unique? What makes it *different* from animal communication? Debra.

Female student

Uh, how about *grammar*? Like, having verbs, nouns, adjectives . . .

Professor

OK, that's another feature and it's a good examp—

Female student

. . . I mean, I mention this 'cause, like, in my biology class last year, I kinda remember talking about a study on *prairie dogs*, where . . .

I *think* . . . the researchers claimed that the warning cries of prairie dogs constitute *language* because they have these different parts of *speech*—you know, like *nouns* to name the type of predator they've spotted, uh, *adjectives* to describe its size and shape, *verbs*, um . . . but now it seems like—

Professor

Alright, hold on a moment . . . I'm familiar with the study you're talking about—and for those of you who don't know, *prairie* dogs are not actual *dogs*; they're a type of *rodent* who-who burrow in the ground in the grasslands of the western United States and Mexico.

And, uh—in this study, the researchers looked at the high-pitched *barks* a prairie dog makes when it spots a predator. And from this they made some pretty—well, they made some *claims* about these calls qualifying as an actual *language*, with its own "primitive" grammar. But actually these warning calls are no different from those found among certain types of monkeys. And—well, let's not even get *into* the question of whether concepts like "noun" and "verb" can be meaningfully applied to animal communication.

Another thing that distinguishes a *real* language is a property we call *discreteness*. In other words, messages are built up out of smaller parts—sentences out of words, words out of individual sounds, etc. Now maybe you could say that the prairie dog's message is built from smaller parts. Like, say for example our prairie dog spots a predator—a big coyote, approaching rapidly. So the prairie dog makes a call that means "coyote," then one that means "large," and then another one to indicate its speed. But do you really suppose it makes any difference what *order* these calls come in? No. *But* the discrete units that make up *language can* be put together in different ways . . . those smaller parts can be used to form an *infinite* number of messages—including messages that are completely novel, that've never been expressed before. For example, we can differentiate between "A large coyote moves fast" and, say, um, hmm . . . "Move the large coyote fast," or "Move fast, large coyote!"—and I truly doubt whether anyone has ever uttered *either* of these sentences before. Human language is *productive*—an open-ended communication system—whereas no other communication system has this property.

And another feature of language that's not displayed by any form of animal communication is what we call *displacement*—that is, language is *abstract* enough that we can talk about things that aren't present here and now—things like, "My friend Joe is not in the room," or "It'll probably rain next Thursday." Prairie dogs may be able to tell you about a hawk that's circling overhead right *now*, but they've never shown any inclination to describe the one they saw *last week*.

TRACK 9 TRANSCRIPT

Narrator

Listen again to part of the lecture. Then answer the question.

Male student

when you talk about *gorilla* language, do you mean, like, those experiments where humans taught them *sign* language, or-or a language like . . .

Professor

OK, wait-wait-wait just a minute—now, who in this class heard me use the word "language"?

Narrator

Why does the professor say this:

Professor

Now, who in this class heard me use the word "language"?

TRACK 10 TRANSCRIPT

Narrator

Some people think that family members are the most important influence on young adults. Others believe that friends are the most important influence. Which do you agree with? Explain why.

TRACK 11 TRANSCRIPT

Narrator

The business studies department at State University is creating a new requirement. You have 45 seconds to read the announcement. Begin reading now.

TRACK 12 TRANSCRIPT

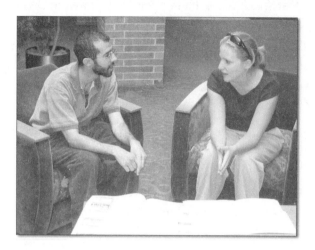

Narrator

Now listen to two students discussing the announcement.

Male student

Did you read this announcement?

Female student

Yeah, and I disagree—I don't think it will actually help students.

Male student

Really? Why not?

Female student

Well, they talked about leadership . . . and organizational skills . . . but that's not really the kind of work you do. Like my older brother's had the kind of jobs they're talking about . . . and typically you're just there to do basic tasks like typing or filing stuff— nothing very meaningful.

Male student

Oh, so you wouldn't actually learn anything new . . .

Female student

Exactly.

Male student

I guess I see what you mean—but what about the other point they make?

Female student

About this helping us after we graduate? I don't agree.

Male student

How come?

Female student

Well, the problem is that there are lots of other universities in our area that have the *same requirement* . . . so there are lots of other students at these positions.

Male student

Yeah, I guess I hadn't thought of that.

Female student

So even if you take a position like this in a company while you're still a student, once you graduate, the competition for permanent jobs will be impossible . . . I mean, there just won't be enough jobs available for all the business graduates in this city who will be looking for full-time work.

Male student

Hmm . . . I see what you're saying.

Narrator

The woman expresses her opinion of the university's new policy. State her opinion and explain the reasons she gives for holding that opinion.

TRACK 13 TRANSCRIPT

Narrator

Read the passage from a film studies textbook. You will have 50 seconds to read the passage. Begin reading now.

TRACK 14 TRANSCRIPT

Narrator

Now listen to part of a lecture on this topic in a film class.

Professor

So, the other day I went to this great new movie. And one of the scenes in particular, I thought, was really set up nicely. At the start of the scene . . . uh, before the action and talking and things started . . . you saw, on the movie screen, an image of a city. You could tell it was a big city . . . there were lots of buildings—tall ones, skyscrapers. And the cars and signs on the city streets looked old-fashioned—like they were from the past, like the 1940s.

The other thing I noticed right away, from this first image, just when the scene started, was that the city seemed, uh, gloomy. You couldn't see much because it was, well, there was mostly darkness rather than sunlight, and there was only just a little bit of light from the streetlamps. On top of that, it was raining, and kinda foggy. All of these details worked together to create a dark, gloomy, mysterious feeling.

So, then, when the action started, and it showed detectives talking to each other in an office, I already knew that the office was located in a tall building in a big city, sometime in the 1940s. And I, uh, had a good idea that the events that'd be taking place would be pretty dark and mysterious, because of the shot, the image, I saw at the beginning of the scene.

Narrator

Using the professor's example, explain what an establishing shot is and how it is used.

TRACK 15 TRANSCRIPT

Narrator

Listen to part of a lecture in a biology class.

Professor

We all know that insects like to eat plants. But some plants have been able to-to develop ways to protect themselves from insects. Today I'm gonna talk about some ways plants defend themselves.

Now, some plants have physical features that prevent insects from landing on them. Like the *passion plant*, for example. Its leaves have little spiky hairs all over them. They're like spikes . . . sticking out of the plant . . . that are so numerous and dense that they prevent insects from landing on the leaves. Basically, there's just no room for the insect to land. And since insects can't land on the leaves, they can't eat them. So, the little hairs serve as a physical feature that helps protect the passion plant from insects.

Alright, but other plants protect themselves using *chemical defenses*. Like the *potato plant*. The potato plant's able to release a chemical throughout its leaf system whenever an insect attacks it—starts eating the leaf. So, say an insect starts eating a potato plant's leaf. That will cause the plant to react by releasing a chemical throughout its leaf system. The insect swallows this chemical as it eats. And this chemical discourages the insect from wanting to eat any more of the plant. How? Well, the substance makes the insect feel full, like it's already had enough to eat. The insect no longer feels hungry. So it stops eating the plant. So, by emitting this chemical, the potato plant protects itself from insects.

Narrator
Using points from the lecture, explain how the passion plant and the potato plant defend themselves from insects.

TRACK 16 TRANSCRIPT

Narrator
Now listen to part of a lecture on the topic you just read about.

Professor
It's quite possible that *R. robustus* actively chased and hunted moving dinosaurs. It was not just a scavenger that ate eggs.

First, about *R. robustus* being too small to hunt dinosaurs. Sure, it would've been too small to have hunted a full-grown psittacosaur, but that doesn't mean it couldn't have hunted baby dinosaurs. *R. robustus* was considerably bigger than a baby psittacosaur would have been, which supports the idea that *R. robustus* was a hunter. Ya see, most predators have at least twice the mass of the animals they prey on, and *R. robustus* was more than twice the mass of the dinosaur in its stomach. Those size relations are exactly what we would expect to find if *R. robustus* hunted baby psittacosaurs and similarly sized dinosaurs.

Second, the length and position of *R. robustus's* legs. Well, there's a *modern* mammal known as the Tasmanian Devil.

Like *R. robustus*, the Tasmanian Devil also has short legs positioned a little to the side, and yet the Tasmanian Devil can achieve speeds of up to 15 kilometers per hour and is an active and successful predator. Clearly, if the Tasmanian Devil can run fast enough to catch prey, an *ancient* mammal with similar legs probably could too.

Third, the absence of teeth marks on the psittacosaur's bones. The reading overlooks some important facts about *R. robustus*. While *R. robustus* had powerful jaws that it used for grabbing and holding onto prey, it didn't use its back teeth for chewing. We've concluded this because there isn't much wear on the back teeth of various *R. robustus* specimens. Given this evidence, it seems that *R. robustus* swallowed its prey whole or in big pieces. So, given the way *R. robustus* consumed meat, we shouldn't expect to find tooth marks on the bones of prey in its stomach.

TRACK 17 TRANSCRIPT

Narrator
Summarize the points made in the lecture, being sure to explain how they respond to the specific points made in the reading passage.

TRACK 26 TRANSCRIPT

Narrator

Listen to a conversation between a student and her photography professor.

Student

Professor Johnson, there's something that's been on my mind . . .

Professor

OK.

Student

Remember last week you told us that it's really important to get our photography into a show, basically as soon as we can?

Professor

Yup, it's a big step, no question.

Student

Thing is, I'm sitting here and I'm just not sure how I'd get there. I mean, I've got some work I like, but is it really what a gallery is looking for? How would I know? How do I make the right contacts to get into a show? I just really don't . . .

Professor

OK, hold on, slow down. Ah, these are questions that . . . well, that just about every young artist has to struggle with. OK, the first thing you should do is: you absolutely have to stay true to your artistic vision . . . uh, take the pictures you want to take. Don't start trying to catch the flavor of the month and be trendy because you think you'll get into a show. That never works, because you wind up creating something you don't really believe in, that's uninspired, and won't make any shows. I've seen it happen so many times. Uh, this doesn't mean that you should go into a cave. Uh, keep up with trends, even think about how your work might fit in with them, but don't mindlessly follow them.

Student

Well, yeah, I can see that. I think, though, that I've always been able to stay pretty true to what I want to create, not what others want me to create. I think that comes through in my work.

Professor

OK, just remember that it's one thing to create work that you really want to create when it's in the classroom—uh, the only thing at stake is your grade. But work created outside the classroom, that can be a different story. I'm not talking about technique, or things like that. It's just that there's so much more at stake when you're out there making art for a living–uh, there's a lot of pressure to become something you're not, and people often surrender to that pressure . . .

Student

But to get stuff exhibited . . .

Professor

Well, you need to be a bit of an opportunist—y'know, common sense things . . . like always having a sample of your work on hand to give to people. You won't believe the kind of contacts and opportunities you can get this way. And try to get your work seen in places like restaurants, bookstores. You'd be surprised how word gets around about photography in places like that.

Student

OK. It's just so hard to think about all of those practical things *and* make good work, you know?

TRACK 27 TRANSCRIPT

Narrator

Listen again to part of the conversation. Then answer the question.

Student

I think, though, that I've always been able to stay pretty true to what I want to create, not what others want me to create. I think that comes through in my work.

Narrator

Why does the student say this:

Student

I think that comes through in my work.

TRACK 28 TRANSCRIPT

European History

Narrator

Listen to part of a lecture in a European history class.

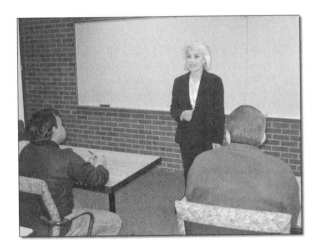

Professor

So would it surprise you to learn that many of the foods that we—uh, *today*—consider traditional European dishes—that their key ingredients were not even known in Europe until quite recently—until the Europeans started trading with the native peoples of North and South America? I mean, you're probably aware that the Americas provided Europe—uh, and Asia—with foods like squash . . . beans . . . turkey . . . peanuts . . . But what about all those Italian tomato sauces, Hungarian goulash or—my favorite—french fries—those yummy fried potatoes?

Male student

Wait—I mean, I knew *potatoes* were from—where, South America—?

Professor

South America, right—the Andes Mountains.

Male student

But you're saying . . . *tomatoes* too? I just assumed, since they're used in so many Italian dishes . . .

Professor

No, like potatoes, tomatoes grew wild in the Andes—although *un*like potatoes, they weren't originally *cultivated* there; that seems to have occurred first in *Central* America. And even *then* the tomato doesn't appear to have been very important as a food plant until the Europeans came on the scene. They took it back to Europe with them around 1550, and Italy was indeed the first place where it was widely grown as a food crop. So, in a sense, it really *is* more Italian than American. And another thing—and this is true of both the potato *and* the tomato—both of these plants are members of the nightshade family.

The nightshade family is a category of plants which also includes many that you *wouldn't* want to eat . . . like oh, uh, mandrake, belladonna, and, uh . . . and even tobacco! So it's no wonder that people once considered tomatoes and potatoes to be inedible too, even poisonous—and, in fact, the leaves of the potato plant *are* quite toxic. So it took both plants quite a while to catch on in Europe, and even *longer* before they made the return trip to North America and became popular food items here.

Female student

Yeah, you know, I remember . . . I-I remember my grandmother telling me that when *her* mother was a little girl, a lot of people still thought that tomatoes were poisonous.

Professor

Oh, sure—people didn't really start eating them here until the mid-1800s.

Female student

But, ah—seems like I heard . . . didn't Thomas Jefferson grow them or something?

Professor

Ah! Well, that's true . . . but, then, Jefferson is known not only as the third president of the United States, but also as a scholar who was way ahead of his time—in many ways! He didn't let the conventional thinking of his day restrain his ideas.

Now, potatoes went through a similar sort of, ah—of a rejection process, especially when they were first introduced in Europe—you know how potatoes can turn green if they're left in the light too long? And that greenish skin can make the potato taste bitter—even make you ill. So that was enough to put people off for over 200 years! Yes, Bill?

Male student

I-I'm sorry, Professor Jones, but—I mean, yeah, OK, American crops've probably contributed a lot to European *cooking* over the years, but . . .

Professor

But have they really played any kind of important role in European *history*? Well, as a matter of fact, yes, I was just coming to that. Let's, uh—let's start with North American *corn*, or *maize*, as it's often called. Now, before the Europeans made contact with the Americas, they subsisted mainly on grains—grains that often suffered from crop failures—and it's largely for this reason that political power in Europe was centered for centuries in the *south*—around the Mediterranean Sea, which was where they could grow these grains with more reliability. But when corn came to Europe from Mexico . . . well, now they had a much heartier crop that could be grown easily in more *northerly* climates, and the centers of power began to shift accordingly.

And *then*—well, as I said, potatoes weren't really popular at first, but when they finally *did* catch on—which they did first in Ireland, around 1780—well, why do you suppose it happened? Because potatoes had the ability to provide an *abundant* and extremely *nutritious* food crop—no other crop grown in northern Europe at the time had anything like the number of vitamins contained in potatoes. Plus, potatoes grown on a single acre of land could feed many more people than say, uh, wheat grown on that same land. Potatoes soon spread to France and other northern European countries, and as a result, the nutrition of the general population improved tremendously, and populations soared in the early 1800s. And so the shift of power from *southern* to *northern* Europe continued.

TRACK 29 TRANSCRIPT

Narrator

Listen again to part of the lecture. Then answer the question.

Male student

I-I'm sorry, Professor Jones, but—I mean, yeah, OK, American crops've probably contributed a lot to European *cooking* over the years, but . . .

Professor

But have they really played any kind of important role in European *history*? Well, as a matter of fact, yes, I was just coming to that.

Narrator

What can be inferred about the professor when she says this:

Professor

But have they really played any kind of important role in European *history*?

TRACK 30 TRANSCRIPT

Narrator

Listen to a conversation between a student and an employee in the university bookstore.

Student

Hi, I bought this book at the beginning of the semester, but something's come up, and I'd like to return it.

Employee

Well, for a full refund, store policy is that you have to return merchandise two weeks from the time it was purchased, but for assigned textbooks or anything having to do with specific courses . . . wait, was it for a specific course?

Student

Yes, but, uh, actually . . .

Employee

Well, for course books, the deadline is four weeks after the beginning of the semester. So for this fall semester, the deadline was October first.

Student

Ouch! Then I missed it. But, uh, why October first?

Employee

I guess the reasoning is that by October first, the semester is in full gear and everyone kinda knows what courses they'll be taking that semester.

Student

I get it. So, it's mainly for people who decide to withdraw from . . . uh, to change to new courses early on . . .

Employee

Exactly. The books have to be in perfect condition of course; they can't be marked up or look used in any way. For the full refund, I mean.

Student

Well, but uh, see, my situation is a little different . . . I-I hoped you might be able to make an exception.

Employee

Well, the policies are generally pretty rigid—*and* the semester is almost over.

Student

OK—here's what happened . . . uh, I think my professor really miscalculated. Anyway, the syllabus was way too ambitious in my opinion. There are only two weeks of classes left in the semester, and there are, like, six books on the syllabus that we haven't even touched.

Employee

I see. So you were hoping to return this one.

Student

Yeah—the professor already announced that we won't be reading this one by Jane Bowles. And all the others I bought used.

Employee

Jane Bowles? Which book of hers?

Student

It's called *Two Serious Ladies*.

Employee

Oh! But you should keep that one! Are you interested in literature?

Student

Well, I am an English major . . .

Employee

You're lucky to have a professor who includes a lesser-known writer like her on the syllabus. You know, not the usual authors we've all read.

Student

So you really think, uh . . . ?

Employee

I do, and especially if you're into literature.

Student

Hmm, well, this I wasn't expecting. I mean, uh, wow!

Employee

I hope you don't think I'm being too pushy. If you prefer, you can return the book and arrange for a store credit. You don't qualify for a refund—policy is policy, after all—but you can make an exchange. And you can use the credit for your books for next semester. The credit carries over from one semester to the next.

Student

Hmm—that's good to know. But now I'm really intrigued. I guess that just because we ran out of time to read this book in class doesn't mean that I can't read it on my own time. You know, I think I'll give it a try.

TRACK 31 TRANSCRIPT

Narrator

What does the man mean when he says this:

Student

Hmm, well, *this* I wasn't expecting. I mean, uh, wow!

TRACK 32 TRANSCRIPT

Ecology

Narrator

Listen to part of a lecture in an ecology class.

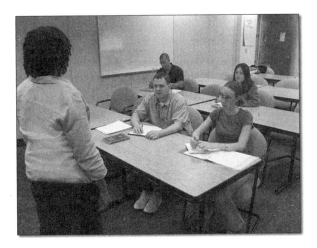

Professor

So we've been talking about *nutrients*, the elements in the environment that are essential for living organisms to develop, live a healthy life, and reproduce. Some nutrients are quite scarce; there just isn't much of them in the environment, but fortunately, they get recycled. When nutrients are used over and over in the environment, we call that a *nutrient cycle*. Because of the importance of nutrients and their scarcity, nutrient recycling is one of the most significant ecosystem processes that we'll cover in this course.

The three most important nutrient cycles are the nitrogen cycle, the carbon cycle, and the one we're gonna talk about today, the phosphorus cycle.

So, the phosphorus cycle has been studied a lot by ecologists because, like I said, phosphorus is an important nutrient, and it's not so abundant. The largest quantities are found in rocks and at the bottom of the ocean. How does phosphorus get there? Well, let's start with the phosphorus in rocks. The rocks get broken down into smaller and smaller particles as they're weathered—they're weathered slowly by rain and wind over long periods of time. Phosphorus is slowly released as the rocks are broken down, and it gets spread around into the soil. Once it's in the soil, plants absorb it through their roots.

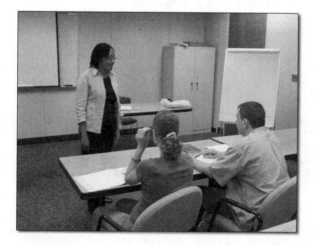

Female student

So that's the reason people mine rocks that contain a lot of phosphorus? To help with agriculture?

Professor

Uh-huh. They mine the rock, artificially break it down, and put the phosphorus into agricultural fertilizers. So humans can play a role in the first part of the phosphorus cycle—the breaking down of rocks and the spreading of phosphorus into the soil—by speeding up the rate at which this natural process occurs, you see?

Now . . . after the phosphorus is in the soil, plants grow, they use phosphorus from the soil to grow. And when they die, they decompose, and the phosphorus is recycled back into the soil. Same thing with the animals that eat those plants . . . or eat other animals that have eaten those plants. We call all of this the *land phase* of the phosphorus cycle.

But, a lot of the phosphorus in the soil gets washed away into rivers by rain and melting snow. And so begins another phase of the cycle. Can anyone guess what it's called? Nancy?

Female student

Uh, well, if the one is called the land phase, then this has to be called the *water* phase, right?

Professor

Yes. That's *such* a difficult point, isn't it? In a normal water phase, rivers eventually empty into oceans, and once in the oceans, the phosphorus gets absorbed by water plants like algae. Then fish eat the algae . . . or eat other fish that have eaten those plants.

But the water phase is sometimes affected by excessive fertilizers. If not all of the phosphorus gets used by the crops, and large amounts of phosphorus gets into the rivers, this could cause rapid growth of water plants in the river, which can lead to the waterways getting clogged with organisms, which can change the flow of the water . . . Several current studies are looking at these effects, and I really do hope we can find a way to deal with this issue before these ecosystems are adversely affected.

OK? Of course another way that humans can interrupt the normal process is fishing. The fishing industry helps bring phosphorus back to land. In the normal water phase, the remaining phosphorus makes its way—settles—to the bottom of the ocean and gets mixed into ocean sediments.

But remember, this is a cycle: the phosphorus at the bottom of the ocean has to somehow make its way back to the surface . . . to complete the cycle, to begin the cycle all over again. After millions of years, powerful geological forces, like underwater volcanoes, lift up the ocean sediments to form new land. When an underwater volcano pushes submerged rock to the surface, a new island is created. Then, over many more years, the phosphorus-rich rocks of the new land begin to erode . . . and the cycle continues.

Male student

What about . . . well, you said that the nitrogen cycle is also an important nutrient cycle. And there's a lot of nitrogen in the atmosphere, so I was wondering: Is there a lot of *phosphorus* in the atmosphere too?

Professor

Good question, George. You're right to guess that phosphorus can end up in Earth's atmosphere . . . it can move from the land or from the oceans to the atmosphere, and vice versa. However, there's just not a substantial amount of it there, like there is with nitrogen. It's a *very* minimal quantity.

TRACK 33 TRANSCRIPT

Narrator

Listen again to part of the lecture. Then answer the question.

Professor

Can anyone guess what it's called? Nancy?

Female student

Uh, well, if the one is called the land phase, then this has to be called the *water* phase, right?

Professor

Yes. That's *such* a difficult point, isn't it?

Narrator

What does the professor mean when she says this:

Professor

That's *such* a difficult point, isn't it?

TRACK 34 TRANSCRIPT

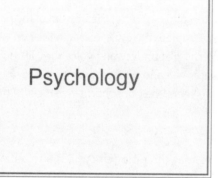

Psychology

Narrator

Listen to part of a lecture in a psychology class.

Professor

OK, if I asked about the earliest thing you can remember, I'll bet for most of you, your earliest memory would be from about age 3, right? Well, that's true for *most* adults . . . we can't remember anything that happened before the age of 3. An-and this phenomenon is so widespread and well-documented it has a name. It's called childhood amnesia and was first documented in 1893.

As I said this phenomenon refers to *adults* not being able to remember childhood incidents. It's not *children* trying to remember events from last month or last year. Of course it follows that if you can't remember an incident as a child you probably won't remember it as an adult. OK? So-so-so why is this? What are the reasons for childhood amnesia . . . Well, *once* a popular explanation was that childhood memories are repressed . . . um, the memories are disturbing, so that as adults we keep them buried. And so we can't recall them . . . and this is based on . . . well-well it's *not* based on-on-on the the kind of solid research and lab testing I want to talk about today, so-so let's put that explanation aside and concentrate on just two. OK? It-it could be that as children we *do* form memories of things prior to age 3, but forget them as we grow older. That's one explanation. Another possibility is that children younger than 3 lack, um, lack some cognitive capacity for memory. And *that* idea . . . um, that children are unable to form memories, um . . . *that's* been the dominant belief in psychology for the past hundred years. And this idea is very much tied to two things: the theories of Jean Piaget and also to language development in children.

So . . . Piaget's theory of cognitive development. Piaget suggested that because they don't have language, children younger than 18-24 months live in the "here and now," that is, they lack the means to symbolically represent objects and events that are not physically present. Everybody get that? Piaget proposed that young children don't have a way to represent things that aren't right in front of them. That's what language does, right? Words represent things, ideas. Once language starts to develop, from about age 2, they *do* have a system for symbolic representation and can talk about things which aren't in their immediate environment, in-including the past. Of course, he didn't claim that infants don't have any sort of memory—uh, it's acknowledged that they can recognize some stimuli, like faces. And for many years, this model was very much in favor in psychology even though memory tests were never performed on young children.

Well, finally, in the 1980s, a study was done. And this study showed that very young children— under the age of two—*do* have the capacity for recall. Now, if the children can't talk, how was recall tested? Well, that's a good question, since the capacity for recall has always been linked with the ability to talk. So the researchers set up an experiment using imitation-based tasks. Adults used props, um, toys or other objects, to demonstrate an action that had two steps. The children were asked to imitate the steps immediately, and then again after delays of 1 or more months. And, even after a delay, the children could-could recall, or replicate the action—the objects used, the steps involved and the order of the steps. Even children as young as nine months! Now, tests showed that there was a faster rate of forgetting among the youngest children . . . but most importantly, it showed that the development of recall did not depend on language development. And that was an important finding. I guess I should add that the findings don't say that there was *no* connection, um no connection between the development of language and memory. There's some evidence that being able to talk about an event does lead to having a stronger memory of that event. But that doesn't seem to be the real issue here . . .

So, back to our question about the cause of childhood amnesia. Well, there is something called the "rate of forgetting." And childhood amnesia may reflect a high rate of forgetting. In other words, children under the age of three do form memories, and do so without language. But they forget the memories at a fast rate, probably faster than adults do. Researchers have set a standard . . . sort of an *expected* rate of forgetting. But that expected rate was set based on tests done on adults. So what is the rate of forgetting for children under the age of three? We expect it to be high but the tests to prove this really haven't been done yet.

TRACK 35 TRANSCRIPT

Narrator

Do you agree or disagree with the following statement? Use details and examples to explain your answer.

All children should be required to learn a second language in school.

TRACK 36 TRANSCRIPT

Narrator

Read a student letter in the university newspaper. You have 45 seconds to read the letter. Begin reading now.

TRACK 37 TRANSCRIPT

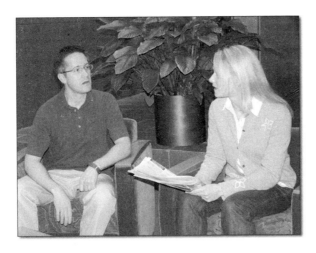

Narrator

Now listen to two students discussing the letter.

Male student

Mary, *you're* an art student—what do you think of this letter?

Female student

I don't like the idea.

Male student

Why not?

Female student

Well, first of all . . . his first point, about a lot of people passing through the student center. That's true, but . . .

Male student

But?

Female student

But it's always really crowded with people coming and going, it's not good for showing artwork. Imagine you're standing there, trying to look at a painting . . . there's gonna be, like, a million people walking through . . . people walking in front of you, blocking your view, distracting you . . .

Male student

Hmm, yeah. I hadn't thought of that.

Female student

You won't be able to appreciate the artwork . . . or get a good look at anything, with so much going on, with so many people moving around.

Male student

Yeah, I see what you mean.

Female student

Plus, he's wrong about the windows.

Male student

But isn't it true that it's good for art to have lots of light?

Female student

In a sense, yeah. But *that* kinda light, all that *natural* light from windows, that's actually *not* good, because if it's really sunny out, it'll be way too bright, if it's cloudy it'll be way too dark.

Male student

Oh.

Female student

What you want is *controlled* light, *consistent* light—the kind you get from electric lightbulbs. Think about in an art museum . . . in an art museum you've got electric lighting, and the light is always carefully controlled, always at the same level.

Narrator

Briefly summarize the proposal in the student's letter. Then state the woman's opinion about the proposal and explain the reasons she gives for holding that opinion.

TRACK 38 TRANSCRIPT

Narrator

Read a passage from a marketing textbook. You have 50 seconds to read the passage. Begin reading now.

TRACK 39 TRANSCRIPT

Narrator

Now listen to a lecture from a marketing class.

Professor

OK, so I've actually got a few different examples of this. You know, ah, when I was a kid a character named Action-hero was really popular with my friends and me. We would always watch the Action-hero program on television every week and, and play games pretending that we were as strong and powerful as he was. Then pretty soon we began seeing these small Action-hero figures in all the stores and . . . well . . . we all just had to have them. I mean, we'd been watching the television show for so long that it seemed only natural to want to own the toys too.

Well, I finally grew up and left the Action-hero television program and toys behind. Ah, but now I have a seven-year-old daughter who watches television a lot and also likes to play with her toys. And lately her favorite toy is a cute little baby doll with a big round face and lots of curly hair named Rosa. All my daughter's friends have Rosa dolls too, and they enjoy going to each other's houses to play with them. Then a few weeks ago my daughter came running up to me all excited because she had just heard there was going to be a new television program on every week with the doll—Rosa—as the main character. So naturally she and all her friends have begun watching the show, and it's already very popular—as popular as the toy doll.

Narrator

Using the examples from the lecture, explain the concept of entertainment merchandising.

TRACK 40 TRANSCRIPT

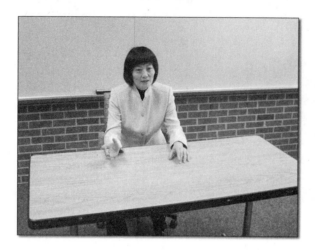

Narrator

Listen to part of a lecture in a psychology class.

Professor

OK, we generally assume that babies can feel only very basic emotions, like happiness, or anger. That is, that babies just react to things that happen directly to them. However, some new research is suggesting that babies may be able to feel concern for *others* . . . to have *empathy* for others. Now, empathy is a complex emotion—it involves a baby relating to someone else's emotions, not just reacting to things happening directly to them. Let's talk about an experiment that may show that babies could be capable of feeling empathy.

OK, for the first part of the experiment . . . Well, we've always known that babies start to cry when they hear other babies crying, right? One baby in a room starts crying, and all the rest join in. We've always assumed that the other babies cried because they were reacting to the *noise* of the crying, that the noise itself was distressing. So, in the experiment, researchers played a tape recording, a tape of babies crying, to another baby. And, sure enough, the baby started crying when he heard the sound of other babies crying. This was no surprise, of course, and the researchers assumed that the baby cried because of the noise.

But the next part of the experiment *was* surprising. The researchers played the baby a tape of his *own* crying. It was just as noisy, so the researchers expected him to cry. However, this time, the baby did *not* cry; he wasn't upset by the sound of his own crying. Why not? Well, maybe it wasn't the *noise* that had made him cry before, when he heard other babies crying. In fact, maybe noise had nothing to do with it. It could be that the baby felt empathy for the other babies, and that was why he got upset when he heard them crying. The researchers concluded that it's indeed possible that babies feel empathy, concern, for others.

Narrator

Using the points from the lecture, explain why researchers think that babies may feel empathy.

TRACK 41 TRANSCRIPT

Narrator

Now listen to part of a lecture on the topic you just read about.

Professor

Well, ongoing investigations have revealed that predation is the most likely cause of sea otter decline after all.

First, the pollution theory is weakened by the fact no one can really find any dead sea otters washing up on Alaskan beaches. That's not what you would expect if infections caused by pollution started killing a lot of otters. On the other hand, the fact that it's so hard to find dead otters is consistent with the predator hypothesis: if an otter is killed by a predator, it's eaten immediately so it can't wash up on shore.

Second, although orcas may *prefer* to hunt whales, whales have essentially disappeared from the area because of *human* hunters. That means that orcas have had to change their diet to survive, and since only smaller sea mammals are now available, orcas have probably started hunting those. So it probably *is* the orcas that are causing the decline of all the smaller sea mammals mentioned in the passage, the seals, the sea lions, and the sea otters.

And third, the uneven pattern of otter decline is better explained by the orca predation theory than by the pollution theory. What happens to otters seems to depend on whether the location where they live is accessible to orcas or not. In those locations that orcas can access easily, the number of sea otters has declined greatly. However, because orcas are so large, they can't access shallow or rocky locations. And shallow and rocky locations are precisely the types of locations where sea otter populations have *not* declined.

TRACK 42 TRANSCRIPT

Narrator

Summarize the points made in the lecture, being sure to explain how they respond to the specific points made in the reading passage.

TRACK 51 TRANSCRIPT

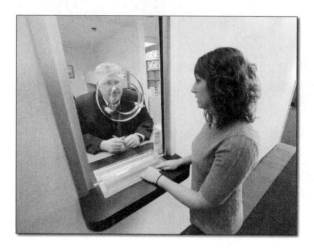

Narrator

Listen to a conversation between a student and a university employee.

Student

Hi, I need to pick up a gym pass.

Employee

OK, I'll need your name, year, and University I.D.

Student

Here's my I.D. card, and my name is Gina Kent and I'm first year.

Employee

OK, Gina, I'll type up a pass for you right away.

Student

Great. This is exciting. I can't wait to get started.

Employee

Oh, this is a wonderful gym.

Student

That's what everybody's been saying. Everyone is talking about the new pool and the new indoor courts, but what I love is all the classes.

Employee

The classes?

Student

Yeah, like the swimming and tennis classes and everything.

Employee

Oh yeah, but this pass doesn't entitle you to those.

Student

It doesn't?

Employee

No, the classes fall into a separate category.

Student

But that's my whole reason for getting a pass. I mean I was planning to take a swimming class.

Employee

But that's not how it works. This pass gives you access to the gym and to all the equipment, and to the pool and so forth, but not when the teams are practicing, so you'd have to check the schedule . . .

Student

But what do I have to do if I want to take a class?

Employee

You'll have to one, register, and two, pay the fee for the class.

Student

But that's not fair.

Employee

Well, I think if you think about it you'll see that it's fair.

Student

But people who play sports in the gym . . . they don't have to pay anything.

Employee

Yes, but they just come in and play or swim on their own. But taking a class, that's a different story. I mean someone has to pay the instructors.

Student

So . . . if I want to enroll in a class . . .

Employee

Then you have to pay extra. The fee isn't very high, but there is a fee. So, what class did you say you wanted to take?

Student

Swimming.

Employee

OK, swimming classes are $30 a semester.

Student

I guess I could swing that, but I'm still not convinced it's fair. So, do I pay you?

Employee

Well, first you need to talk to the instructor. They have to assess your level and steer you to the right class—you know, beginner, intermediate.

Student

You mean, I have to swim for them, show them what I can do?

Employee

No, no, you just tell them a little bit about your experience and skills, so they know what level you should be in.

Student

Oh. OK, so, I guess I'll need an appointment.

Employee

And I can make that for you right now. And then I'll type up your gym I.D. card, you'll need it to get into the building. Now, about that appointment, um, how does Wednesday at 3 sound?

Student

Fine.

Employee

OK, and you'll be meeting with Mark Giddis, he's the swimming instructor. He also coaches the swim team. And, here . . . I've jotted it all down for you.

Student

Great. Thanks.

TRACK 52 TRANSCRIPT

Narrator

Listen again to part of the conversation. Then answer the question.

Employee

Yes, but they just come in and play or swim on their own. But taking a class, that's a different story.

Narrator

What does the man imply when he says this:

Employee

But taking a class, that's a different story.

TRACK 53 TRANSCRIPT

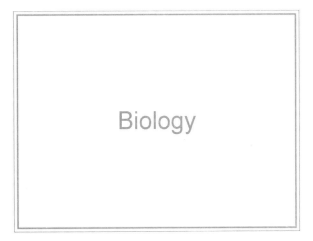

Narrator

Listen to part of a lecture in a biology class. The class has been learning about birds.

Professor

OK. Today we're going to continue our discussion of the *parenting* behaviors of birds . . . And we're going to start by talking about what are known as "distraction displays."

Now if you're a bird, and there's a predator around, what're you going to do? Well, for one thing, you're going to try to attract as *little* attention as possible, right? Because if the predator doesn't know you're *there*, it's not going to try to *eat* you. But sometimes, *certain species* of birds do the exact *opposite*: when a predator approaches, they do their best to *attract* the attention of that predator. Now why would they do that? Well, they do that to *draw* the predator *away* from their *nest*, away from their *eggs* or their *young birds*. And the *behaviors* that the birds engage in to *distract* predators are called "*distraction* displays," and there are a number of different kinds of distraction displays.

Most of the time, when birds are engaging in distraction displays, they're going to be pretending . . . either that they have an *injury* . . . or that they're *ill* . . . or that they're *exhausted* . . . You know, something that'll make the predator think, "Ah, *here's* an *easy* meal."

One pretty *common* distraction display is what's called the *broken-wing* display. And, uh, in a broken-wing display, the bird *spreads* and *drags* a wing or its tail. And while it does that, it slowly moves away from the nest. So it really looks like a bird with a broken wing. And these broken-wing displays can be pretty convincing.

Another version of this kind of distraction display is where the bird creates the impression of a mouse or some other small *animal* that's running along the ground. A good example of that kind of display is created by a bird called a "purple sandpiper."

Now what the purple sandpiper does is, when a predator approaches, it drags its wings—but *not* to give the impression that its wing's *broken*—but to create the illusion that it has a second pair of legs . . . and then it raises its feathers, so it looks like it's got a coat of fur . . . and then it runs along the ground, swerving left and right—you know, like it's running around little rocks and sticks . . . and as it, as it goes along, it makes this little squealing noise, so from a distance it really looks and sounds like a little animal running along the ground, trying to get away. Again, to the predator, it looks like an easy meal.

Now what's interesting is that birds have different levels of performance of these distraction displays. They don't give their top performance, their prime-time performance, every time. What they do is, they save their best performances, their most conspicuous and most risky displays, for the time just before the baby birds become able to take care of themselves. And they time it that way because that's when they'll've made the greatest investment in parenting their young. So they're not going to put on their best performance just after they've laid their eggs, because they haven't invested that much time or energy in parenting yet. The top performances are going to come later.

Now you have some birds that are quite mature, quite capable, almost as soon as they hatch. In that case, the parent will put on the most conspicuous distraction displays just before the babies hatch. Because once the babies are hatched, they can pretty much take care of themselves. And then you have other birds that're helpless when they hatch. In that case, the parent will save its best performances until just before the babies get their feathers.

TRACK 54 TRANSCRIPT

Narrator

Why does the professor say this?

Professor

But sometimes, *certain species* of birds do the exact *opposite*: when a predator approaches, they do their best to *attract* the attention of that predator. Now why would they do that?

TRACK 55 TRANSCRIPT

Narrator

Listen again to part of the lecture. Then answer the question.

Professor

Most of the time, when birds are engaging in distraction displays, they're going to be pretending . . . either that they have an *injury* . . . or that they're *ill* . . . or that they're *exhausted* . . . You know, something that'll make the predator think, "Ah, *here's* an *easy* meal."

Narrator

Why does the professor say this?

Professor

You know, something that'll make the predator think, "Ah, *here's* an *easy* meal."

TRACK 56 TRANSCRIPT

Narrator

Listen again to part of the lecture. Then answer the question.

Professor

Now what the purple sandpiper does is, when a predator approaches, it drags its wings—but not to give the impression that its wing's *broken*—but to create the illusion that it has a second pair of legs . . .

Narrator

Why does the professor say this?

Professor

but *not* to give the impression that its wing's *broken*

TRACK 57 TRANSCRIPT

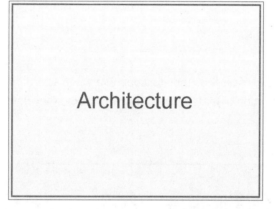

Narrator

Listen to part of a lecture in an architecture class.

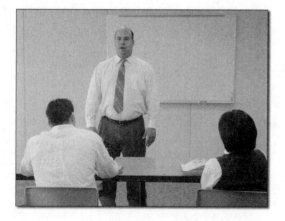

Professor

Today we're taking, uh, a little detour from the grand styles of *public* architecture we've been studying . . . to, uh, look at *residential* architecture in the United States. Since this is something we can all identify with, I, I think it'll help us see the relationship between the *function* of a structure and its, uh, its style, or *form*; this has been an ongoing theme in our discussions, and we'll be getting back to it in just a moment.

Uh, but before we get started, I want you to take a moment to think: Does anyone know what the *single* most popular style for a house in the United States is today? Bob?

Male student

I bet it's the ranch-style house.

Professor

Well, in *this* area, probably—But are we typical? Yeah. Sue?

Female Student

How about the kind of house my grandparents live in? They call it, uh, a Cape Cod . . .

Professor

That's the one. Here's a drawing of a, of what we consider—of a classic Cape Cod house.

Cape Cod house

These days, you see this style all *over* the United States, . . . uh, but it **first** showed up in the U.S. northeast—in the New England region—around the late 1600s. Uh, for those of you who don't know the northeast coastal region—um, Cape Cod is a peninsula, a, a narrow strip of land that juts out into the Atlantic. And um . . . so, so *many* houses in this particular style were built on Cape Cod, that the name of the *place* became the name of the *style*. Uh, now, *why* did the Cape Cod-style house become so popular in the northeast? Well, *one* reason is that it's a great example of form following function. Uh, we've, we've talked about this design principle a lot . . . about form following function . . . and . . . what'd we say it meant? Someone give me an application of this principle. What does this concept, that form should follow function, how would it be applied to housing design?

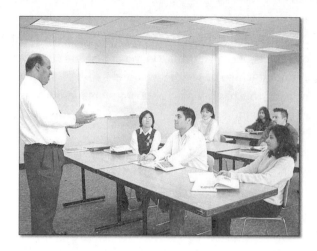

Female student

Well . . . if it means that the *design* of a building should be based on the needs of the people who *use* it. Then . . . well . . . the architect has to be very practical—to think about . . . the people who'll actually be living in the house . . . or working in the office building—whatever . . . So, for the *architect*, it's all about the *users*—*not* about showing off how creative you can be.

Professor

Good! Of course, for a Cape Cod house, it might be even *more* accurate to say that, uh, form *also* follows *climate*.

Who knows what the climate's like on Cape Cod?

Male student

Cold in the winter!

Female student

And whenever I visit my grandparents, it's really wet—it's usually either raining or snowing or foggy . . . and windy, too. I guess because it's so exposed to the ocean?

Professor

That's right. So take another look at this drawing, and, uh, you can imagine how this design might be particularly helpful in that kind of climate.

Cape Cod house

Notice how the house sits fairly low to the ground. Uh, this relatively low, compact structure helps the house withstand the strong winds blowing off the ocean. An-and look at the slope of the roof. The steep angle helps keep off all that rain and snow that accumulates in the winter. A-another thing: Cape Cod houses usually face *south*, to take advantage of, of the sun's warmth through the windows—that's helpful in winter.

Now. What can you tell me about the chimney? A-about its location.

Female student

Well. It's in the middle . . . Because . . . Does that have something to do with heating the houses . . . I mean, since—the heat never has to travel very far.

Male student

That'd mean you can heat the house more efficiently, right?

Professor

Exactly. Now, see how the house has very little exterior decoration? Tha-That's also typical of early Cape Cod houses. The wind was one reason—nothing sticking out that might blow away in the harsh weather. Uh, but there was probably another reason—*not* related to the climate—um, more, um—more a reflection of rural New England *society* back then. You see, Cape Cod houses were not built in the big cities, where all the rich people lived back then. These were modest dwellings; the people who built them simply couldn't afford lots of expensive decorative details. But, it was *more* than just a matter of money. In these rural areas, people depended on each other for survival: uh, neighbors had to help and support each other in a difficult environment. So, you didn't want to appear to be showing off. You'd want to avoid anything that might set you apart from your neighbors—the same people you might need to help you some day. So, so, all this helped to create an attitude of *conformity* in the community . . . and you can see why a modest—a, a very plain style would have become so widely imitated throughout rural New England.

Female student

It *is* plain but, you know, it's nice looking.

Professor

Good point! And, in fact, it's precisely that aesthetic appeal—the um, uh, the purity . . . the nearly perfect proportions of the house—that's another reason for the Cape Cod's enduring popularity—even in places where the climate's so mild that its functional design doesn't matter.

TRACK 58 TRANSCRIPT

Narrator

Listen again to part of the lecture. Then answer the question.

Professor

Does anyone know what the *single* most popular style for a house in the United States is today? Bob?

Male student

I bet it's the ranch-style house.

Professor

Well, in *this* area, probably—But are we typical?

Narrator

Why does the professor say this:

Professor

Well, in *this* area, probably—But are we typical?

TRACK 59 TRANSCRIPT

Narrator

Listen to a conversation between a student and a professor.

Student

Hi Professor Atkins, you wanted to see me?

Professor

Hi Bill, thanks for coming. I wanted to talk to you about . . .

Student

. . . Is there . . . is there something wrong with my research paper?

Professor

No, not at all. In fact, it's very good. That's why I wanted to talk to you.

Student

Oh . . . thanks.

Professor

I *think* you know the department is looking to hire a new professor. Are you familiar with our hiring process?

Student

No . . . but . . . what's that gotta do with me?

Professor

Well, Bill . . . we have several qualified applicants we're serious about. And as part of the interview process, we have them meet with a committee of professors and students in our department. They also have to give a talk.

Student

Do you mean . . . like a lecture?

Professor

Yes. Like a sample lecture on one of their academic interests.

Student

Oh . . . so you can see their teaching style?

Professor

Exactly.

Student

Uh-huh, makes sense.

Professor

So I'd like to know if you'd be willing to join as a student representative on the interview committee. It'd be a good experience for you. You could . . . uh . . . put it on your résumé.

Student

Oh! That'd look good for my grad school application, I guess. So what do I have to do?

Professor

The department secretary will give you a schedule of the applicants' visits. If you're free, we'd like you to attend their talks, and then later you can give us your opinion. Oh, and, we usually serve lunch or snacks, depending on what time the talk is.

Student

Cool! That's another good reason to do this. Um . . . when is the next talk?

Professor

We actually haven't had *any* yet. The first one is next Friday at 10:00 A.M. Then lunch and informal discussion with the applicant right after.

Student

Oh, well I'm free on Fridays. If all the talks are on Fridays, I'll be able to make it to all of them.

Professor

That's great! Now you should know that this job candidate is interested in the life cycles in the forest . . .

Student

That's . . . that's what my research is about!

Professor

Yes, I know. That's why I feel it necessary to point out that even though this applicant's research interests are similar to yours, we want you to tell us what you think about the teaching of all these applicants. Your perspective as a student—how the applicant *teaches* in the classroom—that's what's important to us.

Student

I understand. So, how many applicants are there?

Professor

Let's see . . . we have . . . four—all very good candidates that we'll be looking at over the next few weeks. It's going to be a tough decision. But it'll be a good experience for you—especially if you're going to grad school.

Student

Thank you! It'll be cool to do this. I'll get a copy of the schedule from the secretary on my way out.

Professor

You're welcome! See ya in class this afternoon.

TRACK 60 TRANSCRIPT

Narrator

Listen again to part of the conversation. Then answer the question.

Professor

I *think* you know the department is looking to hire a new professor. Are you familiar with our hiring process?

Student

No . . . but . . . what's that gotta do with me?

Narrator

Why does the student say this:

Student

what's that gotta do with me?

Environmental Science

Narrator

Listen to part of a lecture in an environmental science class.

Professor

When land gets developed for human use, the landscape changes . . . we don't see as many types of vegetation . . . trees . . . grasses . . . and so forth . . . this in turn leads to other losses . . . the loss of animals that once lived there . . . uh, but these are the *obvious* changes . . . But there are also *less* obvious changes, like the *climate*. One interesting case of this . . . uh . . . of changes in the local land use causing changes in climate, specifically the temperature, is in Florida. Now, what comes to mind when you think of the state of Florida?

Male student

Sunshine! Beaches . . .

Female student

Warm weather and oranges . . .

Professor

Yes, exactly. Florida has long had a great citrus industry—large groves of oranges, lemons, and the like. Florida's winter is very mild; the temperature doesn't often get below freezing. But there are some areas of Florida that do freeze, so in the early 1900s farmers moved even further south in

Florida to areas that were even less likely to freeze. Obviously, freezing temperatures are a danger to the crops. A bad bout of cold weather . . . a long spell of frosts . . . could ruin a farmer's entire crop. Anyway, before the citrus growers moved south, much of the land in south Florida was what we call "wetlands."

Wetlands are areas of marshy . . . swampy land . . . areas where water covers the soil, or is present either at or near the surface of the soil, for a large part of the year.

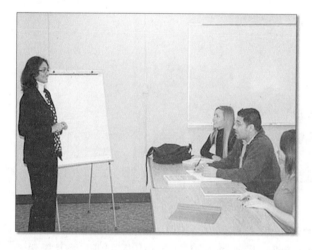

Wetlands have their own unique ecosystems with plants and animals with special and interesting adaptations—very exciting, but it's not what we're talking about today—Ummm . . . where was I?

Male student

Farmers moved south?

Professor

Oh yes . . . farmers moved south, but the land was not suitable for farming . . . you can't grow oranges in wetlands . . . so farmers had to transform the wetlands into land suitable for farming. To do that, you have to drain the water from the land, move the water elsewhere, and divert the water sources, such as rivers. Hundreds of miles of drainage canals were built in the wetlands. Now these areas . . . the new areas the farmers moved to . . . used to be warm and unlikely to freeze, however, recently the area has become susceptible to freezes . . . and we are trying to understand why.

Female student

Is it some global temperature change or weather pattern . . . like El Niño or something?

Professor

Well, there are two theories. One idea, is as you suggest . . . that major weather patterns . . . something like El Niño . . . are responsible. But the *other* idea, and this is the one that I personally subscribe to, is that the changes in the temperature pattern have been brought about by the loss of the wetlands . . .

Male student

Well, how would loss of wetlands make a difference?

Professor

Well, think about what we've been studying so far. We've discussed the impact of landscapes on temperature right? What effects does a body of water have on an area?

Male student

Oh yeah, uh, bodies of water tend to absorb the heat during the day . . . and then they release the heat at night.

Professor

Yes, exactly! What you just said is what I want you all to understand. Bodies of water *release* heat—and moisture back into the environment. So places near large bodies of water are generally milder . . . uh, slightly warmer . . . than those without water. And what I . . . and others think is that the loss of the wetlands has created a situation where the local temperatures in the area are now slightly different, slightly *colder*, than they were a hundred years ago before the wetlands were drained.

Female student

Hmmm . . . do we know what the temperature was like back then?

Professor

Well, we were able to estimate this: We have data about south Florida's current landscape, uh, the plant cover, and we were able to *reconstruct* data about its landscape prior to 1900. Then we entered those data . . . information about what the landscape looked like before and after the wetlands were drained, we entered the data into a computer weather model. This model can predict temperatures . . . and when all of the data were entered . . . an overall *cooling* trend was predicted by the model.

Female student

How much colder does it get now?

Professor

Well, actually, the model shows a drop of only a few degrees Celsius . . . but this is enough to cause dramatic damage to crops. If temperatures overnight are already very *close* to the freezing point, then, this drop of just a few degrees can take the temperature below freezing . . . and freezing causes frosts, which kill crops. These damaging frosts wouldn't happen if the wetlands were still in existence. Just a tiny temperature difference can have major consequences.

TRACK 62 TRANSCRIPT

Narrator

Listen again to part of the lecture. Then answer the question.

Professor

Wetlands have their own unique ecosystems with plants and animals with special and interesting adaptations . . . very exciting, but it's not what we're talking about today . . . Ummm . . . where was I?

Male student

Farmers moved south?

Narrator

Why does the student say this:

Male student

Farmers moved south?

TRACK 63 TRANSCRIPT

Narrator

Some people think that children should be allowed to watch whatever television programs they choose to. Others think that parents should exercise control over the television programs their children watch. Which do you agree with? Explain why.

TRACK 64 TRANSCRIPT

Narrator

Central College is planning to renovate its dormitories. Read the article in the college newspaper about the plan. You will have 45 seconds to read the article. Begin reading now.

TRACK 65 TRANSCRIPT

Narrator

Now listen to two students discussing the college's plan.

Female student

The college is making a mistake with this new plan.

Male student

What do you mean? I think it'll really help accomplish the college's goals.

Female student

Don't be so sure. All that construction—for *two* years—it's gonna create a lot of noise.

Male student

Oh you mean in the beginning, for students still living in the dorms . . .

Female student

Yeah, students who are trying to sleep or do work are constantly going to be disturbed. So people will try to get as far away as possible—probably by moving off campus. So they'll lose even more people.

Male student

Huh. I hadn't thought of that. But still, once all the construction's over, more people will probably want to live in the dorms, right? I mean, the living conditions will be so much better.

Female student

If they can afford to . . . Do you know how the college is planning on paying for this plan? By raising the cost of campus housing.

Male student

Oh, I didn't realize that.

Female student

Yeah. So if it's more expensive, why would people want to move back into the dorms if they can rent an apartment for less money?

Narrator

The woman expresses her opinion about the college's plan. State her opinion and explain the reasons she gives for holding that opinion.

TRACK 66 TRANSCRIPT

Narrator

Now read a passage about Outsider Art from a modern art textbook. You will have 45 seconds to read the passage. Begin reading now.

TRACK 67 TRANSCRIPT

Narrator

Now listen to part of a lecture in an art history class.

Professor

Alright, so let's consider the work of the Outsider Artist Henry Darger. Darger lived by himself in a tiny apartment in Chicago in the 1900s. He had no friends and spent all his spare time there alone, creating hundreds of paintings and drawings. He had never formally studied art and kept his work completely private, so no one ever saw it or responded to it during his lifetime.

And so when you see Darger's work, you notice how unique it is—it doesn't remind you of anything you've ever seen before—it's very much his own. For example, one piece—it's a watercolor painting . . . in this piece he illustrates a story . . . about the adventures of seven children. But see, Darger had a really hard time drawing human figures . . . yet he managed to come up with his own rather unique solution for the problem. He simply cut out pictures of children from newspapers and magazines and pasted them into his own painted illustration of trees, flowers, and grass. The results look . . . uh . . . a little strange. Darger's picture looks more cluttered . . . more crowded with details . . . than the pictures of other artists because its entire surface is painted and there are no spaces left empty. It's also a lot longer than the pictures of most other artists—about nine feet long.

Narrator

Explain why Henry Darger is considered an Outsider Artist.

TRACK 68 TRANSCRIPT

Narrator

Listen to part of a lecture in an interior design class.

Professor

So, we're talking about interior design, er, specifically the basic principles typically used in home and office decoration in the United States. Effective designs create a delicate balance between two things. You need unity *and* you also need contrast, which is essentially a break in unity. Now this might seem a little contradictory, but let me explain why we need both of these for an effective design.

So for the first principle . . . we need *unity* in our design . . . think of it as, hmm, *consistency*. Well, an easy and very effective way to do this is by bringing together similar elements—a common example is by matching colors. You pick a color and use it for different parts of the room. Say, you pick green, and then use a light shade of green for the walls, and maybe a somewhat darker shade for the fabric on the sofa, and finally complement that with a matching green in the rug. When elements match, the room is unified and gives its residents a sense of order and comfort.

OK, but there is such a thing as *too much* unity. Remember, you need a balance of unity and contrast. If all you do is focus on unity, the result will be a booooring room. So, what do you do? Well, you apply the second basic principle of design, which is *contrast*. Contrast serves to disrupt, or, er, break up, the unity in places, but in a careful, intentional way. Uhmmm . . . well let's continue using color as an example . . . to create contrast, color contrast, you need to abruptly change your color scheme once in a while. Ah let's see . . . you could um . . . throw bright red cushions on your dark green sofa, for example. Contrast makes things stand out: the green will look even greener next to the red. So, now your room is more interesting, not completely the same. But watch out, too much contrast is also dangerous, just like too much sameness is . . . too much contrast will make the room feel busy, chaotic.

Narrator

Using the points and examples from the lecture, explain what unity and contrast are, and how they make interior design more effective.

TRACK 69 TRANSCRIPT

Narrator

Now listen to part of a lecture on the topic you just read about.

Professor

It is often said that people are reading less literature today than they used to. What should we make of this?

Well, first, a book doesn't have to be *literature* to be intellectually stimulating. Science writing, history, political analysis, and so forth aren't literature, perhaps, but they're often of high quality. And these kinds of books can be *just* as creative and well-written as a novel or a play—they can stimulate the imagination. So don't assume that someone who isn't reading literature isn't reading a good book.

But let's say that people aren't just spending less time with literature, they're also spending less time with books in general. Does that mean that the culture is in decline? No. There's plenty of culturally valuable material that isn't written: music and movies, for example. Are people wasting their time when they listen to a brilliant song or watch a good movie? Do these non-literary activities lower cultural standards? Of *course* not. Culture has changed. In today's culture there are many forms of expression available other than novels and poems, and some of these creative forms speak more directly to contemporary concerns than literature does.

Finally, it's probably true that there's less support for literature today than in earlier generations. But don't be too quick to blame the *readers*. Sometimes it's the *author's* fault. Let's be honest: a lot of modern literature is *intended* to be difficult to understand. There's not much reason to suppose that *earlier* generations of readers would have read a lot of today's literature *either*.

TRACK 70 TRANSCRIPT

Narrator

Summarize the points made in the lecture, being sure to explain how they cast doubt on specific points made in the reading passage.

TRACK 79 TRANSCRIPT

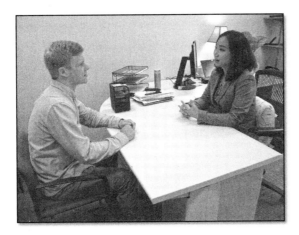

Narrator

Listen to a conversation between a student and a professor.

Student

So, Professor Tibbits, your note said that you wanted to see me . . . about my Hemingway paper? I have to say, that grade wasn't what I was expecting. I thought I'd done a pretty good job.

Professor

Oh, you did. But do you really want to settle for *pretty* good when you can do something *very* good?

Student

You think it can be *very* good?

Professor

Absolutely.

Student

Would that mean you'd, I could get a better grade?

Professor

Oh sorry, it's not for your grade; it's . . . I think you could learn a lot by revising it.

Student

You mean rewrite the whole thing? I'm really swamped; there's deadlines wherever I turn, and . . . and I don't really know how much time I could give it.

Professor

Well, it *is* a busy time . . . with spring break coming up next week. It's your call, but I think that with a little extra effort you can really turn this into a fine essay.

Student

No, yeah, I mean, after I read your comments—I can see how it tries to do too much.

Professor

Yeah, it's just too ambitious for the scope of the assignment.

Student

So I should cut out the historical part.

Professor

Yes, I would just stick to the topic, anything unrelated to the use of nature imagery has no place in the paper; all that tangential material just distracts from the main argument.

Student

I never know how much to include, you know, where to draw the line.

Professor

Tell me about it. *All* writers struggle with that one. But it's something you can learn, that'll become more clear with practice. But I think if you just cut out the, uh . . .

Student

The stuff about the history . . . but, if I cut out those sections, won't it be too short?

Professor

Well, better a short, well–structured paper than a long paper that's poorly structured and wanders off topic.

Student

So, all I have to do is delete those sections?

Professor

Well, not so fast. After you cut out those sections you'll have to go back and revise the rest . . . to see how it all fits together. And of course, you'll have to revise the introduction, too, to accurately describe what you do in the body of the paper. But that shouldn't be too difficult; just remember to keep the discussion focused. Do you think you can get it to me by noon tomorrow?

Student

Wow . . . um, I have so much . . . uh, but I'll try.

Professor

OK, good, do try. But if you can't, we'll shoot for after spring break, OK?

TRACK 80 TRANSCRIPT

Narrator

Listen again to part of the conversation. Then answer the question.

Student

I never know how much to include, you know, where to draw the line.

Professor

Tell me about it.

Narrator

What does the professor mean when she says this:

Professor

Tell me about it.

Biology

Narrator

Listen to part of a lecture in a biology class.

Professor

As we learn more about the DNA in human cells . . . and how it controls the *growth and development of cells* . . . then maybe we can explain a very important observation—that when we try to *grow* most human cells in a laboratory, they seem programmed to divide only a certain number of times before they die. Now this differs with the type of cell; some cells, like nerve cells, only divide seven to nine times in their total life. Others, like skin cells, will divide many, many more times. But finally the cells stop renewing themselves and they die. And in the cells of the human body itself, in the cells of every organ . . . of almost every type of tissue in the body, the same thing will happen eventually.

OK. You know that all of a person's genetic information is contained on very long pieces of DNA called chromosomes—46 of them in a *human* cell, that's 23 pairs of these chromosomes—of various lengths and sizes.

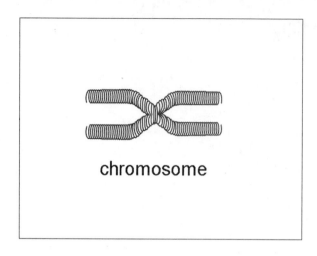

chromosome

Now, um, if you'll look at this rough drawing of one of them—one chromosome about to divide into two—you'll see that it sort of looks like . . . well actually it's much more complex than this . . . but it reminds us of a couple of *springs* linked together . . . two coiled up pieces of DNA and, if you stretch them out, you'll find they contain certain genes, certain sequences of DNA that help determine how the cells of the body will develop. When researchers looked really carefully at the DNA in chromosomes, though, they were *amazed*—we *all* were—to find that only a fraction of it, maybe 20 to 30 percent, converts into meaningful genetic information. It's *incredible*, at least it was to *me*, but if you . . . if you took away all the DNA that codes for genes, you'd still have maybe 70 percent of the DNA left over . . . That's the so-called *"junk* DNA," though the word "junk" is used sort of tongue in cheek. The assumption is that, even if this DNA doesn't make up any of the *genes*, it must serve some other purpose. Anyway, . . . if we examine the *ends* of these coils of DNA . . . , we'll find a sequence of DNA at each end of every human chromosome . . . called a "telomere."

telomere

Now, a *telomere* is a highly *repetitious* . . . and genetically *meaningless* sequence of DNA, what we were calling "junk DNA." But it does have an important purpose. It's sort of like the plastic tip on each end of a shoelace. It may not help you tie your shoe, but that little plastic tip keeps the rest of the shoelace . . . the shoestring . . . from unraveling into weak and useless threads. Well, the telomeres at the ends of chromosomes seem to do about the same thing—protect the genes, the genetically *functional* parts of the chromosome, from being damaged.

Every time the chromosome divides—every time one cell divides into two—pieces of the ends of the chromosome, the telomeres, get broken off. So after each division, the telomeres get shorter; and one of the things that may happen after a while is that pieces of the genes themselves get broken off of the chromosomes . . . so the chromosome is now losing important genetic information and is no longer functional. But as long as the telomeres are a certain length they keep this from happening. So it seems that when the . . . by looking at the length of the telomeres on specific chromosomes, we can actually predict, pretty much . . . how long certain cells can successfully go on dividing.

Now there are *some* cells that just seem to keep on dividing, regardless . . . which may not always be a good thing if it gets out of control . . . , but when we analyze these cells chemically, we find something very interesting—a chemical in them, an enzyme called *"telomerase."*

As bits of the *telomere* break off from the end of the chromosome, this chemical—this *"telomerase"*—can rebuild it . . . can help reassemble the protective DNA, the telomere, that the chromosome has lost. Someday, we may be able to take any cell and keep it alive, functioning and reproducing itself essentially forever, through the use of telomerase. And in the future we may have virtually immortal nerve cells and immortal skin cells or whatever, because this chemical, *telomerase*, can keep the *telomeres* on the ends of the chromosomes from getting any shorter.

TRACK 82 TRANSCRIPT

Narrator

Listen to part of a lecture in a business class.

Professor

OK, as we've talked about, a key aspect of running a successful business is knowing . . . um, getting a good sense of what the customer actually wants. And how they perceive your product. So with that in mind, I want to describe a very simple method of researching customer preference. And it's becoming increasingly common . . . and it's called MBWA, which stands for Managing By Wandering Around.

Professor

Now, MBWA, that's not the most technical-sounding name you've ever heard, but, ah, it describes the process pretty accurately. Here's how it works. Basically, um, the idea is that business owners or business managers just, just go out and actually talk to their customers and ah, to learn more about how well the business is serving their needs. And, and try to see what the customer experiences. Cause that's a great way to discover for yourself how your product is perceived, what its strengths and weaknesses are . . . you know, how you can improve it, that sort of thing. You know Dalton's, they make soup and canned vegetables and such? Well, the head of the company had Dalton's top executives walk around supermarkets, um, asking shoppers what they thought of Dalton's soups, and he used that data to make changes to the company's product. I mean, when Dalton's, of all companies, embraces something as radical as MBWA, it really shows you how popular the theory has become. Yes, Lisa?

Female student

But isn't it dangerous to base decisions on information from a small sample of people? Isn't large-scale market research safer, getting data on a lot of people?

Professor

That's a good question. And, ah, well I don't want to pretend that W, MBWA, uh, is some sort of replacement for other methods of customer research. Now, market research data definitely can give you a good idea of, ah . . . the big picture. But MBWA is, is really useful at kind of filling in the blanks, getting a good on-the-ground sense of how your products are used and how people respond to them. An-and yes, the numbers of opinions you get is small, so, yes, you need to be careful. But, good business managers will tell you that the biggest fear they have, and, and one of the most frequent problems they come across, is, well, becoming out of touch with what their customers really want and need. You know, surveys, and market research . . . stuff like that, they can only tell you so much about what the customers actually want in, in their day-to-day lives. Managing By Wandering Around, on the other hand, well that gets you in there and gives you a good sense of what customers need. So, so when used in combination, then, MBWA and market research, well, there're powerful tools. Oh, here's another example—senior executives for a clothing manufacturer, it was, um ah, Elkin . . . Elkin jeans, you know? They went and worked in a store for a few days selling Elkin's clothes. Now that gave them a very different idea about their product—they saw how people responded to it. They, they could go up to customers in the store and ask them questions about it. Ah, yes, Mike?

Male student

Well, I would think that a lot of customers would be bothered by, you know, if I'm shopping, I don't know if I'd want some business representative coming up to me and asking me questions. It's, it's like when I get phone calls at home from market researchers—I just hang up on them.

Professor

Well, it's certainly true that, well, no one likes getting calls at home from market researchers or, or people like that. But I'll tell you something—most customers have the exact opposite reaction when it comes to MBWA. Now, don't ask me why, because I, I really have no idea, but the fact is that customers tend to respond really well to MBWA, which is the key reason for its success. In fact, the techniques of MBWA work so well, they've actually been extended to all kinds of different contexts. Like politics, for instance. A few years back, the mayor of Baltimore . . . um, ah, I think his name was Schaefer, or something like that . . . anyway, he decided that the best way to serve the people of the city, of his city was to actually get out there and experience the things *they* experienced. So he'd ride around the city, and well, you know, in all parts of it, and he'd see all the potholes, he'd see how trash was sometimes, ah, not picked up off the side of the street, and he'd go back to his office write these memos. They were memos to his staff about the problems he'd seen and how they needed to be fixed, now, that sort of thing. But the thing is he got all this information just by going around, and seeing all the different Baltimore neighborhoods, and talking to people. He called it smart politics. We'd call it MBWA, or just plain good customer service!

TRACK 83 TRANSCRIPT

Narrator

What does the professor imply when she says this:

Professor

I mean, when Dalton's, of all companies, embraces something as radical as MBWA, it really shows you how popular the theory has become.

TRACK 84 TRANSCRIPT

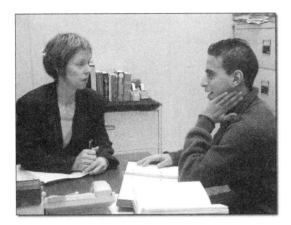

Narrator

Listen to a conversation between a student and a department secretary.

Student

Hi, Miss Hendricks.

Secretary

Hi Brad. How are you?

Student

I'm fine except I have a question about my paycheck.

Secretary

Sure, what's up?

Student

Well, it's already been several weeks into the semester, and my paycheck was supposed to go directly into my bank account, but there haven't been any deposits.

Secretary

That's odd.

Student

Yeah, I thought graduate teaching assistants were automatically put on the payroll at the beginning of the semester.

Secretary

They *are* . . . let's see . . . did you complete all the forms for payroll?

Student

I filled in whatever they sent me, and . . . I returned it, like, at the end of August.

Secretary

Hmm. Well you definitely should've been paid by now. At least two pay periods have passed since then.

Student

I asked at the bank, and they didn't know anything. Who should I talk to about this? Payroll?

Secretary

I'm gonna contact them for you. There was a problem in processing some of the graduate student payroll paperwork, 'cause their computer program crashed after all the information was processed, and some people's information couldn't be retrieved.

Student

Oh . . . but . . . why didn't anyone let me know?

Secretary

I don't know how they work over there, cuz they couldn't even figure out whose information was missing. And this isn't the first time: Seems like something like this happens every semester.

Student

So . . . how do I find out if my information was lost?

Secretary

I'll contact them tomorrow morning to see if you're in the system, but you're probably not.

Student

Well, then what'll I need to do?

Secretary

Sorry, but you'll need to fill out all those forms again, and then I'll fax them over to the payroll office.

Student

And then what? . . . well . . . what I really need to know is . . . how long till I get some money? I'm already a month behind in my bills, and my tuition's due soon.

Secretary

They'll get you into the system the same day they receive your paperwork, so if you do that tomorrow, you'll get paid next Friday.

Student

That's a long time from now. Will that paycheck include all the money I'm owed?

Secretary

It should. I'll double-check with the payroll department.

Student

And another thing: Is there any way I could get paid sooner? I have been teaching all these weeks . . .

Secretary

I know it's not fair but . . . I don't think they can do anything. All the checks are computed automatically in the system. They can't just . . . write checks.

Student

But . . . they're the ones that made a mistake . . . and . . . they never told me.

Secretary

I understand how you feel. If I were you, I'd be upset too . . . I'll tell you what. When I call them, I'll explain the situation and ask if there's any way you could be paid sooner. But I have tell you that, based on past experience, you shouldn't count on it.

Student

I understand. Thanks. I know it's not your fault, and that you're doing everything you can.

Secretary

Well, what I *can* do is make sure that your first check is for the total amount that the university owes you.

Student

That'd be great. Thank you. I'll be on campus about ten tomorrow morning, and I'll come by to see you then.

TRACK 85 TRANSCRIPT

Architecture

Narrator

Listen to part of a lecture in an architecture class.

Professor

OK, so as we've consistently seen over the past week, architecture's, uh, traditional approach has often been to design first, then figure out how to make it work. So what I'd like to talk about now is a structure—a facility that totally reverses that mind-set. For this project, engineers started out by imposing an energy-consumption limit on the facility, and architects built all the design plans around that number. In other words, energy considerations determined the design. And it did so in ways that are so advanced that the facility really raises the standard for energy efficiency.

It's a research facility in Colorado—the first of its size to achieve the goal of net zero in the United States. Meaning it creates as much energy as it uses.

Let's take a look at the basic footprint . . . just an outline of the foundation to start.

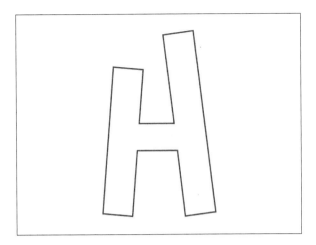

Professor

So you see, there are two long buildings connected at their centers . . . forming kind of a crooked letter H. And these aren't typical buildings. As you can see from the footprint, they're long as well as thin. Can anyone think of a reason why that decision was made?

Female student

So that there'd be more surface area for solar panels on the roof?

Professor

Well, that's the right kind of thinking . . . Certainly, solar panels were used for this facility—they supply electricity. But, you know, the shape of the buildings has even more to do with the sun than just that! It was carefully designed to make an abundance of natural light available throughout the entire facility. First, the architects decided to narrow the width of those rectangular buildings—50 percent thinner than the average modern office building—so that light could penetrate through the many windows into the middle of each building. And, secondly, they consciously positioned the buildings on the site to maximize their exposure to daylight . . . so the long sides get the most sun.

Female student

Hmmm. OK . . . so lots of light . . . but, um, from what I've read, windows are a primary source of both heat loss and heat gain for a building. I mean, how can having so many windows be energy efficient?

Professor

Well, the architects used particular kinds of windows.

Male student

You mean insulated windows? The kind with multiple layers of glass, and gas between each layer?

Professor

Um, as I mentioned earlier, this facility sets the standard . . . . That's old technology.

For instance, throughout much of the facility, they've installed electrochromic windows. Electrochromic windows use a single pane of glass that darkens automatically and blocks out the sunlight as the temperature rises. An electric current actually changes the tint. They're placed where the buildings' windows get the most sun.

Male student

Innovative!

Professor

And it only gets better . . .

Professor

You see, under each of the buildings, architects designed a broad, shallow basement space—that's kind of like a maze. Air—either from within the building or from the outside—is pulled into the basement space through air ducts, and then forced to move slowly around concrete barriers . . . the air is sort of guided through the maze. Now, these concrete barriers, they absorb heat from the air if the air is warm. Or, if the air is cold, the cold is absorbed into the concrete. So, it could be either way. Uh, let's say it's hot air—hot waste air being pulled in from the computer rooms, say. Well, that air moves slowly back and forth around these barriers. In this particular situation then, the heat from the incoming air is transferred to the concrete, which then holds onto it, storing the heat until later when it's slowly released throughout the building. That's the concept of thermal mass in a nutshell.

Male student

OK—so, um, the air . . . it could be hot or cold? So, then it'd be like, um, walking into an old stone—like, an old stone castle during summertime. It's so much cooler inside the castle during the day, 'cause the walls had retained the cold from the night air . . .

Professor

That's right. It's precisely the same thing—thermal mass! As a matter of fact, the outer walls of the facility consist of large panels of concrete—nearly a foot thick—for that very reason. And they play a huge role in maintaining the temperature of each building.

TRACK 86 TRANSCRIPT

Narrator

Listen again to part of the lecture. Then answer the question.

Professor

Well, the architects used particular kinds of windows.

Male student

You mean insulated windows? The kind with multiple layers of glass, and gas between each layer?

Professor

Um, as I mentioned earlier, this facility sets the standard . . .

Narrator

What does the professor imply when he says this?

Professor

Um, as I mentioned earlier, this facility sets the standard . . .

TRACK 87 TRANSCRIPT

Narrator

Some people believe it's essential for a person's education to learn to play a musical instrument. Others don't believe music education is important. Which view do you agree with? Explain why.

TRACK 88 TRANSCRIPT

Narrator

Read the article about a college radio station. You will have 45 seconds to read the article. Begin reading now.

TRACK 90 TRANSCRIPT

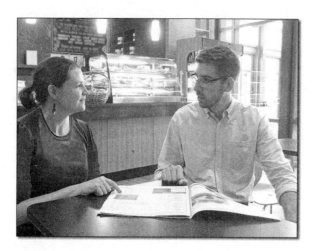

Narrator

Now listen to two students discussing the article.

Male student

What d' you think of the proposal?

Female student

I think it'll work. I mean, the range of the station now is basically limited to the campus and so it's basically just a few programs, mainly for students . . .

Male student

Yeah.

Female student

Well, if this proposal goes through, there will be more programs and it'll give the students more professional experience as they experiment with programming for a much larger . . . you know . . . "real-life" audience. And stuff like that'll give them a better shot at getting a job after they graduate.

Male student

Of course.

Female student

Besides, the whole university will benefit from it.

Male student

What d' you mean?

Female student

Well, you know my friend Tony, right? He told me that the radio station at his university did something like this about five years ago . . .

Male student

And . . .

Female student

Well. It's a success. They are making a lot of money out of commercials and they are using it to offer more scholarships and to help fund projects to renovate the facilities of other programs.

Male student

That sounds really good!

Narrator

The woman supports the proposal described in the article. Explain why she thinks it will achieve the university's goals.

TRACK 90 TRANSCRIPT

Narrator

Now read the passage about subliminal perception. You will have 50 seconds to read the passage. Begin reading now.

TRACK 91 TRANSCRIPT

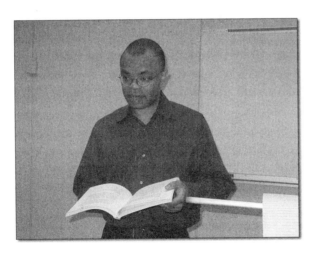

Narrator

Now listen to part of a lecture on this topic in a psychology class.

Professor

Consider this experiment: two groups of people were asked to watch TV and while they were watching, a picture flashed on the screen, less than a second—very quickly, so it was barely noticeable.

The picture was of a boy with a birthday cake. Now, like I said, there were two groups and each group saw a slightly different version of the picture. One group got the boy looking angry; in fact, he was actually throwing the cake on the floor. The other group got a picture of the boy smiling, happy, holding out the cake like he was offering it. Same boy . . . same cake . . . but different emotions expressed in each picture.

Everyone was then asked to look at a different image—now this is a third image, right? Again it's the boy and the cake, but this time the image stayed on the screen. In this picture, the boy's just holding the cake, basically no emotion on his face—everything very neutral. Now remember, nobody knew they'd already seen a picture of this boy. After a minute, everyone was asked to describe the boy's personality. Those who'd been exposed to image of the angry boy, they generally described the boy's personality negatively. Those who'd earlier seen the happy boy described him, well, positively.

Narrator

Describe what subliminal perception is and explain how the experiment discussed by the professor illustrates this phenomenon.

TRACK 92 TRANSCRIPT

Narrator

Listen to part of a lecture from a history of photography class.

Professor

So, um, continuing our review of photographic history, let's turn to the influence of industrialism on photography. Industrialism involved the development of modern machines . . . you see, they were playing a growing role in people's lives as they flocked to cities to work in factories there. Well, photographers reacted to industrialism in very different ways. Nineteenth-century photographers reacted against the machines of their industrial age, while modern, twentieth-century photographers celebrated—and ah even glorified—them.

In the nineteenth century, photographers kept machines out of their pictures altogether. It was a reaction against the growth of industry at that time, Instead, photographers emphasized peaceful scenes of oh humans living close to nature and performing traditional rural activities or trades. For example, one photograph shows farmworkers pulling handheld carts piled with gathered hay. The photographer is trying to emphasize the simplicity of ah of the old-fashioned equipment they used . . . and most importantly the absence of machines.

But around the turn of the century photographers began to think about machines very differently, especially in the United States, where industrial technology was spreading. These twentieth-century photographers, um, instead of playing down their connection to machines, as the nineteenth-century photographers had, they developed a fascination with machines and celebrated them in their art. For example, this one photograph from the 1920s shows the inside of an automobile factory—quite a different scene from a farmer working in his field. In fact, there are no human figures at all. The photograph shows this beautiful sunlight shining in through the big factory windows and ah lighting up all the machines inside, making them sparkle and gleam. Anyway, the effect is basically to glorify technology and industrial production.

Narrator

Using the examples from the lecture, explain how industrialism influenced both nineteenth-century and twentieth-century photographers.

TRACK 93 TRANSCRIPT

Narrator

Now listen to part of a lecture on the topic you just read about.

Professor

The evidence linking this portrait to Jane Austen is not at all convincing. Sure, the painting has long been somewhat loosely connected to Austen's extended family and their descendants, but this hardly proves it's a portrait of Jane Austen as a teenager. The reading's arguments that the portrait is of Austen are questionable at best.

First, when the portrait was authorized for use in the 1882 publication of her letters, Jane Austen had been dead for almost *70* years. So the family members who asserted that the painting was Jane had never actually seen her themselves. They couldn't have known for certain if the portrait was of Austen or not.

Second, the portrait could very well be that of a *relative* of Austen's, a fact that would explain the resemblance between its subject and that of Cassandra's sketch. The extended Austen family was very large, and many of Jane Austen's female cousins were teenagers in the relevant period, or had children who were teenagers. And some of these teenage girls could have resembled Jane Austen. In fact, many experts believe that the true subject of the portrait *was* one of those relatives, Mary Ann Campion, who was a distant niece of Austen's.

Third, the painting has been attributed to Humphrey only because of the style, but other evidence points to a later date. A stamp on the back of the picture indicates that the blank canvas, you know, the actual piece of cloth on which the picture was painted, was sold by a man named William Legg. Records show that William Legg did not sell canvasses in London when Jane Austen was a teenager. He only started selling canvasses when she was 27 years old. So, it looks like the canvas was used for the painting at a time when Austen was clearly older than the girl in the portrait.

TRACK 94 TRANSCRIPT

Narrator

Summarize the points made in the lecture, being sure to explain how they respond to the specific arguments made in the reading passage.

TRACK 103 TRANSCRIPT

Narrator

Listen to a conversation between a student and his psychology professor.

Professor

Good afternoon, Alex. Can I help you with something?

Student

Well, I wanted to talk with you about the research project you assigned today. I, um, hoped you could clarify a few things for me.

Professor

I'll certainly try.

Student

OK, all we have to do is do two observations and take notes on them, right?

Professor

That's a start—but you'll need to do some research, too. Then you'll write a paper that's not so much about the *observations*, but a synthesis of what you've observed and read.

Student

OK . . . and what about the children I'm supposed to observe?

Professor

Not 'children'—a single child, observed twice.

Student

Oh! OK. So I should choose a child—with the permission of the child's parent, of course—and then observe that child a couple of times and take good notes. Then?

Professor

Actually, after your *first* observation, you'll go back and look through your textbook or go to the library and find a few sources concerning the stage of development this particular child is in. And then with *that knowledge*, you'll make a *second* observation of the same child to see if the expected developmental behaviors are exhibited.

Student

Can you give me an example?

Professor

Well, um, if you observed a four-year-old child—uh, for example, my daughter is four years old—you might read up on Piaget's stages of cognitive development. We covered those in class.

Student

Uh-huh.

Professor

Most likely, what stage would a child of that age be in?

Student

Um . . . the preoperational stage?

Professor

Exactly. If that's the case, her language use would be maturing, and her memory and imagination would be developed.

Student

So she might play pretend! Like, she can pretend when driving her toy car across the couch that the couch is actually a bridge or something.

Professor

That's right. In addition, her thinking would be primarily egocentric.

Student

So she'd be thinking mostly about herself and her own needs and might not be able to see things from anyone else's perspective.

Professor

Um hmm.

Student

But . . . what if she doesn't? I mean, what if she doesn't demonstrate those behaviors?

Professor

That's fine. You'll note that in your paper. See, your paper should compare what is expected of children at certain stages of development with what you actually observe.

Student

OK. I have one more question, though.

Professor

And what's that?

Student

Where can I find a child to observe?

Professor

Um, I'd suggest you contact the education department secretary. She has a list of contacts at various schools and with certain families who are somehow connected to the university. Sometimes they are willing to help out students with projects like yours.

Student

OK, I'll stop by the education department office this afternoon.

Professor

And if you have any trouble or any more questions, feel free to come by during my office hours.

TRACK 104 TRANSCRIPT

Narrator

Listen again to part of the conversation. Then answer the question.

Student

OK, all we have to do is do two observations and take notes on them, right?

Professor

That's a start—

Narrator

What does the professor mean when she says this?

Professor

That's a start—

TRACK 105 TRANSCRIPT

Narrator

Listen again to part of the conversation. Then answer the question.

Student

OK, all we have to do is do two observations and take notes on them, right?

Professor

That's a start.

Narrator

What does the professor mean when she says this:

Professor

That's a start.

TRACK 105 TRANSCRIPT

City Planning

Narrator

Listen to part of a lecture in a city planning class.

Professor

In the last 50 years or so, many American cities have had difficulty in maintaining a successful retail environment. Business owners in the city centers, or, uh, the downtown areas, have experienced some financial losses because of a steady movement of people out of the cities and into the suburbs. In general, downtown areas just don't have that many residential areas; uh, not that many people *live* there. So, what have city planners decided to do about it? Well, one way they've come up with some ways to attract more people to shop downtown was by creating *pedestrian malls*.

Now, what *is* a pedestrian mall? It's a pretty simple concept, really. It's essentially, um, an outdoor shopping area designed just for people on foot. And—uh, well, unlike many other shopping malls that are built in the suburbs nowadays—these pedestrian malls are typically located in the downtown area of the city and, well, they have features like wide sidewalks, comfortable outdoor seating, and, uh, maybe even fountains and, you know, art.

Uh, there are variations on this model, of course, but the common denominator is always the idea of-of creating a shopping space that will get people to shop in the city without needing their cars. So I'm sure you can see how having an area that's off-limits to automobile traffic would be ideal for a heavily populated city, where, uh, well, the streets would otherwise be bustling with noisy, unpleasant traffic congestion.

Now, the concept, which originated in Europe, was adopted by American city planners in the late 1950s. And since then, a number of United States cities have created pedestrian malls, and many of them have been highly successful. So what have city planners learned about making these malls succeed? Well, there are two critical factors to consider when creating a pedestrian mall: *location* and *design*. Both of which are equally important.

Now, let's start with the location. In choosing a specific location for a pedestrian mall, there are, in fact, two considerations: proximity to potential customers—uh, that's we would call a "customer base"—and accessibility to public transportation, which we'll get to in just a moment. Now, for a customer base, eh, the most obvious example would be a large office building—since the employees could theoretically go shopping after work or during their lunch hour, right? Uh, another really good example is a convention center, which typically has a hotel and large meeting spaces to draw visitors to the city for-for major business conferences and events. Uh, but ideally, the pedestrian mall would be used by local residents, not just people working in the city or-or visiting the area. So that's where access to public transportation comes in. Either, um, either the designers plan to locate the mall near a central transportation hub—uh, like a bus terminal, a major train, or subway station *or* they work with city officials to create sufficient parking areas not too far from the mall. W-Which makes sense, because if people can't drive into the mall area, well, then they need to have easy access to it.

OK. So that's location, but-but what about design? Well, design doesn't necessarily include things like sculptures, or decorative walkways, or-or even eye-catching window displays—you-you know—art . . . Although, I'd be the first to admit those things are *aesthetically* appealing . . . However, visually pleasing sights, well, they're *not* a part of the pedestrian mall design that-that matter the most. The key consideration is *a compact and convenient layout*—uh, one which allows pedestrians to walk from-from one end of the mall to the other in just a few minutes . . . so they can get to the major stores, restaurants, and-and other central places, eh, without having to take more than one or two turns. Now, this takes careful and creative planning.

Eh, but, now, what if one ingredient to this planning recipe is missing? There could quite possibly be long-lasting effects. And, eh, I think a good example is the pedestrian mall in Louisville, Kentucky, for instance.

Now when the Louisville mall was built, oh, it had lots of visual appeal. It was attractively designed right in a small part of downtown, and it pretty much possessed all of the other design elements for success. But, uh, now here's where my point about location comes into play . . . there wasn't a convention center around to-to help draw in visitors, and, uh, well, the only nearby hotel eventually closed down for that same reason. Well, you can imagine how this must've affected local and pedestrian mall business owners. Sort of, what we call, a chain reaction. It wasn't until a convention center and a parking garage were built, uh, about decade later that the mall started to be successful.

TRACK 106 TRANSCRIPT

Narrator
What does the professor mean when she says this:

Professor
Well, design doesn't necessarily include things like sculptures, or decorative walkways, or-or even eye-catching window displays—you-you know—art . . . Although, I'd be the first to admit those things are *aesthetically* appealing . . .

TRACK 107 TRANSCRIPT

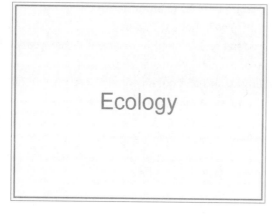

Narrator

Listen to part of a lecture in an ecology class.

Professor

So—uh, continuing our discussion of ecological systems, whole systems . . . the main thing to keep in mind here is the *interrelationships*. The species in a system, uh—and even the landscape itself—they're interdependent. Let's take what you read for this week, and see if we can't apply this interdependence idea. Mike?

Male student

Well, um, how about *beavers*—ecosystems with beavers and waterways.

Professor

Good, good. Go on.

Male student

Like—well, you can see how it's so important, 'cause if you go back before Europeans settled in North America, like before the 1600s, back when Native Americans were the only people living here—well, back then there were a lot of beavers. But later on, *after* Europeans—

Professor

OK, wait—I see where you're heading with this, but before we go into how European settlement affected the ecosystem, tell me this: what kind of environment do beavers live in? Think about what it was like *before* the European settlers came. We'll come back to where you were headed . . .

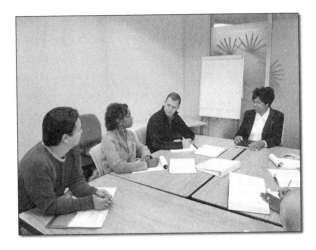

Female student

OK, well, beavers live near streams and rivers . . . And they *block up* the streams and rivers with, like, logs, and sticks, and mud, you know, they build *dams*, that really slow down the flow of the stream. So then the water *backs up* and creates, like, a pond that floods the nearby land.

Professor

And that creates *wetlands*. OK, tell me more.

Female student

Well, with wetlands it's like there's more *standing* water, more *still* water around. And that water's a lot *cleaner* than swiftly flowing water because the dirt and sediment and stuff has a chance to sink to the bottom.

Professor

More important for our discussion: Wetland areas support a lot more varieties of life than swiftly flowing water. For example, there are more varieties of fish, of insects, lots of frog species. And then species that rely on *those* species start to live near the wetlands, too.

Female student

Yes. Like birds and mammals that eat the fish and insects. And you get trees and plants that begin to grow near the standing water that can't grow near running water. Oh, and there's something about wetlands and groundwater, too . . .

Professor

OK. Good. Wetlands have a big effect on groundwater—the amount of water *below* the surface of the land. Think of wetlands as . . . um, like a giant sponge. The earth soaks up a lot of this water that's continually flooding the surface, which increases the amount of water below. So, where there are wetlands, you get a lot of groundwater. And *groundwater* happens to be a big source of our *own* drinking water today. All right. So back to the beavers. What if the beavers weren't there?

Male student

You'd just have a regular running stream, 'cause there's no dam. So the ecosystem would be completely different—there'd be fewer wetlands.

Professor

Exactly. So, now let's go back where you were headed before, Mike. Uh, you mentioned a change that occurred after Europeans came to North America . . .

Male student

Yeah—well, there used to be beavers all over the place . . . um, something like 200 million beavers, just in the continental United States. But when Europeans came, they started hunting the beavers for their fur . . . 'cause beaver fur, it's really warm—and it was really popular for making hats in Europe. So the beavers were hunted a lot, overhunted—they were almost extinct by the 1800s. So . . . that meant fewer wetlands—less standing water.

Professor

And what does that mean for the ecosystem? Kate.

Female student

Well, if there's *less standing* water, then the ecosystem can't support as many species, because a lot of insects and fish and frogs *can't live* in *running* water. And then the *birds and animals* that eat *them* lose *their* food supply.

Professor

Precisely. So the beaver, in this ecosystem, is what we call a *keystone species*.

The term "keystone" kind of explains itself: in architecture, a *keystone* in an archway or doorway is the stone that holds the whole thing together, and keeps it from collapsing. Well, that's what a keystone species does in an ecosystem—it's the crucial *species* that keeps the system going.

Now, beaver populations are on the rise again, but there's something to think about: consider humans as part of these ecosystems. You've probably heard about water shortages or, uh, restrictions on how much water you can use, especially in the summertime, in recent years. And remember what I said about groundwater. Imagine if we still had all those beavers around, all those wetlands. What would our water supply be like *then*?

TRACK 108 TRANSCRIPT

Narrator

Listen again to part of the lecture. Then answer the question.

Professor

So the beaver, in this ecosystem, is what we call a *keystone species*.

The term "keystone" kind of explains itself: in architecture, a *keystone* in an archway or doorway is the stone that holds the whole thing together, and keeps it from collapsing.

Narrator

Why does the professor say this:

Professor

The term "keystone" kind of explains itself: in architecture, a *keystone* in an archway or doorway is the stone that holds the whole thing together, and keeps it from collapsing.

TRACK 109 TRANSCRIPT

Narrator

What does the professor imply when she says this:

Professor

Imagine if we still had all those beavers around, all those wetlands. What would our water supply be like *then?*

TRACK 110 TRANSCRIPT

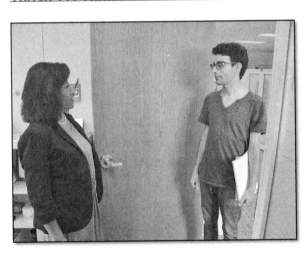

Narrator

Listen to a conversation between a student and an employee in the financial aid office.

Employee

Good morning. Can I help you . . . ? Oh, you look familiar . . . Didn't you play in the concert last Thursday?

Student

Y-yeah . . .

Employee

I took my daughter to that concert—she's just started learning the saxophone—and we both loved your performance!

Student

Well, thanks—that-that's nice to hear. In fact, I've just decided to switch my major from English to music, so now I'm eligible for the Atwood Music Scholarship. Uh, if there's still time to apply . . . ?

Employee

Well, the deadline's next Friday for that one.

Student

Oh, that's what I was afraid of. I'm not going to have time to get everything together, am I?

Employee

Well, you would need a complete transcript of your coursework and grades, and that alone could take . . . mm, depending on how busy the office is . . . they usually say to expect it to take two weeks. You'd also need two letters of recommendation.

Student

Uh could the letters be from anyone? Like, from the director of the Springfield Community Orchestra—she's known me for years. And-and would I bring everything in to you?

Employee

Yes to the first question, but no to the second. The Atwood Scholarship isn't sponsored by the university, so you'd have to mail all your materials directly to the selection committee. So you'll need to get your letters of recommendation pretty fast. Plus, and, uh, this might be even trickier for you to obtain in time . . . um, you'll need to send in an audition recording of your playing.

Student

Oh, actually, that part's no problem. I can just send in recordings of the works I played in the concert. Uh, by the way, do you happen to know who'll be judging it?

Employee

The selection committee's made up of five people: three members of the Atwood family—they're all musicians—and two members of the Greenwood Symphony. But as for the audition recording . . . they're pretty specific about what they want to hear you play—there's a list in the informational flier they provide, but someone took the last flier this morning, so I need to print out some more—if you can give me about ten minutes to do that . . . ?

Student

Sure, no problem.

Employee

You know, uh, have you thought about applying for anything else? Because we just got some information about something called the Gorman Music Fund. There's still over a month to complete the application for that. And the amount's significant—enough to cover a year's tuition!

Student

Oh wow!

Employee

Yeah. Check their Web site for more information—but everything you send in for the Atwood can probably be used for the Gorman too. And there'll be more opportunities coming up soon, so I'd check back here if I were you.

Student

Thanks!

TRACK 111 TRANSCRIPT

Poetry

Narrator

Listen to part of a lecture in a poetry class. The professor is discussing medieval poetry.

Professor

OK, so, the two poems we're looking at today fall into the category of, uh, medieval times, which was how long ago?

Female student

Almost a thousand years ago, right?

Professor

Yes, that's right—

Female student

But professor, are you sure these are poems? I mean, I thought poems were shorter. These are more like long stories. I mean, one of 'em was all about love, but the other one, the chan—chan—whatever it's called, that other one, well, it was all about fighting and battles. I mean, can both of them be considered poems?

Professor

Well, think back to the very beginning of this course.

Female student

Uh-huh.

Professor

Remember how w-w-we defined poetry? In the very broadest sense, we said it's written to evoke, uh, to make *you*, the audience, have some kind of emotional experience through the use of imagery, uh, some kind of predictable rhythm, and-and usually, but not always, there's more than one meaning implied with the words that are used. Let's start with chanson poetry first. That's chanson.

Chanson poems became popular in Europe, particularly in France, and the term is actually short for a longer French phrase that translates to, uh, *songs* of *deeds*. Ah, now, they were called songs of deeds because, strangely enough, they were written to describe the heroic deeds or actions of . . . of warriors, the knights during conflicts. We don't know a lot about the authors . . . it's still contested somewhat, but we're pretty sure about *who* the chanson poems were written *for*. That is, they were written for knights and the lords, the, uh, nobility that they served. The poems were sung, uh, performed by a minstrel, a singer who traveled from castle to castle, singing to the local lord and his knights . . . Well, would, uh, would someone summarize the main features of the chanson poem you read?

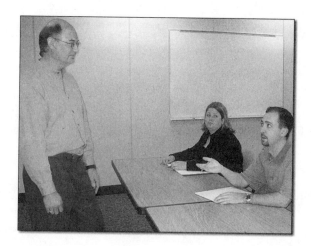

Male student

Well, there's a hero, a knight, who goes to battle, and he's admired for his courage, bravery, and loyalty, loyalty to the lord he serves, his country, and his fellow warriors in the field. He's—he has . . . uh, he's a, he's a skilled fighter willing to face the most extreme dangers, uh, sacrificial, uh, willing to sacrifice anything and everything to protect his king and country.

Professor

OK, now, given that the intended audience for these poems were knights and lords, what can we say about the purpose of chanson poetry? What kinds of feelings was it meant to provoke?

Female student

Well, I guess they must've been really appealing to those knights and lords who were listening to them, hearing the songs probably made 'em feel more patriotic, made 'em feel like it was a good and noble thing to serve their countries in whatever way they could.

Professor

Good. We've got a pretty good picture of what the chanson hero was like. Now let's compare that to the hero in the *other* poem. The other poem is an example of what's called romance poetry. And the hero in the romance poem was also a knight. But what made the knight in romance poetry different from the knight in chanson poetry?

Well, first, the *purpose* of the hero's actions was different. The hero in romance poetry is independent, purely solitary in a way, not like the chanson poet who was always surrounded by his fighting companions. He doesn't engage in conflict to protect his lord or country. He does it for the sake of adventure, to improve himself, to show he's worthy of respect and love from his lady. He's very conscious of the particular rules of social behavior he has to live up to somehow, and-and all of his actions are for the purpose of proving that he is an-an upright, moral, well-mannered . . . well-behaved individual. You may have noticed that in chanson poetry there isn't much about the hero's feelings . . . the focus is on the actions, the deeds. But the romance poetry describes a lot of the inner feelings, the motivations, uh, psychology, you could say, of a knight trying to improve himself, to better himself so that he's worthy of the love of a woman.

What explains this difference? Well, digging into the historical context tells us a lot. Um, romance poetry emerged a few generations after chanson and its roots were in geographic regions of France that were calmer, where conflict wasn't central to people's lives. More peaceful times meant there was more time for education, travel . . . more time for reflection. Another name for romance poetry that's often synonymous with it is *troubadour* poetry.

Troubadours were the authors of these new romance poems. And we know a lot more about the troubadours than we do about the chanson authors because they often had small biographical sketches added to their poems that gave pretty specific information about their social status, geographical location, and a small outline of their career. This information wasn't particularly reliable because they were sometimes based on fictitious stories of great adventure, or scrapped together from parts of different poems, *but* there is enough there to squeeze, mmm, *infer* some facts about their social class.

The political climate had settled down enough so that troubadours had the luxury of being able to spend most if not all of their time creating, crafting, or, uh, composing their love songs for their audiences. And yes, these poems were also sung. Many troubadours were able to make a living being full-time poets, which should tell you something about the value of that profession during medieval times.

TRACK 112 TRANSCRIPT

Narrator

Listen again to part of the lecture. Then answer the question.

Female student

But professor, are you sure these are poems? I mean, I thought poems were shorter. These are more like long stories. I mean, one of 'em was all about love, but the other one, the chan—chan—whatever it's called, that other one, well, it was all about fighting and battles. I mean, can both of them be considered poems?

Professor

Well, think back to the very beginning of this course.

Narrator

Why does the professor say this:

Professor

Well, think back to the very beginning of this course.

TRACK 113 TRANSCRIPT

Narrator

When looking for information for a research project, some students prefer to get their information mainly from the Internet. Others prefer to mainly use printed materials such as books and academic journals. Which do you prefer, and why?

TRACK 114 TRANSCRIPT

Narrator

The university is considering building a new athletic stadium. Read the article in the student newspaper. You will have 45 seconds to read the article. Begin reading now.

TRACK 115 TRANSCRIPT

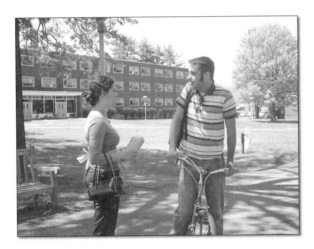

Narrator

Now listen to two students discussing the article.

Male student

So, what do you think of the university's new plan?

Female student

Oh, I don't know. I don't think it's gonna work.

Male student

No?

Female student

I mean, I can't imagine top students being too thrilled about some of the conditions on this campus.

Male student

What do you mean?

Female student

Like, the science laboratories having such old, outdated equipment, and the library needing more books, and the student center being so small. I think that the two million could be spent in better places if the university is really serious about achieving its goal.

Male student

OK. But what about the other reason for building the stadium? I mean, right now, we have so little contact with the town . . .

Female student

Yeah, but this won't help relations. Look, people from town hardly ever come to games because our teams always lose and they're not suddenly going to improve overnight. Besides, adding seats won't make a difference. I mean, if people from town didn't come before, they won't come now just because the place is bigger.

Narrator

The woman expresses her opinion about the university's plan. State her opinion and explain the reasons she gives for holding that opinion.

TRACK 116 TRANSCRIPT

Narrator

Now read the passage from a psychology textbook. You have 50 seconds to read the passage.

TRACK 117 TRANSCRIPT

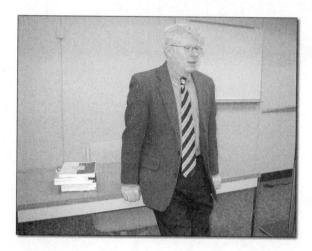

Narrator

Now listen to part of a lecture on this topic in a psychology class.

Professor

Let's take an everyday example, an ordinary round plate like you'd find in a kitchen. If you hold the plate directly in front of your face and look at it, what shape do you see? A perfect circle, right? Suppose you tilt the plate to a different angle, to a horizontal position—like you're planning to put food on it. Still a perfect circle? No. The circle is now stretched out, flattened into an oval. Do you conclude the plate has actually changed shape? Or—that it's a different object, not the same plate? Of course not. It looks different, but we perceive it as still being the same.

Here's a different example. This classroom we're in . . . it's fairly large, right? Now, from up close, from the front row, I appear to be relatively big—bigger than if you were in the last row, right? But let's say you're sitting in the front row today, but tomorrow you're sitting in the back row. From back there I'm going to look smaller, but you don't think I've actually gotten smaller. You don't think you're seeing a different professor, a guy who looks like me except he's smaller. No matter where you are—up close or far away, you understand, without even thinking about it, that I'm the same size, the same person.

Narrator

Explain what is meant by perceptual constancy, using the examples provided by the professor.

TRACK 118 TRANSCRIPT

Narrator

Now listen to part of a lecture in a biology class.

Professor

Now, many sea animals, in order to hide from predators, have over time, developed different kinds of *camouflage* to help them blend in with their environment and avoid detection by predators.

Picture the surface of the seafloor—it's as varied as the land we live on. It's got peaks and valleys, vegetation, rocky areas. And some sea animals have developed permanent colors or shapes to resemble these environmental features. This camouflage helps disguise them from predators by enabling them to blend into a-a *specific part* of the sea. For instance, take a kind of fish like the *leafy sea dragon*. Well, the name says it all: it resembles a small green dragon, with leaf-like protrusions sticking out like arms. Now, because of its color and shape, it blends in extremely well with green sea plants. So when the leafy sea dragon is swimming through these plants, predators have trouble seeing it. But when it enters other environments, without these green plants, its camouflage doesn't work anymore.

Now, other sea animals are difficult to spot *anywhere* in the sea because their type of camouflage enables them to change color. Take the cuttlefish, an animal that's closely related to the squid and octopus. Unlike leafy sea dragons, cuttlefish have not developed any particular shape to hide from predators, but, uh, they have a lot more mobility because their camouflage allows them to blend into any environment. Because cuttlefish have shifting pigments that allow them to change color in a matter of seconds. And so they can almost instantaneously match the color of their surroundings. If they're swimming by green sea plants, they'll turn green and if they're swimming over the brown seafloor, they'll turn brown.

Narrator

Using the examples of the leafy sea dragon and the cuttlefish, describe two kinds of camouflage and the benefits they provide.

TRACK 119 TRANSCRIPT

Narrator

Now listen to part of a lecture on the topic you just read about.

Professor

Of course there's some negative consequences of selling fossils in the commercial market, but they've been greatly exaggerated. The benefits of commercial fossil trade greatly outweigh the disadvantages.

First of all, the public is likely to have *greater* exposure to fossils as a result of commercial fossil trade, not *less* exposure. Commercial fossil hunting makes a *lotta* fossils available for purchase. And as a result, even low-level public institutions, like-like public schools and libraries, can now routinely buy interesting fossils and display them for the public.

As for the idea that scientists will lose access to really important fossils, that's not realistic either. Before anyone can put a value on a fossil, it needs to be scientifically identified. Right? Well, the only people who can identify fossils—who can really tell what a given fossil is or isn't—are *scientists*, by performing detailed examinations and tests on the fossils themselves. So, even if a fossil's destined to go to a private collector, it has to pass through the hands of scientific experts first. This way, the scientific community is not gonna miss out on anything important that's out there.

Finally, whatever damage commercial fossil collectors sometimes do, if it weren't for them, many fossils would simply go undiscovered, because there aren't that many fossil collecting operations that're run by universities and other scientific institutions. Isn't it better for science to at least have *more* fossils being found—even if we don't have all the scientific data we'd like to have about their location and surroundings—than it is to have many fossils go completely undiscovered?

TRACK 120 TRANSCRIPT

Narrator

Summarize the points made in the lecture, being sure to explain how they oppose specific points made in the reading passage.

Notes

Notes